VIETNAM MEDAL OF HONOR HEROES

EDWARD F. MURPHY

PRESIDIO
PRESS

BALLANTINE BOOKS • NEW YORK

A Presidio Press Book
Published by The Random House Publishing Group

Published in the United States by Presidio Press, an imprint of The Random House Publishing Group, a division of Random House, Inc., New York, and simultaneously in Canada by Random House of Canada Limited, Toronto.

Presidio Press and colophon are registered trademarks of Random House, Inc.

Map of Vietnam from *The Hill Fights* by Edward F. Murphy, copyright © 2003 by Edward F. Murphy

ISBN 978-0-345-47618-0

Printed in the United States of America

www.presidiopress.com

First Edition: July 1987
First Mass Market Edition: April 2005

OPM   9   8   7   6   5   4   3   2

VIETNAM MEDAL OF HONOR HEROES

To Kay, who has made it all possible.

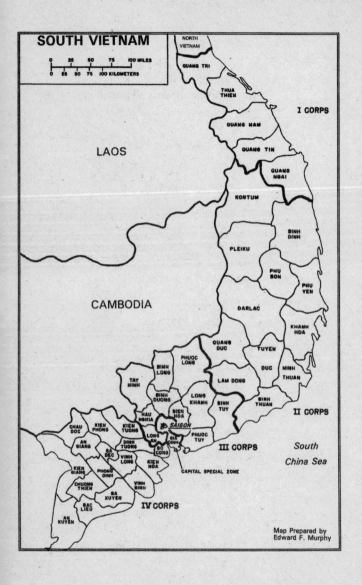

Contents

Preface

Since this book was published in 1985 there has been such a large increase in information about the Medal of Honor and its Vietnam War recipients that the need for a revised, expanded, and up-to-date edition was obvious. In the last twenty years material about the war and the experience of its combatants has been produced in massive quantities in print and visual media. Included among these are a number of Medal of Honor recipients' autobiographies that have substantially expanded our knowledge of how those men earned their awards and how the medal has affected their lives. In addition, detailed histories of specific campaigns and battles have been written that have shed new light on the events that resulted in Medals of Honor being earned, including a number of valorous deeds originally identified as having occurred in South Vietnam but that actually occurred in either Laos or Cambodia. Many of the living recipients have completed their careers and either retired or moved into new careers. Regrettably, a number of recipients have died since this book was originally released.

Six additional awards of the medal have been made since 1985. Although the armed forces have clear regulations that govern the time limits for submission of a Medal of Honor recommendation, the discovery of lost records, additional eyewitness accounts, congressional acts to waive the time limits, and the determination of wartime comrades to see these heroes recognized have made these late awards possible.

Since 1985 an unusual change in society's view of the Vietnam War veteran has occurred: Once disparaged by much of the public for their service, these same veterans now find themselves frequently praised and repeatedly thanked for their service. The nonveteran American citizen has come to understand and recognize the tremendous sacrifices the Vietnam combat veteran experienced.

Unfortunately, this newfound appreciation has created another problem. Untold numbers of nonveterans have presented themselves as Vietnam veterans. Even veterans who did not serve in the war zone have passed themselves off as hardened combat veterans. Regrettably, many of these "wannabes" claim to have been awarded the Medal of Honor. More times than not they have said that their medals were awarded in secret because their action occurred behind enemy lines while they were members of the elite navy SEALs or army Special Forces. Thus, they said, their names are not included on the official roster. Many gullible Americans, in their zeal to lessen their guilt for having disparaged the true Vietnam veteran for so long, accepted these fabrications without question, often elevating the pretender to a position of responsibility within veterans organizations, civic groups, academia, private companies, and even the government. The problem became so severe that in the late 1990s, Congress passed a law specifically aimed at punishing fraudulent Medal of Honor recipients and the Federal Bureau of Investigation has vigorously pursued the pretenders. One Vietnam veteran, B. G. Burkett, became so disgusted at the many phony veterans he encountered at veteran-related functions that he began to document their deceit and eventually published a book, *Stolen Valor,* exposing many of them.

As a result of all this new material and other changes, and because the original edition of this book has been out of print since 1990, I went to work on the new edition. That product is now in your hands. I hope it will not only serve to document the tremendous levels of heroism demonstrated by those American servicemen who served their country so well in Southeast Asia, but will also be the definitive reference for verifying authentic Medal of Honor recipients from the Vietnam War.

* * *

America's military involvement in South Vietnam polarized this country as have few other events in our history. Despite the deep political divisions brought about by that involvement, most of the young American men who were eligible to serve in the armed forces accepted their government's call to arms and acquitted themselves extremely well.

While the United States may not have won the war in Vietnam, its soldiers never lost a battle. Individual soldiers demonstrated tremendous competence—even heroism—in pursuit of their country's uncertain military goals.

In brief but bitter firefights in isolated rice paddies and in savage urban house-to-house gun battles that rivaled the European campaign of World War II, American soldiers, marines, sailors, and airmen routinely proved they could take the best that the Viet Cong and North Vietnamese regulars could dish out and still emerge winners. Gen. William C. Westmoreland, commanding general of U.S. forces in Vietnam from 1964 to 1968, called them, "fighters" and "tough combatants."

Leading these youngsters was a solid cadre of senior enlisted men and officers, men who had devoted their lives to the defense of their country. Beneficiaries of the finest military training in the world, these dedicated career professionals provided a level of leadership and inspiration unprecedented in the history of warfare.

Two hundred and forty-four U.S. servicemen in Vietnam fought so bravely that their grateful nation awarded them its highest accolade, the Medal of Honor, for their "conspicuous gallantry and intrepidity above and beyond the call of duty." (One naval officer, Capt. William McGonagle, was awarded the Medal of Honor for his gallantry in June 1967 when Israeli planes attacked his spy ship, USS *Liberty,* off the coast of Israel. He is not counted in these totals.) One hundred and fifty-three died performing the valorous act that earned them the medal. Others received permanently crippling injuries; several never fully recovered from the mental anguish caused by the war.

America's youth fought the enemy in Vietnam as well as, if not better than, their fathers fought World War II or their grandfathers fought World War I.

Unlike heroes from earlier wars, though, the returning Vietnam heroes received scant public attention.

When Audie Murphy received the Medal of Honor for his World War II exploits, his picture graced the cover of *Life* magazine—but no Vietnam Medal of Honor hero was accorded the same recognition.

During World War II, newspapers, magazines, and newsreels were full of stories about how our heroes had killed a large number of enemy troops or shot down scores of enemy planes. World War II heroes sold war bonds, toured manufacturing plants, kissed movie stars, received job offers, and had their pictures taken with civic leaders. An admiring public made them objects of adulation. Men like Jimmy Doolittle, Joe Foss, and "Commando" Kelly became familiar names and had movies made about their exploits. They were treated like heroes.

Heroes of the Vietnam War were not so lucky.

Being a hero of an unpopular war was often a burden. Friends and even family members felt uncomfortable in their presence. Strangers wanted to know how many Vietnamese babies they had killed or women they had raped to earn their medal. "Hey," someone asked one Vietnam War Medal of Honor recipient, "if you're so brave, why didn't we win over there?"

No one wanted to hear about the heroism of the soldiers from America's longest and most frustrating war.

Most of the surviving Medal of Honor recipients from the Vietnam War quickly settled into a lifestyle of obscurity. Few sought public recognition. A surprisingly large number—nearly sixty—of the ninety-one living recipients decided to remain in or return to the military. Such a career offered them an anonymity—and acceptance from their peers—not found on the "outside."

By the time Saigon fell to North Vietnamese forces in April 1975, almost all of the war's Medal of Honor heroes had retreated into the security of working on their careers, raising families, and paying mortgages. Few took part in community affairs. Few led parades. The graves of posthumous recipients went unacknowledged, except by relatives.

American society had said, in effect, "The war is over. We lost it. Let's forget it—and forget the men who fought there. If we ignore them, maybe the painful memories will go away."

"Time heals all wounds" is a well-worn cliché, but it is a strikingly appropriate description of America's reaction to the Vietnam War. As the years have passed, the agony of the war—and the disputes and recriminations that followed—has faded from most citizens' minds.

Today there are millions of Americans who had not even been born while the war was raging—and millions more are too young to remember it. It has become ancient history.

With enough distance from the war, people have begun to respect Vietnam War veterans for the sacrifices they made. The veterans themselves have begun to play a more visible role in society.

The dedication of the Vietnam Veterans Memorial in Washington, D.C., on November 11, 1982, catalyzed national recognition of the Vietnam veteran. It had taken the American public over ten years to realize that it was all right to hate the war, but not to hate their warriors.

From this beginning, the true story of the Vietnam combat soldier began to be told. History books and memoirs have appeared that reveal the unbelievable hardships American troops experienced during the war—and the uncommon valor and heroism with which they responded.

Only now can the most neglected group of warriors in our history receive the public praise they deserve. The stories of the incredible heroism they displayed in fighting an unpopular war can finally be told.

Their deeds of valor equal and sometimes surpass the heroics of soldiers from earlier wars. Their achievements deserve an equally respected place in American history.

A note on sources: As the founder of the Medal of Honor

Historical Society, I began to gather information on Vietnam War Medal of Honor recipients in the early 1970s. In addition to studying the contemporary literature, including books, government documents, newspaper accounts, and magazine articles, I have interviewed dozens of recipients, their families, and the men who fought with them.

Since war is by nature a confusing event, few combatants are able to recall exactly what happened, what was said, by whom, or why. The actual words spoken by an individual are often lost forever in the heat of combat.

Therefore, rather than simply reproduce the official Medal of Honor citations—which are often terse and dry—I have reconstructed battle scenes based on the available information, adding dialogue where necessary for dramatic purposes. Whenever possible events are depicted as the participants recall them.

EDWARD F. MURPHY
Mesa, AZ

CHAPTER ONE

A History of the Medal of Honor

When President Lyndon B. Johnson placed the blue ribbon of the Medal of Honor around Capt. Roger H. C. Donlon's neck on December 5, 1964, the army Special Forces officer became the 3,154th person so honored and the first to earn the medal for service in the Vietnam War.

Since its birth during the Civil War, many men have coveted the medal; only a few have earned it. President Harry S. Truman enjoyed telling recipients, "I'd rather have this medal than be president." Gen. George S. Patton once remarked, "I'd give my immortal soul for that medal."

In all, 3,440 recipients have received 3,459 medals. Nineteen Americans have received the august decoration twice.

The Medal of Honor can be earned only by a member of the United States armed forces through a display of the most conspicuous gallantry and intrepidity above and beyond the call of duty—in the presence of an armed enemy. There must be a clear risk of life. It must be a deed that would not subject the candidate to criticism if it had not been performed. A minimum of two eyewitnesses must attest to the action. These strict guidelines reserve the Medal of Honor for the "bravest of the brave."

But it was not always that way.

Civil War navy secretary Gideon Welles was looking for a way to motivate his more reluctant sailors when he hit upon the idea of an honor medal. By rewarding those who exhibited courage in front of the enemy, maybe he could inspire others to new heights of daring. At Welles's urging, Iowa senator James W. Grimes proposed a congressional bill "to promote the efficiency of the navy." One clause of the bill authorized the creation of a "medal of honor" for sailors and Marines who distinguished themselves through gallantry in action. The bill—and the Medal of Honor—was signed into law by President Abraham Lincoln on December 21, 1861.

Not to be outdone, the army convinced Massachusetts senator Henry Wilson to introduce a similar proposal in February 1862. That law was signed into effect on July 12, 1862.

Both medals were originally reserved for enlisted men and limited to the "present insurrection." Additional legislation the following year extended the life of the medal beyond the Civil War. Also, army officers were made eligible; naval officers remained ineligible until 1915. The army limited its award to heroism in combat while the navy permitted theirs to be awarded for heroism in "the line of one's profession."

The original medal was designed by a Philadelphia silversmith firm, Wm. Wilson & Son. The piece was described as:

A five-pointed star, one point down. On the obverse the foul spirit of Secession and Rebellion is represented by a male figure in crouching attitude holding in his hands serpents, which, with forked tongues, are striking at a large female figure (portrayed by Minerva, the Roman goddess of wisdom) representing the Union of Genius of our country, who holds in her right hand a shield, and in her left, the fasces. Around these figures are thirty-four stars, indicating the number of states in the Union. ("The Medal of Honor of the United States Army," GPO, 1948)

Both the army and navy medals would be suspended from identical ribbons: a blue horizontal top bar above alternating vertical stripes of red and white, with only the suspension devices differing. The navy's medal connected to the ribbon with a rope-foiled anchor; the army's via an eagle, wings spread, astride crossed cannons and cannonball stacks.

The first Medals of Honor to be awarded went to six soldiers from Ohio who survived the legendary "great locomotive chase." This ill-fated mission to disrupt Confederate rail lines in Georgia in April 1862 ranks as one of the most daring of the Civil War. When six of the survivors were paroled from a Confederate prison in March 1863, they were taken to an audience with Secretary of War Edwin M. Stanton in Washington, DC, on March 25.

After listening to the group's hair-raising tales, Stanton praised their courage and devotion to duty. He then said, "Congress has recently created a special medal to honor the brave defenders of the Union. None have yet been awarded. I have the honor of presenting you the first." He pinned the first medal to the tunic of the group's youngest member, nineteen-year-old Jacob Parrott. The others receiving medals that day were: William Bensinger, Robert Buffum, Elihu Mason, William Pittinger, and William H. Reddick.

A few weeks later the navy awarded its first medals. There was no formal ceremony for these heroes, though. Instead, their medals were forwarded to their respective commanding officers, who handled the presentations on an individual basis.

After the Civil War, medals continued to be awarded to soldiers who fought Indians and outlaws in America's West and to sailors and Marines exploring the far reaches of the globe. Medals went to the brave men who stormed San Juan Hill, who battled the Chinese at Tientsin, and who fought the insurrectionists in the Philippines.

Just after the turn of the century, living recipients of the Medal of Honor—who had formed a Medal of Honor Legion in 1890—became concerned about the growing number of imitation Medals of Honor being issued as membership badges by various veterans groups. At the legion's urging, Brig. Gen. Horace Porter, ambassador to France and a Civil War Medal of Honor recipient, had the Parisian jewelry firm of Messrs. Arthur, Bertrand, and Berenger prepare several proposals for a new medal for the army. One was approved by the members of the legion and Secretary of War Elihu Root. On November 22, 1904 a patent was issued to protect the medal.

The new design retained the chief feature of the old medal, the five-pointed star. At its center appears the head of Minerva surrounded by the words UNITED STATES OF AMERICA. An open wreath enameled in green encircles the star. Green oak leaves fill the prongs of the star. Above the star is a bar bearing the word VALOR. Atop the bar sits a gold eagle, wings spread.

The medal's new ribbon was a light blue watered silk material spangled with thirteen white stars, representing the original colonies. At first the medal was pinned to the left breast of the recipient's uniform. Later a neck ribbon was added.

The navy elected to retain its original design. They did change the suspension ribbon to the light blue of the army in 1913 and to the neck ribbon in 1917. In 1919 the navy adopted a gold cross *pattee* (the cross's arms are narrower at the center than at the ends) design for a second Medal of Honor to be used to reward combat heroism; the original design would be used for noncombat heroism. The two-medal system proved too confusing, however, and the practice was dropped in 1942. The navy went back to the original design to recognize both combat and noncombat heroism, and noncombat heroism continued to be recognized with a Medal of Honor through the Korean War.

Because of claims from the Medal of Honor Legion alleging abuses in the awarding of the Medal of Honor, in 1916 the army convened a special board to review all of its Medal of Honor awards.

Out of all the medals awarded by the army up to that time, the Civil War alone accounted for 1,519 medals—nearly half of all those awarded—under rules that were much less strict. Many of the medals awarded for Civil War service were based on sketchy information—often submitted by the intended recipient himself. A large number of Civil War medals were awarded for deeds that would not be considered worthy today. However, the army had no other medals that could be used to recognize heroism, regardless of its degree.

It was the Medal of Honor or nothing. Too often, it was the Medal of Honor.

Following the board's recommendations, the army rescinded 911 Medals of Honor for not being merited. The board further recommended the creation of additional medals to properly recognize heroism in its varying degrees. Not all displays of bravery warrant a Medal of Honor—the board recommended that it be reserved for only the most outstanding displays of bravery. New eligibility rules would clearly spell out the criteria for each new medal.

During World War I the army created several new decorations. The Distinguished Service Cross would rank immediately below the Medal of Honor, honoring deeds of a lesser degree. Below the DSC was the Silver Star. Originally a small device attached to the ribbon of the campaign medal during which it was earned, it became an actual medal with a suspension ribbon in 1932. The navy created the Navy Cross to be on par with the DSC and also used the Silver Star. These new decorations assured that only the top heroes of the American Expeditionary Force would receive the Medal of Honor.

As a result of the board's insight, the Medal of Honor was elevated to the pinnacle of a so-called "pyramid of honor." Since then the Medal of Honor has become the most prestigious of all decorations. A strict review process ensures that the medal will not be conferred upon unworthy candidates. The standards are so high that over 55 percent of the medals awarded since World War I have been posthumous. During the Korean and Vietnam Wars nearly 70 percent of the awards were posthumous. Those who wear the Medal of Honor are a special breed.

Only 124 Medals of Honor were awarded for World War I (all figures are as of January 1, 2004): 96 in the army (including a late award in 1991), 21 in the navy, and 7 to Marines (five of those Marines also received the army medal for the same deed; these men are also counted in the army's total). For the first time, posthumous awards accounted for a large percentage of the total—thirty-two recipients died performing the act that earned them the medal.

It was during World War II that the Medal of Honor truly came into its own, achieving the prominence it holds today. To ensure that only the most deserving acts of heroism received the top medal, the different service branches created internal decorations boards to review award recommendations. Each recommendation had to pass several levels of scrutiny. The higher the proposed award, the longer and more thorough the process. Recommendations for both army and navy Medals of Honor went all the way to Washington, DC, where senior, combat-tested officers reviewed the required documentation. They or any intermediate board could downgrade a recommendation for the Medal of Honor to a lesser award.

So exacting were the standards that only 464 medals were awarded for World War II: 324 army (this total includes late awards made en masse to 7 black WWII veterans in January 1997 and to 22 Pacific Islanders in June 2000), 57 navy, 82 Marines, and 1 lone Coast Guardsman. For the first time posthumous awards outnumbered living awards—only 211 of the 464 men survived to have their medals placed around their necks.

Unlike World War I, when most Medal of Honor presentation ceremonies were held at Gen. John J. Pershing's headquarters at Chaumont, France, during World War II every effort was made to bring the heroes who survived their actions to Washington for the presentation. President Franklin D. Roosevelt delighted in presenting the medals. He often delayed more pressing matters in order to attend the ceremony and chat with the recipient afterward. President Truman's World War I combat experience gave him a deep appreciation for Medal of Honor heroes. As a combat veteran, he understood how most men's accomplishments paled in comparison to their heroic acts, and he viewed his participation in presentation ceremonies as a humbling experience. Subsequent presidents have continued the practice of presenting the Medal of Honor to living recipients, or to the survivors of deceased heroes.

Although World War II was thought to be the war to end all wars, reality soon proved different. Five short years later, America found itself embroiled in its first limited-commitment war—in Korea. Although the military strategy in Korea was one of holding actions rather than the mass movements of earlier wars, the opportunities for heroic action did not disappear. The valor displayed by American fighting men in Korea was incredible; 131 of them earned Medals of Honor during the three years of the Korean War (78 army, 7 navy, 42 Marines, and 4 members of the newly created U.S. Air Force). Over 70 percent of the awards were posthumous—only thirty-seven men survived their gallant deeds.

In the years after the Korean War the U.S. military recognized changes in the style of warfare it was likely to face. The global political situation decreased the likelihood of the United States again participating in great land battles as seen in the two world wars. Instead, it would probably continue to become involved in limited warfare as an ally to governments threatened by uprisings or insurgencies. American soldiers would be fighting alongside troops of other nations or serving in advisory roles. It was to be a very different kind of warfare, to be sure, but the fighting could be just as deadly.

To properly recognize the bravery of its troops in these new situations, the military revised the conditions under which the Medal of Honor could be granted. On July 25, 1963, Congress amended the U.S. Code to permit awarding the Medal of Honor for distinguished service:

(1) while engaged in an action against an enemy of the United States;
(2) while engaged in military operations involving conflict with an opposing foreign force, or;
(3) while serving with friendly forces engaged in an armed

conflict against an opposing armed force in which the United States is not a belligerent party.

With these new provisions, which also applied to other combat decorations, the United States was well prepared to honor distinguished gallantry on the part of its troops wherever they might be sent.

Since its designation as a separate branch of the armed forces in 1947, the air force had used the army's Medal of Honor. In 1965 it announced its own design. The five-pointed star was retained, as were the green-enameled wreath and the oak leaf–filled prongs. The main change was the replacing of Minerva with the head of the Statue of Liberty, looking now left instead of right, as had Minerva. The eagle was gone, too. In its place a bar bearing the word VALOR was placed above an adaptation of the thunderbolt sprays from the air force's coat of arms. Also, the medal is about 50 percent larger than its army and navy counterparts, giving it a heavier appearance.

The 244 Medals of Honor awarded for Vietnam War service went to 159 soldiers, 15 sailors, 57 Marines, and 13 airmen. Like their comrades from earlier wars, these men were characterized by their willingness to sacrifice themselves so that others might live to fulfill their mission and defeat the enemy.

CHAPTER TWO

The First Hero

ROGER H. C. DONLON

The attack was coming tonight. *Capt. Roger H. C. Donlon* could smell it in the air. All of his finely tuned senses told him that tonight would be the night the Viet Cong would try to overrun his Special Forces camp at Nam Dong. The attack had been imminent for the past week. Intelligence reports from Donlon's headquarters at Da Nang had reported the presence of an unusually large number of VC in the nearby mountains. Reports from local sources told Donlon that the local VC commander had decided he needed to test the Americans' resolve.

Two days earlier, July 3, 1964, one of Donlon's patrols had radioed back from a village far up the valley from the camp: "The villagers are scared, but they won't tell us why." Sgt. Terry Terrin had returned from a three-day patrol that morning to report he had found the corpses of two village chiefs who had been friendly to the Americans. That afternoon several fistfights broke out between the camp's contingent of South Vietnamese soldiers and the Nungs (ethnic Chinese who fought as mercenaries for the Americans). Donlon was sure that dissension was being sown by enemy agents.

As the sun moved lower on the horizon that Sunday night, Donlon cautioned his team sergeant, M.Sgt. Gabriel R. "Pop" Alamo, "Get everyone buttoned up tight tonight, Pop. The VC are coming. I can feel it. I want everyone ready."

For the better part of the previous ten years, Donlon had

been preparing for this moment. He was determined that he and his men would survive and prevail over the enemy.

Donlon was born January 30, 1934 in Saugerties, New York, just up the Hudson River from the U.S. Military Academy at West Point. One of eight children, he attended the local parochial school before graduating from Saugerties High School with the class of 1952.

As far back as he could remember, Donlon had wanted to be a soldier. This goal had its roots in his involvement with the Boy Scouts. He joined the local troop as soon as he was eligible and excelled at scouting, earning every merit badge he could and holding every position of leadership in his troop. He loved the challenge of being a scout. A military career seemed a logical choice.

His mother, though, had other plans. She wanted her son to continue his education. At her urging, Donlon enrolled at the New York State College of Forestry at Syracuse University. He stayed a year but was never happy, and decided not to return for his sophomore year. On December 18, 1953, with his mother's blessing, he enlisted in the U.S. Air Force.

Donlon liked the air force, but quickly decided that the only way for him to make the most of a military career was as an officer. On July 4, 1955 he entered West Point as a cadet. He attended until April 1957, when he resigned for personal reasons.

Donlon's exposure to the air force and the harsh regime at West Point did not dampen his enthusiasm for a military career. He enlisted in the army on February 5, 1958 and one year later was selected to attend the Infantry Officer Candidate School at Fort Benning, Georgia. He received his commission as a second lieutenant on June 24, 1959.

Four years later Donlon began his training with the army's new elite troops, the Special Forces. When he graduated from the Special Warfare School at Fort Bragg, North Carolina, in September 1963, he was entitled to don the distinctive headgear of these counterinsurgency experts, the green beret.

Donlon was given command of Special Forces Team A-726, with orders to prepare it for deployment to the Republic of Vietnam. They were ready in May 1964.

At that time the American involvement in South Vietnam was technically limited to an advisory role. Special Forces teams worked with Army of the Republic of Vietnam commanders to provide a level of training unavailable to ARVN officers. The Americans could not lead men into combat. They could not give orders to their ARVN counterparts. All they could do was "strongly suggest" a course of action. The Americans were allowed to fire their weapons only when directly fired upon.

In reality the Americans even then carried the brunt of the fighting. Incompetence and pure cowardice on the part of some ARVN officers forced the Americans to assume leadership positions. Many ARVN officers and enlisted men lacked an aggressive fighting spirit. Their senior officers would not motivate them. Some field commanders were known to be on the payrolls of both the South Vietnamese government and the Viet Cong. Their lack of enthusiasm for battle made winning the war a difficult task.

Upon his arrival in South Vietnam, Donlon and his eleven-man team were assigned to relieve another A-team at Camp Nam Dong. Thirty miles west of Da Nang and about the same distance directly south of Hue, Nam Dong was in the high plateau country along the border of Thua Thien and Quang Nam Provinces. It was actually two camps in one. The inner camp was manned by the Americans and their Nungs. The outer camp, surrounded by a double barbed-wire fence, was the responsibility of the South Vietnamese. Much of the nearby country was heavily wooded and sparsely populated, ideal country for guerrilla operations.

The camp's ARVN commander had 311 soldiers organized into three companies. The Special Forces had about sixty Nungs on their payroll. Many of the Vietnamese had their families with them. The camp contingent was completed by two other Westerners: Australian army WO (Warrant Officer) Kevin Conway, who represented his country at this lonely outpost, and Dr. Gerald C. Hickey, an American anthropologist studying the Vietnamese mountain tribes.

Just before two o'clock in the early morning hours of July 6, 1964, Captain Donlon relieved Conway from guard duty. As was his custom, Donlon made a circuit of the oval-shaped inner perimeter. It took him about twenty-five minutes to make a complete round of the football field–sized area as he checked the sandbagged mortar positions and the fighting holes manned by the Nungs. He moved slowly, assuring himself that all was in readiness for the attack he was sure was coming. Donlon finished his rounds with an inspection of the four 81mm mortar positions spaced evenly around the inner perimeter. All stood ready. His team members and the Nungs were awake and alert. As he headed for the mess hall to check the guard roster, Donlon thought that it might be a quiet night after all.

Donlon's watch read 2:26 A.M. when he opened the mess hall's screen door. At that moment the building erupted in a brilliant white flash. The blast blew him back outside.

Donlon instantly realized that an enemy mortar round had come through the building's roof and exploded; he scrambled into his command post next door. There he found two team members already fighting back.

A curtain of mortar rounds crashed down on the camp, spewing out death and destruction. The lesser explosions of hand grenades added to the din. Tracers from automatic weapons crisscrossed the night sky. A fire blazing in the mess hall quickly spread to the adjoining command post. Donlon routed some Vietnamese soldiers huddled in a corner of the CP. "Put the fire out," he shouted at them. "Put the fire out in the mess hall."

With Pop Alamo's help, Donlon battled the flames that threatened to consume the CP. Unmindful of the shrapnel flying through the air, the two men dragged weapons and ammo out of the burning structure. Donlon did not worry about his men; he knew they would take up their battle stations without orders from him. He was right. The other Green

Berets manned mortars, threw grenades, or fired their automatic weapons at the fleeting shadows of the attacking VC.

Sgt. Michael Disser fired an illuminating round from his mortar, then peeked over the rim of his pit. The light from the flare revealed hundreds of men moving on the camp. He later called it, "The most frightening sight of my life." What he witnessed was the main assault force of two reinforced battalions—800 to 900 men—ringing Nam Dong.

Once Donlon had salvaged all the equipment and supplies from the CP that he could, he hurried to help his men throw back the VC. He raced across the open ground, acutely aware of the exploding grenades and mortars. He stopped at the mortar pit manned by S.Sgt. Mervin Woods. Suddenly a VC mortar round went off at Donlon's feet, hurtling him through the air like a rag doll. Dizzy from the concussion and minus a boot, Donlon stumbled into Woody's fighting hole. He hardly had time to gather his thoughts when Sgt. John Houston called from a nearby position, "They're over here! By the ammo bunker." Houston turned back and fired a burst from his light machine gun into the bunker enclosure.

Donlon moved to help Houston. The blast of a third mortar round picked the young captain up and slammed him down. Donlon lost his pistol belt, his other boot, and all his equipment except his AR-15 rifle and two ammunition magazines.

With blood streaming from wounds in his left forearm and stomach, Donlon diverted to Disser's mortar pit when he picked up several more magazines of ammunition.

"Conway's dead and Alamo's hit. Hit bad," Disser reported.

God, thought Donlon, it had only been a few minutes since he'd left Pop.

Donlon started to say something to Disser when movement by the main gate only twenty yards away caught his eye.

"Illuminate the main gate, Mike!" Donlon yelled.

Disser fired an illumination round. In its light Donlon saw three VC scurrying alongside a fallen log. They were already inside the wire, he realized. Donlon swore, then fired. Two VC dropped. The third crawled into the grass. Donlon threw a grenade. The VC stopped crawling.

Donlon looked back to where he had left Houston. Two VC had snuck up and killed him. Their continued heavy fire pinned Donlon down. While he watched, two Nungs killed the VC. Donlon could now move to the rear of the camp to check on his men manning positions there.

Once on the other side of the camp, Donlon called for his medic. Sgt. Thomas L. Gregg answered from his position in SFC (Sergeant First Class) Thurman R. Brown's mortar pit. Ducking and dodging, Donlon made his way to them.

"How're you doing?" he shouted above the noise.

"Okay, so far," they responded.

Donlon ordered Gregg to check on the wounded. Gregg first wanted to treat the captain's wounds, but Donlon refused. "Tend to the others first," he said, and Gregg took off.

A second later the team's communications man, S.Sgt. Keith Daniels, stumbled into the hole.

"Did you call Da Nang, Dan?" Donlon wanted to know.

Daniels said he had. Donlon could not understand where the reaction force was. The battle had been raging for over an hour. He questioned Daniels again. The sergeant assured his captain that the message had gone out. Donlon did not know that the commo bunker had been destroyed in the opening minutes of the battle, cutting off further communications and delaying the needed air support. Daniels did not tell him, either. He thought Donlon had seen the wrecked building burning in the night.

"I'm going over to Beeson's pit to see how he's doing," Donlon announced. He left Brown's position and tried to cover the forty yards to SFC Vernon Beeson's bunker. Mortar shells crashed around him. Automatic weapons fire twice drove him to the ground. On his third try, pain stabbed his foot. Donlon looked down. A nail protruded from the top of his foot and a piece of plywood was clamped to its sole. He had stepped on the board and moved several yards before the pain registered. In disgust he tore it off and made his way back to Brown's mortar pit.

A few minutes later, Medic Gregg bounced back into the

position. "Captain, you're badly wounded. Let me fix you up," he said.

"I'm all right," Donlon said. "Take care of the others."

Gregg left again. Donlon, assured that Brown was handling his mortar well, headed again to Disser's position to see how the situation was at the front gate. Just as he passed the supply room, fire reached the ammunition stored there. It blew up with a tremendous roar. For the fourth time that night Donlon was slammed to the ground. This time, shrapnel painfully ripped through his left leg. Bleeding profusely and racked with pain, Donlon continued to Disser's position.

It was a mess.

The VC had overrun the ARVN troops manning the outer perimeter in front of Disser's pit. The enemy formed up just outside the inner barbed wire. Only heavy small-arms fire from the Nungs prevented them from attacking. They still threw grenades, though. Six or seven at a time exploded around Disser's position.

Disser fired his mortar as fast as he could drop shells down the glowing barrel. He did not take time to aim, he just knew the shells were landing among the enemy. Alamo fired an AR-15 from the front rim of the pit while a ragged hole in his shoulder streamed blood. Lt. Jay Olejniczak stood next to him firing an M-79 grenade launcher at the enemy. As Donlon watched, an enemy soldier jumped up on the parapet, set to fire his machine gun into the pit. Donlon fired first and the VC fell backward. A split second later a fragmentation grenade landed with a thud. It went off at Olejniczak's feet.

Fortunately the VC grenade did not pack the punch of an American grenade. The blast broke the lieutenant's foot but did not stop him. He kept on firing his M-79.

So many grenades landed in the next five minutes that the defenders could do nothing but ignore them. But each explosion cut a little more flesh. Alamo fell, fresh wounds sending new rivulets of blood coursing down his body. Olejniczak was a mass of wounds. Disser watched in amazement as a grenade explosion peppered his left leg and foot with shrapnel.

Fighting off fatigue—caused by loss of blood from his old wounds and the shock of the new ones—Donlon fired his AR-15 at the wire, trying to disrupt any attempt by the VC to exploit their grenade barrage.

In spite of his efforts, grenades continued to rain into the hole. In desperation, Donlon picked up the missiles and threw them back at the enemy. The others joined in. But the grenades were too plentiful. The men reached the same conclusion at the same time.

"Let's get out of here," Donlon yelled.

"Right," the others responded.

At that instant a concussion grenade exploded between Donlon and Disser and knocked them both down. Donlon staggered to his feet, helped Disser up, and passed him along to the others. As they raced to safety, Donlon covered their withdrawal with quick bursts from his rifle.

Pop Alamo was crouched in the corner of the pit, blood running from his face, shoulder, and stomach. Donlon went to him, got one of the sergeant's arms around his neck, and stood up. He was about halfway up when a tremendous blast went off in his face. A mortar shell had exploded on top of the sandbags in front of him. He felt himself falling backward. "You're dead," Donlon told himself.

Disser, too, thought Donlon was dead. He did not see how anyone could survive that blast.

Miraculously, Donlon was still alive, but badly damaged.

Blood ran from fresh wounds on Donlon's arm and face. His stomach wound was bleeding again. But he was still full of fight; he was not about to give up.

A quick glance told Donlon that Alamo had not survived the blast. Donlon grabbed the 60mm mortar, then evacuated the position. Thirty yards away, he stumbled on four wounded Nungs lying beside a brick wall. In pidgin English he urged them to return the enemy's fire, but they were too shocked to fight. Donlon used pieces of their clothing to bind their wounds. He stuffed a leftover piece of the cloth into his own stomach wound to staunch the bleeding.

"Come on, you'll be all right," Donlon told the Nungs. "Get your weapons and fight."

Donlon propped them up, put weapons in their hands, and then went back to Disser's pit for mortar shells. The intense pain from his multiple wounds forced him to walk in a crouch. Donlon returned to the Nungs with the ammunition, got the 60mm mortar back into action, then made three more trips to the mortar pit, stripping it of anything that could be of value to the enemy should they overrun the position. On his last trip, shrapnel from an exploding grenade tore yet another hole in his leg.

Satisfied that the Nungs were now responding well, Donlon once again made his way through the carnage to Woods's 81mm mortar pit. He spent time there helping the sergeant drop the deadly rounds on the enemy. Assured that Woods was holding his own, he returned to where he had left Disser and the others. Another mortar blast knocked him down.

The effects of the multiple wounds and repeated concussions began to tell on Donlon. He had been fighting nonstop for more than two hours. He was moving more slowly, thinking less clearly. He kept asking himself, "Did I do this? Did I say that?" He shook his head, groggy and tired, but remained determined to stay in command and drive off the VC.

Donlon scurried through the explosions to where Gregg had set up an aid station in an area protected from gunfire by the terrain. The medic had done a good job of patching up the many wounded. When he saw his CO, he insisted on checking him over.

"I'm all right," Donlon said. "I'll be okay, just a little tired is all. I want to make sure the others are taken care of."

"You're all shot up," Gregg said. "I'll fix you up."

"No," Donlon said. "I haven't got time."

Before Gregg could say more, Donlon was on his way back to the front gate. Donlon thought the VC would be making a determined assault there and he wanted to direct the effort to drive them away. He also wanted to know again where the air support requested by Daniels was. It should not have taken the aircraft two hours to get there.

As Donlon reached Disser's position, the drone of an airplane could be heard above the battle. At last, a flare ship. Suddenly the sky lit up. It was just after 4:30 A.M.

The arrival of the flare ship brought a momentary lull to the battle as the VC sought cover. They knew, too, that the arrival of the plane signaled the beginning of the end of the battle.

In the eerie light of the flares, a loudspeaker suddenly boomed forth with a chatter of Vietnamese. Donlon grabbed one of his interpreters. "What's he saying?" he demanded.

The shaking ARVN soldier responded, "He say put down weapons. VC take camp and we all be killed."

Those around Donlon resolved to go down fighting. As they lay there in the silence waiting for the expected attack, the loudspeaker crackled again, this time in English.

"Can you pick up the direction of the loudspeaker?" Donlon asked Disser.

"Yes, sir."

"Drop a volley of rounds that way and let's see if we can't knock the damn thing out."

With Donlon directing his fire, Disser put a round on the loudspeaker, destroying it. The field of battle was silent for a few seconds. Then one of the Nungs shot at a shadow, signaling the renewal of the fight. Almost instantly the air was filled again with the crack of bullets, the sharp explosions of grenades, and the deep thump of mortars.

For the remaining two hours of the battle, Donlon continued to make his rounds, checking on men. He was everywhere, doing everything. He threw grenades, shot at VC running through the night, and helped man mortars. He brought up ammunition supplies. He continued to offer encouragement to his troops. Seemingly invincible to the shrapnel slashing through the air, Donlon stood as upright as he could, a tower of strength to those who witnessed his inexhaustible courage.

As the sun broke across the morning sky, Donlon was manning a mortar with Woods. In the growing light he spotted four or five VC hiding in some tree stumps about fifty yards away, throwing grenades everywhere.

"Think we can drop a round on them that close?" Donlon asked.

"I don't know, sir, but we can try," Woods replied.

Manhandling the heavy steel tube to a nearly vertical position, the two dropped a round down the barrel. It landed on target, but was a dud.

Cursing, Donlon fed the weapon another round. The stumps blew sky-high, taking the enemy with them. Except for occasional small-arms fire that continued for several more hours, the battle for Nam Dong was over. It was almost 7:00 A.M.

One hundred fifty-four Viet Cong died during the fight. Over fifty ARVN and Nungs were killed. Two Americans died; seven were wounded. Donlon refused evacuation until his wounded men were treated. Only when assured that they had received the necessary medical attention would he allow his own wounds to be tended. Later that day he was evacuated. He spent over a month in a hospital in Saigon, where his visitors included General Westmoreland and Ambassador Maxwell Taylor. In his first battle Donlon had led a magnificent fight, and word of his exploits quickly spread.

When he recovered from his wounds, Donlon rejoined the surviving members of his A-team. They completed their six-month tour in South Vietnam in November 1964 and flew home together.

The nine survivors gathered with Donlon at the White House on December 5, 1964, where President Johnson presented Captain Donlon with the Medal of Honor for his "conspicuous gallantry and intrepid leadership" in defending Nam Dong.

Donlon was justifiably proud of his team members. "The medal belongs to them, too," he told the president.

Donlon remained in the army, wrote a book about his experiences, and served another tour in South Vietnam. He retired in 1988 as a colonel after a distinguished career that included command of the 3d Battalion, 7th Special Forces in Panama, the United Nations Command in Japan, and several tours as an instructor at the Command and General Staff College at Fort Leavenworth, Kansas. Today he is a much sought after public speaker.

CHAPTER THREE

America Goes to War

One month after the attack on Donlon's jungle encampment, on August 2, 1964 the U.S. Navy destroyer *Maddox* was on patrol off the coast of North Vietnam on an electronic surveillance assignment. Unknown to the *Maddox*'s crew, ARVN commandos were conducting raids on two nearby North Vietnamese islands, Hon Me and Hon Ngu. Although the *Maddox* had no role in the raids, the electronic eavesdroppers aboard the vessel recorded increasingly frequent references to their ship among the North Vietnamese radio traffic. Comdr. Herbert L. Ogier, captain of the *Maddox,* was sufficiently alarmed to request clarifying instructions from his headquarters. The reply was terse: "Resume itinerary."

Just after 2:00 P.M. that afternoon, the *Maddox*'s radio center intercepted a North Vietnamese message: Three PT boats were ordered out from Hon Me to attack the *Maddox.* The North Vietnamese had assumed that the *Maddox* was in control of the covert operation. The enemy PT boats raced toward the lone destroyer at a speed of fifty knots. Commander Ogier sounded battle stations. "This is not a drill," he announced.

At 3:08 P.M. two of the destroyer's six five-inch guns fired. The PT boats remained on course. Three minutes later the *Maddox* opened up with all six guns. The exploding shells raised huge plumes of ocean water around the enemy craft. The PT boats spread out and spit torpedoes at the *Maddox.* The destroyer zigged and zagged to evade the deadly underwater missiles. *Maddox*'s gunners continued to fire. One of their rounds connected with a PT boat. It stopped dead in the water. A second PT boat slowed, damaged by a near hit.

At that moment four F-8 Crusaders from the carrier USS *Ticonderoga* appeared overhead in response to Ogier's earlier request for help. With their 20mm cannons blazing away, the jets drove off the PT boats. The entire engagement lasted but eight minutes.

The deliberations over a proper response to the attack involved top government officials, including President Johnson. It was decided to continue the patrols. The American government took the position that their ships were in international waters and that they had every right to cruise the Gulf of Tonkin free from harassment. To emphasize that position, a second destroyer, the *Turner Joy,* was added to the patrol. Also, constant air cover would protect the vessels. The gauntlet had been thrown down to the North Vietnamese, but no one told Commander Ogier about the commando raids.

On the night of August 4, a pitch-black, stormy night, the *Maddox*'s radar picked up unidentified surface blips approaching the two destroyers. The blips appeared and disappeared, possibly due to the effects of the adverse weather. At 9:30 P.M. the blips seemed to gather speed as they bore down on the *Maddox*. The *Turner Joy* also reported that it had picked up the blips.

When the blips approached the four-thousand-yard range, the two destroyers opened fire. The inky blackness prevented the sailors from seeing either the enemy vessels or the explosions of their own shells. There were those aboard the two destroyers who doubted whether the enemy vessels really existed. They thought the blips were due to the effect of the nearby storms on their radar, a not uncommon event. Yet some crewmen aboard the *Turner Joy* reported that they had seen a torpedo pass within one hundred feet of the ship.

Eight jets from the *Ticonderoga* appeared overhead but found no evidence of enemy surface craft. The *Maddox* and *Turner Joy* continued to fire at the blips while they took evasive action against reported enemy torpedoes, but still had no visual contact with the enemy. Within thirty minutes the "attack" was over. The two destroyers broke off the "engagement" and resumed their patrol. The presence of the enemy vessels was never confirmed.

On the basis of this second attack, President Johnson ordered retaliatory air strikes against North Vietnamese torpedo boat bases. He also told his key advisers to draft a congressional resolution that endorsed his action and allowed him wide latitude in his responses to any further hostilities in Vietnam. On August 7, Congress approved these measures with the Gulf of Tonkin Resolution.

The first major step toward committing the United States to the war in South Vietnam had been taken.

The second major step came six months later, after the Viet Cong attacked a U.S. Army installation near Pleiku in South Vietnam's Central Highlands. On February 7, 1965, four hundred soldiers of the 52d Combat Aviation Battalion were retired for the night when enemy 82mm mortar rounds crashed down on their barracks. VC sappers raced through the camp, blowing up helicopters and planes with satchel charges and firing automatic weapons at the Americans.

The GIs reacted instantly. They manned defensive positions. Firemen doused fires on the aircraft. Uninjured soldiers carried their wounded comrades to safety.

In fifteen minutes the attack was over. It had cost the Americans seven dead and more than one hundred wounded.

The next morning, presidential assistant McGeorge Bundy, who happened to be in South Vietnam on a factfinding mission for President Johnson, visited the base accompanied by General Westmoreland. In Westmoreland's words, once Bundy "smelled a little gunpowder he developed a field marshal's psychosis." Bundy, a former army captain, sent a message to the White House with one suggestion: Strike back.

Twelve hours after the attack on Pleiku, forty-nine navy bombers attacked Dong Hoi, a guerrilla training camp forty miles north of the seventeenth parallel—in North Vietnam.

On February 10, 1965, near Qui Nhon, the Viet Cong blew up a barracks that housed members of the U.S. Army's 140th

Maintenance Detachment. Twenty-three Americans died and twenty-two were wounded in the attack.

The next day, 160 U.S. and South Vietnamese planes streaked northward to strike VC staging areas in North Vietnam. Further, President Johnson agreed on February 13 to execute a program of "measured air action" against North Vietnamese targets. Under the code name Rolling Thunder, twice weekly air raids would hit selected targets in North Vietnam.

Because the air force base at Da Nang provided most of the support for Rolling Thunder, General Westmoreland became concerned about the base's security. He had no faith in the South Vietnamese troops that guarded it. Westmoreland cabled the Pentagon asking for two battalions of U.S. Marines to guard the complex. Four days later the approval was granted. The final step toward major U.S. involvement in South Vietnam had been taken.

At 9:18 A.M. on March 8, 1965, the 3d Battalion, 9th Marines, 9th Marine Expeditionary Brigade, began to land at Red Beach Two just north of Da Nang. Two hours later the 1st Battalion, 3d Marines, arrived by aircraft from Okinawa. The Marines deployed to defensive positions around Da Nang.

Justification for Johnson's actions came on March 29 when a car bomb exploded outside the U.S. embassy in Saigon, killing and wounding dozens of embassy employees. Two more Marine infantry battalions and one Marine air squadron were deployed to South Vietnam. By April 6, twenty-seven thousand American fighting men were in South Vietnam. The United States was there for keeps.

During their first few weeks in-country, the newly arrived forces were generally limited to purely defensive roles. The bulk of the actual fighting was still the exclusive work of isolated Special Forces detachments.

In the Viet Cong attack on the camp at Dong Xoai, fifty-five miles north of Saigon, on June 10–13, 1965, two men earned the war's second and third Medals of Honor.

During the fourteen-hour initial assault on the camp, thirty-one-year-old second lieutenant *Charles Q. Williams* assumed command of the camp after its CO was seriously wounded in the early minutes of the battle. The South Carolinian repeatedly dashed through heavy gunfire to rally the outnumbered defenders. He received five wounds during the fight.

At one point the American forces were pinned down by a VC machine gun. Williams grabbed a 3.5-inch rocket launcher and asked for a volunteer to help him go after the gun. *Marvin G. Shields,* a twenty-six-year-old member of the camp's navy construction battalion who had already been wounded three times, stepped forward.

The intrepid duo completely ignored the extremely heavy enemy fire to creep toward the enemy gun position. In full view of the VC, the pair knelt together, Shields loading, Williams firing. With one well-placed shot they destroyed the enemy gun and broke the back of the attack. Unfortunately, on the way back to safety, Shields was mortally wounded.

In the words of Williams's citation, he "continued to rally his men, to protect the wounded, and to hold off the enemy until help arrived."

When President Johnson presented the medal to Williams on June 23, 1966, the gallant father of three said, "I had a mission to perform and I did it. The thought that I was a hero didn't occur to me. I just wanted to protect my men."

Joan Elaine Shields accepted her husband's posthumous Medal of Honor from President Johnson on September 13, 1966. The president called Shields "a new kind of fighting man, forged and tempered in a new kind of war, who gave his life for his country, his comrades, and a good cause." Shields is the only Seabee to have earned his country's highest award.

The U.S. Marine Corps had never trained for a defensive mission. It seemed unlikely that their assigned role as security guards around the air force base at Da Nang would last too long. The young, aggressive Marines were not content to sit idle while they waited for the Viet Cong to attack them. Within weeks of their landing, the Marines were on the offensive. They sent out patrols that ranged several miles from the base, on the lookout for any guerrillas intent on attacking the air base. It was not long before the two forces clashed.

On July 11 a platoon of Company D, 3d Reconnaissance Battalion, became embroiled with VC forces just south of Da Nang where Highway 1 crosses the Cau Do River. The Marines were heavily outnumbered. Reinforcements were fed into the fight and the battle raged throughout the afternoon before the VC pulled back. Battalion headquarters decided to send a small force out the next day to land south of the battlefield and sweep north, looking for the VC. Company A, 3d Reconnaissance Battalion, received the mission.

FRANK S. REASONER

A platoon from Company A—seventeen Marines, one navy corpsman, and an ARVN dog handler and his animal—stepped off helicopters outside the village of Dai Loc about ten air miles south of Da Nang about noon on July 12. Accompanying the small force was the company commander, *1st Lt. Frank S. Reasoner*. It was a little unusual for the CO to join such a small patrol, but Reasoner had been in command of Company A for only two weeks. This mission would give him a chance to get to know his troops better. That was important to him.

At twenty-nine Reasoner was old for a lieutenant, but he had already been in the Marine Corps for twelve years. Born in Spokane, Washington, on September 16, 1937, Reasoner moved with his family to Kellogg, Idaho, when he was ten. Just after graduation from high school in 1955 he enlisted in the Marines.

Reasoner served three years before he received a special congressional appointment to the U.S. Military Academy. At

West Point he excelled in baseball, wrestling, and boxing. In 1962 he was designated the academy's outstanding boxer, winning an unprecedented four straight brigade championships in four different weight classes.

When Reasoner graduated in June 1962, he was appointed a Marine Corps second lieutenant. His first and only assignment was with the 3d Reconnaissance Battalion. He joined them in Hawaii in January 1963 and went with Company B to Da Nang in April 1965.

A short, stocky man, Reasoner often spoke of his wife Sally and their young son Mike back in Idaho. After a difficult day's work, he liked to retire to his tent to spend several hours writing to his wife about his life in the war zone. A common topic was the young men in his charge. As a former enlisted man, Reasoner exhibited a tremendous concern for his Marines. He went out of his way to see to their welfare. He would not rest until his men had settled in. He refused to eat until his men had had their chow. He saw to it that none of his officers had any "creature comforts" not shared by the enlisted men.

Reasoner was well respected by his Marines, and he in turn respected them. It pained him deeply when one of his men was wounded. It was difficult for him to write a letter to a casualty's next of kin. He tried to write as comforting a letter as he could in hope of easing a mother's or wife's pain.

The lieutenant's performance as a platoon leader in Company B impressed his superiors so much that when the command of Company A became available, they did not hesitate to put Reasoner in charge. The patrol south of Da Nang would be his first since taking command.

Helicopters inserted the patrol into a landing zone (LZ) near Dai Loc. After setting up a radio relay team at the ARVN fort there, Reasoner led his men down a dirt road that headed north out of the village. The first three hours passed uneventfully. Then as the men approached the small hamlet of An My 4 several rounds of poorly aimed sniper fire cracked overhead. Reasoner sent the platoon commander, 2d

Lt. William Henderson, and eight men on a flanking movement to the west; he and the rest of the patrol would continue into the village.

The village was ominously quiet as the little band moved cautiously through it. No villagers were in evidence. Beyond the village the two point men spotted a pair of armed Viet Cong in a tree line about two hundred yards to their left front. The Marines got off several shots at the figures and almost immediately came under fire from an enemy machine gun emplaced on a small knoll west of the tree line. As the Marines hit the deck, the enemy fire built rapidly as dozens of VC in the tree line and on the knoll opened up. It was later estimated that a force of 75 to 100 enemy soldiers had ambushed the platoon.

From his position a few yards behind the point men and completely exposed to the building enemy fire, Reasoner organized the men around him. He had them put out a base of fire that would allow the point men to pull back.

"Come on, Marines," he shouted. "Give 'em hell! Pick your targets. Don't waste any ammo."

Inspired by Reasoner's courage, the isolated Marines began to return the fire. Over the next three hours Reasoner repeatedly exposed himself to the enemy fire to guide his men. He personally killed two VC and knocked out an enemy automatic weapon that had prevented the evacuation of a wounded man. He pointed out targets, directed the fire of his men, and encouraged them through his words and actions.

Because the radios carried by the patrol did not have much range, Reasoner could not call in supporting arms. Lieutenant Henderson had entered the village from the west, but could not link up with Reasoner and the forward elements due to the enemy fire. Reasoner and his men were trapped.

When his radio operator, L.Cpl. (Lance Corporal) James Shockley, was wounded, Reasoner ignored the enemy fire to move to the youngster's side. "Take it easy," Reasoner spoke calmly. "You'll be okay. We'll get you out of here."

With cool determination, Reasoner applied a battle dressing to the wound. When finished, he gave Shockley a reassuring pat. "You're going to make it," Reasoner told him.

Reasoner moved away from Shockley and shouted encouragement to his men. As he did, Shockley began to crawl toward a nearby ditch. When the VC spotted the movement, they concentrated their fire on him. Shockley screamed in pain as he was hit again.

Reasoner ignored the wall of enemy fire and ran to Shockley's side. His only thought was to get the radio operator to safety. He had just reached Shockley when a burst of enemy machine gun fire ripped into Reasoner's belly, killing him instantly. He crumpled alongside Shockley.

As night approached, one of the radiomen was able to contact a flight of H-34 helicopters flying nearby. The pilots instantly agreed to extract the patrol. Lieutenant Henderson ordered everyone to pull back to the south side of the village. Two men went forward and retrieved Reasoner's body and Shockley.

By the time the helicopters arrived it was 9:00 P.M. and dark. Someone tossed an illumination grenade onto the LZ to guide the helicopters in. As the battered platoon members climbed aboard, enemy rounds smacked into the aluminum aircraft. When the helicopters landed at Da Nang, a young corporal sobbed uncontrollably as he jumped off. "My skipper's dead. He should be covered up. Will someone get a blanket?"

Navy secretary Paul H. Nitze presented Reasoner's posthumous Medal of Honor to his widow and son in ceremonies at the Pentagon on January 31, 1967. Nitze said of Reasoner, "[His] complete disregard for his own welfare will long serve as an inspiring example to others."

Back in South Vietnam, the 3d Reconnaissance Battalion named its post at Da Nang in honor of the gallant officer.

Five weeks after Lieutenant Reasoner died, twenty-two-year-old corporal *Robert E. O'Malley* became the first Marine to survive his Medal of Honor exploits in South Vietnam.

In early August 1965, Marine intelligence received word that the VC intended to attack the isolated Marine base at Chu Lai, south of Da Nang. The Marine operations officer recommended a spoiling attack to prevent that from happening. The offensive was dubbed Operation Starlite. It would be the first major engagement between U.S. and Viet Cong forces.

In the early morning hours of August 18, O'Malley's unit, Company I, 3d Battalion, 3d Marines, made an amphibious landing near the village of An Cuong 1. The Marines' mission was to push north and clear the area of any VC. The operation proceeded smoothly until the company tried to clear An Cuong 2 of enemy snipers. Without warning, a blast of enemy small-arms fire forced the Marines to withdraw. As Capt. Bruce D. Webb tried to reorganize his command, he was killed. Webb's executive officer, 1st Lt. Richard M. Purnell, assumed command of Company I.

While Purnell prepared the company for a counterassault, O'Malley spotted a trench that held an enemy squad. With complete disregard for his own safety, O'Malley raced across an open rice paddy to the trench. He jumped in and used his rifle and hand grenades to kill eight VC. He then returned to his squad and led it to the relief of a pinned-down platoon.

"It was like watching the U.S. cavalry come over the hill," Purnell recalled. "Under Corporal O'Malley's expert leadership, the threatened Marines were able to drive off a fanatical enemy attack."

Ignoring three wounds he received in this action, O'Malley personally assisted several wounded Marines to an evacuation point. Next, he took his squad to the area of heaviest fighting. There, he helped repel another VC assault.

Ordered by Purnell to secure a landing zone for a medevac, O'Malley led his besieged and badly wounded squad members to the LZ. Although himself eligible for evacuation, O'Malley refused to climb aboard the chopper. Instead, he moved to an exposed position and delivered telling suppressive fire against the enemy until all the other wounded were removed. Only then did he allow his injuries to be treated. Fortunately, his wounds were not serious enough to incapacitate him.

O'Malley, a native of Woodside, Queens, New York, received his medal from President Johnson in an impressive ceremony at the Texas White House on December 6, 1966.

The first major army combat unit to arrive in South Vietnam was the elite 173d Airborne Brigade. Formed on Okinawa in May 1963, the 173d began as a test unit and developed many of the tactics it would later put to good use in South Vietnam. It also was designated as the U.S. Army's ready-reaction force for the Pacific Theater. It was thus inevitable that the Sky Soldiers would be tapped for duty in the war zone.

On May 7, 1965 the 173d came ashore at Vung Tau, at the mouth of the Saigon River. The unit's initial assignment was for ninety days temporary duty; they stayed in-country more than six years. The brigade set up headquarters at Bien Hoa, twelve miles north of Saigon, where their mission was to guard the U.S. Air Force base there. Like the Marines at Da Nang, though, it was only a matter of time before the paratroopers went on the offensive.

The brigade's first significant contact with the Viet Cong came on June 10, 1965 when one of its battalions was sent to aid the ARVN unit trying to secure the area around the embattled Special Forces camp at Dong Xoai. On June 28–30, the paratroopers conducted the first officially announced search-and-destroy mission of the Vietnam War. Held within the notorious War Zone D, twenty miles northwest of Saigon, the initial effort was inconclusive. The sixty-square-mile area, also known as the Iron Triangle, would be visited many times by the Sky Soldiers.

MILTON LEE OLIVE III

He was an unlikely-looking hero. A kind, delicate face was *Milton Lee Olive*'s chief feature. He was a soft-spoken, gentle youth who grew up in a middle-income black neighborhood on Chicago's South Side. Olive's mother died when he was a youngster, leaving a void quickly filled by his stepmother, Antoinette, a Chicago public school teacher. His father and Antoinette raised Milton as their own natural son.

A desire for adventure caught young Milton between his junior and senior years at Saints Junior College High School. He had had his fill of school. There was a whole world beyond Chicago's South Side that he wanted to see. Father and son sat down one evening and talked. Although he wanted his son to finish high school, Milton Olive II understood the need to fulfill one's dreams. In addition, blacks were beginning to reap the benefits of President Johnson's Great Society programs. A three-year tour in the army might do young Olive more good than another year of high school. The senior Olive consented to his son's enlistment.

Olive entered the U.S. Army on August 17, 1964, three months short of his eighteenth birthday. Basic training followed at Fort Knox, Kentucky. After basic, Olive was assigned to advanced training at the Artillery School at Fort Sill, Oklahoma. The lure of fifty dollars a month extra pay, however, drew Olive to the Airborne infantry. In April 1965 he reported to the Airborne School at Fort Benning, Georgia. Upon graduation from the course he was assigned to the 173d's 2d Battalion, 503d Infantry, then already deployed in South Vietnam.

By the time the summer of 1965 was over, Private First Class Olive was a hardened combat veteran. Though not yet nineteen years old, he had participated in the heavy fighting in War Zone D as well as in numerous firefights with the VC. He had witnessed more death in those four months than most adults see in a lifetime. He understood what fear was and had learned how to overcome it. He was well respected by both the officers and enlisted men of his unit, Company B. In spite of the numerous hardships encountered by the Sky Soldiers, Olive maintained a positive sense of humor that inspired the members of his platoon. Some called him "Preacher" because he frequently read from his well-worn Bible. No task was too hard for him. He did what needed to be done without complaint. He was a good soldier.

On October 22, 1965, Olive's company was on a routine patrol near Phu Cuong, about thirty-five miles northwest of Saigon on the southern fringes of the Iron Triangle. As the unit moved through the thick jungle, it was subjected to varying degrees of enemy fire. Several times the company was pinned down temporarily. Each time the men rallied to drive off the VC.

Private First Class Olive was in the forefront of most of these counterattacks. Without hesitation he repeatedly exposed himself to hostile fire to repulse the enemy.

Late in the afternoon Olive and four other soldiers, including his platoon commander, 1st Lt. James Sanford, moved through dense jungle foliage in pursuit of a band of VC. As the grunts moved stealthily through the thick jungle, a VC threw a hand grenade into their midst.

Although he knew full well the risk, Olive dashed forward, scooped up the deadly missile, and moved away from the others. "I've got it," he yelled as he tucked the grenade into his middle and fell on it to absorb the full, deadly blast.

"It was the most incredible display of selfless bravery I ever witnessed," Lieutenant Sanford later said.

Eighteen-year-old Milton Lee Olive's willingness to sacrifice his own life saved the lives of four other soldiers.

Six months later, when he was notified of the Medal of Honor awarded to his only son, Milton Olive II penned a letter to President Johnson. In it he said:

It is our dream and prayer that some day the Asiatics, the Europeans, the Israelites, the Africans, the Australians, the Latins, and the Americans can all live in One-World. It is our hope that in our country the Klansmen, the Negroes, the Hebrews, and the Catholics will sit down together in the common purpose of goodwill and dedication; that the moral and creative intelligence of our united people will pick up the chalice of wisdom and place it upon the mountaintop of human integrity; that all mankind, from all the earth, shall resolve "to study war no more."

The city of Chicago honored its deceased warrior hero by naming in his memory a junior college, a lakefront park, and a portion of its McCormick Place convention center.

Two weeks after Olive died, a twenty-year army veteran became the first living African American to earn the Medal of Honor since the Spanish-American War. (Two blacks had died earning their medals during the Korean War. In 1991, Congress approved a posthumous Medal of Honor for an African American veteran killed in World War I. In 1997, Congress granted seven black World War II veterans the Medal of Honor; only one of these men was alive at that time.)

Sp5. (Specialist Fifth Class) Lawrence Joel was a medic with the 1st Battalion, 503d Infantry, 173d Airborne Brigade, when that unit was attacked in the Iron Triangle by a numerically superior and well-concealed enemy force on November 8, 1965.

In spite of a severe leg wound suffered in the early stages of the battle, Joel moved from man to man and administered first aid. He was wounded a second time, the bullet lodging deep in his thigh, but continued to treat his wounded comrades, completely oblivious to the battle raging around him. At one point the thirty-eight-year-old father of two saved a man's life by placing a discarded plastic bag on the casualty's sucking chest wound.

Even after the twenty-four-hour battle had subsided and 410 VC had been killed, Joel never lost sight of his mission. He continued to comfort and treat the wounded until his own evacuation was ordered.

On March 9, 1967, President Johnson presented the Medal of Honor to Joel in ceremonies held on the South Lawn of the White House. That much room was needed to accommodate Joel's wife and children, his beaming parents, his nine brothers and sisters, his foster parents, and his five foster brothers and sisters.

By the end of the summer of 1965, the United States was fully committed to the ever-expanding war in Southeast Asia. General Westmoreland had received permission to use U.S. troops "in any situation." With that dictum, his next request was predictable: Send more troops.

There were no more maneuver battalions available in the Pacific Theater. It was time to deploy an entire division directly from the United States. Just the unit Westmoreland wanted was waiting at Fort Benning, Georgia.

Organized in July 1963 as a test division, the 11th Airborne Division had spent the next year and one-half perfecting the new "airmobile" tactics championed by Secretary of Defense Robert S. McNamara. Fully trained in the new doctrine of the helicopter, the unit was eager to prove itself under fire. When it was ordered to South Vietnam, the division swapped colors with a unit based in Korea. In September 1965 the newly designated 1st Cavalry Division (Airmobile) relocated to South Vietnam.

The division set up its headquarters at An Khe in Binh Dinh Province, a part of the II Corps Tactical Zone in central South Vietnam. The unit barely had time to acclimate itself to the brutally hot environment of Southeast Asia when one of its battalions was sent to the aid of an ARVN unit under attack near Pleiku, in the Central Highlands along the Laotian border. Once the siege at the isolated camp at Plei Me had been broken, division commander Maj. Gen. Harry W. B. Kinnard received permission from General Westmoreland to "find, fix, and defeat the enemy forces that had threatened Plei Me." The cavalrymen would meet the enemy in a one-thousand-square-mile area southwest of Pleiku known as the Ia Drang Valley for the river that drained the region. It would be the first major battle between American forces and members of the North Vietnamese Army (NVA).

As part of the U.S. offensive operation, Lt. Col. Harold G. Moore's 1st Battalion, 7th Cavalry, 1st Cavalry Division (Airmobile), aggressively swept its assigned section—only to find it empty of the enemy. Determined to close with the NVA, Moore requested and received permission to move his battalion farther west, near the Chu Pong Massif that straddled the border. By noon of November 14, 1965, most of his men had choppered into LZ X-ray. The companies fanned out in search of the enemy.

Moore was spoiling for a fight. His men had been in the Ia Drang Valley for five days, with only sporadic contact with the foe. Moore wanted more.

So did the local NVA commander. From his position in the Chu Pong Massif, the North Vietnamese officer watched the helicopters deposit the largely untried American soldiers. He knew that the only way to find out how these Americans would fight was to attack them. He gave the order. Two full regiments, the 33d and 66th, of North Vietnamese regulars started down the hill.

Moore's Company B had advanced only a short distance beyond LZ X-ray when it came under fire from the NVA. Within minutes the unit was pinned down. Moore ordered Company A to relieve the isolated troops.

WALTER J. MARM, JR.

2d Lt. Walter J. "Joe" Marm, Jr. was a platoon leader in Company A. A twenty-three-year-old native of Washington, Pennsylvania, Marm had enlisted in the army the previous June after receiving a degree in business from Duquesne University in Pittsburgh. He joined the 7th Cavalry upon completion of his officer candidate school and arrived in South Vietnam in September 1965.

As Marm's platoon moved through the thick scrub brush toward Company B, it was subjected to increasingly heavy enemy fire. Marm quickly realized that this was no ordinary fight. The NVA were well organized. Their fire was deliberate and well controlled, not the sporadic volleys the Americans had seen in earlier contacts. The NVA were determined to keep Marm's platoon from reaching its objective.

Marm took cover under a withering hail of fire and directed his squad into a tight defensive perimeter. Seconds later he detected four NVA moving to flank him. Shouting "I'll take 'em," Marm moved forward under heavy fire and killed all four.

Marm next saw that his men were receiving heavy fire from an enemy machine gun. Unable to pinpoint its exact location, he deliberately exposed himself to draw the NVA's fire so that his men could spot the gun. Once the weapon's position was known, Marm tried to destroy it with an anti-tank weapon. His fire caused casualties among the enemy crew but did not silence the weapon.

Frustrated by his ineffectiveness but still determined to destroy the gun, Marm moved across thirty yards of open ground to a better position behind a tall anthill. From there he hurled grenades into the enemy position, killing several of the NVA who manned the gun.

As Marm prepared to move forward to finish off the position, an enemy rifle round tore into his face. Severely wounded, the young officer fell to the ground. Momentarily stunned by the blow and the resulting pain, Marm resumed his mission. He crawled forward, determined to relieve the pressure on his platoon. Armed with only an M-14 rifle, Marm picked off the remaining gun crew one by one. Only when assured that his platoon was safe did Marm consent to have his wounds treated. His selfless actions had reduced the fire on his platoon, broken the enemy assault, and allowed his company to continue its mission.

The battle at LZ X-ray raged into the night and the next day before the NVA withdrew. Casualties were heavy on both sides; the Americans lost 79 dead and 121 wounded. The NVA left more than 634 bodies in the jungle. It was an expensive but valuable lesson for both commanders.

Marm was evacuated from the battlefield before the fight

ended. He spent four months in the hospital recovering from his wound, then returned to active duty.

Marm received his Medal of Honor on December 19, 1966. He remained in the army and retired as a colonel. He then began a new career as a schoolteacher in North Carolina.

HARVEY C. BARNUM, JR.

The last Medal of Honor earned in 1965 went to twenty-five-year-old Marine first lieutenant *Harvey C. Barnum, Jr.* A native of Cheshire, Connecticut, Barnum was commissioned in 1962 through the platoon leaders class at Saint Anselm College in Manchester, New Hampshire. Trained as an artillery officer, Barnum was the guard officer at the Marine Barracks at Pearl Harbor, Hawaii, in 1965 when the Marine Corps announced a new program designed to broaden the experience level of junior officers and staff noncommissioned officers. Selected officers would be temporarily assigned to duty in South Vietnam for two months. Upon their return to their duty station, they could then share their experiences and new knowledge with other Marines, preparing them for their eventual tours of duty in the war zone. Barnum immediately volunteered for the program. He arrived in Da Nang on December 4, 1965 and was assigned to Company H, 2d Battalion, 9th Marines, as an artillery forward observer.

Company H was temporarily attached to the 2d Battalion, 7th Marines, then in the final stages of Operation Harvest Moon. The four-company battalion was sweeping eastward toward Tam Ky, on Highway 1, along the Khang River, about eight miles south of Que Son in Quang Tin Province. Heavy monsoonal rains had plagued the battalion for several days. The ground was so saturated that fifty-four men with immersion foot were evacuated during a temporary break in the weather on the morning of December 18. After the medevac, Company G, 2/7, headed out in the point position. It was followed by Company F; then came Headquarters and

Service Company. Company H, 2/9, brought up the rear. The column moved along a narrow dirt road that snaked its way through hedgerow-lined rice paddies.

Shortly after noon Company G passed through the little hamlet of Ky Phu, about eight miles west of Tam Ky. As they proceeded east, harassing enemy fire broke out along their south flank. The battalion commander, Lt. Col. Leon N. Utter, traveling with H&S Company, ordered Company G to deploy along the south side of the trail while Company F advanced into supporting positions.

No sooner had Utter issued these orders than enemy mortar rounds dropped on H&S Company, which was still west of Ky Phu in the middle of some rice paddies. Suddenly two companies of Viet Cong intent on isolating H&S charged out of the nearby tree lines. Utter radioed Company F to reverse direction and support H&S.

With this help, H&S fought its way clear of the VC and made it into Ky Phu. This now left Barnum and Company H isolated some five hundred yards west of Ky Phu. The VC turned its forces in that direction. Simultaneous attacks from both flanks and the rear pinned down the Marines of Company H. The opening blast of enemy rifle fire killed the company commander and his radio operator.

Barnum, under fire for the first time, was only yards away from the fallen company commander. A quick assessment of the situation told Barnum that the company's platoon leaders were scattered and busy with their own segments of the battle. He noticed several young Marines nearby looking at him for instruction. He later said, "This is what being a Marine is all about. You train and train and when you have to do something, you do it right. I was too busy for fear. You do what has to be done at the time."

Barnum pulled the radio from the dead operator's back and went to work. He advised Utter of the company's situation and, with the battalion commander's sanction, took command. Rallying the decimated company, he organized a tight defensive perimeter. For the next five hours the company fought a well-disciplined and entrenched enemy. This artillery officer, so new to the war, rose to the occasion. He first directed the fire of supporting artillery on the enemy positions. Then, when a pair of UH-1E "Huey" helicopter gunships came on station, Barnum directed their fire by radio. At one point he stood completely exposed atop a small hill to personally direct the gunships' fire on a pesky enemy automatic weapons position. It was destroyed in the attack.

With the resultant letup in enemy fire, Barnum called for a medevac. Again ignoring enemy fire, he stood in the open to direct the helicopters in and supervise the evacuation of casualties. With this task completed, he turned his attention back to the VC.

Because the battalion's other companies were still engaged with the enemy around Ky Phu, there was no one to help Company H. If the company were to break out of the ambush, it would have to do so on its own. That meant fighting its way across five hundred yards of open rice paddy. Barnum knew it had to be done.

Barnum ordered the survivors to lighten their loads. After blowing up all of the extraneous matériel, Barnum ordered his Marines toward Ky Phu. They fought a running gun battle as they dashed across the open ground, picking up and carrying any new casualties. No one was left behind. As darkness neared, what was left of Company H burst through the cordon of Marines around Ky Phu.

Now faced with attacking a tight, well-organized Marine perimeter, the VC broke contact. They left 104 of their comrades on the battlefield. The Marines lost 11 killed and 71 wounded.

Barnum completed his two-month tour in February 1966 and returned to his post in Hawaii. One year later he was presented his Medal of Honor. In October 1968 he returned to South Vietnam and took command of an artillery battery in the 12th Marines. During this tour he added two Bronze Stars and a Purple Heart to his awards.

In August 1989, Barnum retired as a colonel. He worked in a number of civilian and government jobs before being appointed deputy assistant secretary of the navy for reserve affairs in 2001. Barnum also has served two terms as president of the Congressional Medal of Honor Society, composed solely of living recipients of this august decoration.

By the end of 1965, 184,000 American military personnel were in South Vietnam. Their presence indicated the U.S. government's strong commitment to assisting the South Vietnamese in their struggle against external aggression. It would be the courage of the individual fighting man, though, that would have to enforce that commitment.

CHAPTER FOUR

Search-and-Destroy Operations

After testing each other's resolve in the latter part of 1965, U.S. and North Vietnamese forces spent the next few months consolidating their positions and building up their troop strength. Military Assistance Command, Vietnam (MACV) started 1966 with three divisions—the 3d Marine, 1st Infantry, and 1st Cavalry—and two separate brigades—the 1st Brigade of the 101st Airborne Division, and the 173d Airborne Brigade. Over the next twelve months, four additional divisions—the 1st Marine, 4th Infantry, 9th Infantry, and 25th Infantry—plus three more brigades—the 11th Armored Cavalry Regiment and the 196th and 199th Infantry Brigades—poured into South Vietnam.

These new units, composed of mostly green, conscripted troops, arrived in-country anxious for combat with the NVA, eager to save the little country from communism. Filled with visions of the large-scale attacks used in World War II and Korea, the new troops quickly had their hopes dashed when they learned that the traditional military strategy of seizing and holding terrain objectives was not being used in South Vietnam.

Shortly after General Westmoreland took command of MACV in 1964, he defined the American military's overall strategy as one whereby units would "find, fix in place, fight, and destroy" enemy forces and their base areas. It was in essence a war of attrition. According to Westmoreland's doctrine, if his soldiers simply killed enough of the enemy, the VC and NVA would lose their will to fight. To an army—

and a nation—accustomed to liberating towns to the riotous cheers of once-captive people, this slow, costly program of "search and destroy" would prove frustrating. In addition, Westmoreland never considered that the loss of national will to pursue the war because of high casualties and no victory could work against him.

The fresh American troops soon learned too that they had to fight this war of attrition according to rules that differed from those used by the enemy. United States forces and their allies were generally prohibited from attacking the enemy in his base camps across the borders in North Vietnam, Laos, or Cambodia. They could not even pursue fleeing enemy troops that crossed these borders. They could not call in supporting arms on enemy positions across these borders. Allied forces could not unilaterally fire their small arms or supporting weapons at suspected targets. In many cases, permission to fire had to come from the local South Vietnamese province chief and/or from a higher level in the military's chain of command.

The North Vietnamese regulars and the Viet Cong were free to do what they wanted, whenever and wherever they wanted.

Westmoreland's primary campaign effort for 1966 was to secure base areas for the incoming units, open and secure lines of communications, and acclimate the arriving units to the area warfare practiced in South Vietnam. To search out and destroy the enemy, new units went on "reconnaissance-in-force" missions. A small force, occasionally as large as a battalion, would conduct patrols in hopes of clashing with the enemy. If a firefight developed, the superior American firepower would be brought to bear and the enemy destroyed.

It was a tough way to fight a war because the ground troops were essentially pawns. But the tactics produced numerous instances of unusual bravery.

JAMES A. GARDNER

On February 7, 1966, the 1st Battalion, 327th Infantry, 101st Airborne Division, was on a routine reconnaissance-in-force mission near the village of My Canh in Pleiku Province when superior enemy forces in well-fortified positions pinned down one of its companies. The company commander tried to move his platoons forward, but to no avail. Attempts to outflank the village also failed due to heavy fire from enemy automatic weapons and mortars. He called for air strikes and artillery, but their combined effort still failed to dislodge the enemy.

Battalion headquarters dispatched several other companies to attack the village from another direction, but unless they moved quickly, the pinned-down company would be destroyed.

1st Lt. James A. Gardner led one of the relief platoons from the battalion's Headquarters and Headquarters Company. A native of Dyersburg, Tennessee, Gardner had briefly attended West Point in 1961, then spent a year at the University of Tennessee before enlisting in the army. After basic training at Fort Polk, Louisiana, Gardner went to the Infantry Officer Candidate School at Fort Benning, Georgia. When he was commissioned, he was assigned to the 101st Airborne Division at Fort Campbell, Kentucky. When that unit sent a brigade to South Vietnam in July 1965, Gardner went with it.

Lieutenant Gardner was ordered to take his platoon around behind My Canh and attack the enemy from the rear. No sooner had the platoon commenced its movement than it was pinned down by heavy small-arms fire from a series of supporting bunkers. Gardner pressed his men hard and they advanced a few yards, but the intense enemy fire stymied his mission.

"Stay here and give me covering fire," Gardner told his platoon sergeant.

The young officer ran through the withering fire. He splashed across a rice paddy then reached the first enemy bunker. Without a moment's hesitation he flipped a grenade into the position. It erupted with a roar.

Even before the smoke cleared from that attack, Gardner was on his way to a second bunker. Another grenade was tossed and a second enemy position was destroyed.

To avoid the enemy fire now concentrated on him, Gardner low-crawled through the paddy water to reach the third position. Although the berm around the paddy offered some protection from the enfilading fire, the splashes of water erupting around Gardner gave evidence that the enemy knew he was coming. Once in position, Gardner readied a third grenade. Suddenly the enemy gunner darted out of his bunker and made straight for Gardner. Gardner raised his M-16. The enemy gunner fired. He missed. Gardner did not. From a distance of six feet he shot and killed the NVA.

With that bunker cleared, enemy resistance weakened. Gardner's brave action allowed the main body of troops to move forward. They neutralized the center of the enemy's fortifications. Gardner returned to his platoon and led his men forward to continue his mission. Before the platoon had moved very far, automatic weapons fire from a previously unseen bunker pinned them down.

Gardner called for the grenades that remained among his men and repeated his earlier solo assault. He dropped a grenade into the bunker and vaulted over it. As the grenade erupted, yet another enemy position opened up on Gardner. The lieutenant rolled into a nearby drainage ditch for cover and crawled down it toward the source of the fire.

A few yards from his objective, Gardner leaped from the ditch, an armed grenade in one hand, his rifle in the other. When he was mere feet from the bunker, a blast of enemy fire tore into his chest. He staggered forward. With his last dying effort, he flipped the grenade into the bunker. It exploded as Gardner fell forward. It was his twenty-third birthday.

Gardner's display of raw courage so inspired his men that they resumed the attack and completely routed the enemy.

A posthumous Medal of Honor was presented to Gardner's parents on October 19, 1967.

The 2d Brigade, 25th Infantry Division, arrived in South Vietnam on January 19, 1966 from its base at Schofield Barracks, Oahu, Hawaii. The proud unit, which had earned an outstanding combat record in both World War II and Korea, took up positions west of Saigon, where they guarded Tay Ninh and Hau Nghia Provinces from Viet Cong and NVA forces holed up across the nearby Cambodian border. One of the brigade's primary responsibilities was to secure the area around Cu Chi, the capital of Hau Nghia.

On a routine patrol outside Cu Chi on February 18, 1966, *Sp4. Daniel Fernandez,* Company C, 1st Battalion, 5th Infantry, of Albuquerque, New Mexico, earned the 25th Infantry Division's first Medal of Honor in South Vietnam. Twenty-one-year-old Fernandez, a sergeant, and two others fought through heavy enemy fire to locate a wounded comrade isolated by a VC ambush.

As the other three men administered first aid to the casualty, an enemy hand grenade landed among them. Fernandez realized that one man had not seen the missile. Determined to protect him, Fernandez vaulted over the sergeant and threw himself on the hand grenade just as it exploded. He was killed; the others survived.

The 1st Infantry Division, which had sent one of its brigades to South Vietnam in August 1965 (the rest of the division did not arrive until October), also took up positions north and west of Saigon to protect the city. The division's various infantry units sent out patrols and ambushes every day. Nearly every one made contact with the enemy.

2d Lt. Robert J. Hibbs, Company B, 2d Battalion, 28th Infantry, set up a fifteen-man ambush on the night of March 5, 1966 outside of Don Dien Lo Ke in War Zone D. Soon after the men were in place, one of them radioed that a company of VC was moving toward Hibbs's CP. The Cedar Falls, Iowa, native quickly set up two claymore mines along the enemy's likely avenue of approach. When the VC entered the kill zone, Hibbs detonated the mines and destroyed half the enemy force. He then provided a base of covering fire with his M-16 while the rest of the patrol withdrew back toward the company's main defensive perimeter.

Halfway back to friendly lines, the small band of Americans ran into another VC company intent on attacking the Americans' main perimeter. Without hesitation, Hibbs led his men into the enemy formation, disrupted them, and stalled their attack.

Even though they were just minutes away from the relative safety of their perimeter, Hibbs and a sergeant went back through the scattered VC to locate a missing patrol member who had been wounded and wandered off by himself. Hibbs found the stricken soldier, turned him over to the sergeant, then advanced on two enemy machine guns that were sweeping the ground between the sergeant and the friendly lines. Alone, Hibbs attacked the positions. He died but wiped out the machine guns. Somehow, as he lay dying, he found the strength to destroy the classified "Starlight" rifle scope he carried to prevent it from falling into enemy hands.

The U.S. Air Force was tasked with a myriad of different missions in the Vietnam War. From B-52 bombers that dropped high explosives on enemy positions from great altitudes to helicopters that ferried supplies and evacuated the wounded, the air force contributed significantly to the war effort.

One vital job the air force pilots performed was to provide close air support for ground troops. When friendly forces were in close contact with the enemy, it took pinpoint accuracy to spray machine gun fire effectively from a fast-moving airplane. The mission was fraught with danger, but the American air force pilots saved many lives, some in unexpected ways.

BERNARD F. FISHER

Early on the morning of March 10, 1966, *Maj. Bernard F. Fisher* and his wingman, Capt. Francisco Vazquez, flew their planes from the runway at Pleiku Air Base. Their mission lay 150 miles north at an isolated Special Forces camp in the A Shau Valley, adjacent to the Cambodian border. The four hundred defenders, including twenty Green Berets, had been under siege by more than two thousand NVA for two days. On this, the second full day of the siege, the Allied defenders had been driven into a single bunker on the camp's northern perimeter. Without American air support the NVA would quickly overrun the beleaguered defenders.

To the air force pilots, the mile-wide, six-mile-long valley was "the Tube." The terrain forced the pilots to fly their prop-driven World War II–vintage A-1E Skyraiders straight down the valley, deliver their ordnance while in a left turn, continue the turn into a tight 180-degree maneuver, and race back up the valley to start the procedure all over again. To further complicate matters, the NVA had placed twenty anti-aircraft guns and hundreds of automatic weapons in the surrounding hills. One Skyraider pilot said it was like "flying inside Yankee Stadium with all the people in the stands firing at you with machine guns."

That morning Fisher and Vazquez rendezvoused with four other Skyraiders over the A Shau Valley. They let down through an 8,000-foot-thick layer of clouds and broke out just 800 feet above the valley's floor.

The six planes flew straight up the valley, strafed, and continued around to the starting point. On his second run, Lt. Col. Dafford W. "Jump" Myers felt his plane shudder. He was hit. Flames streamed back from the engine compartment. Too low to bail out, Myers glided the injured aircraft to an emergency landing on the camp's little runway. When the plane came to a stop, Myers leaped overboard and ran into the nearby underbrush to escape the NVA.

Fisher had called for a rescue helicopter as soon as he received word that Myers was going in. The other four planes strafed the area where Myers was hiding to hold off the enemy.

Ten minutes later Fisher received a radio call that advised that the rescue helicopter was still at least twenty minutes away. Fisher did not think Myers could evade the NVA that much longer. In the next instant he decided to land himself and rescue Myers, a decision that would change his life forever. "I knew it wasn't wise. It wasn't a very good thing to do," he said later. "But it was one of those situations you get into. You don't want to do it, but you've got to, because he's part of the family; one of our people. You know you have to get him out of there."

Debris littered the twenty-five-hundred-foot runway. Tin roofs from nearby buildings, buckets, fifty-five-gallon-drums, unexploded rocket pods, and other rubble all made landing very hazardous. In addition, the strip's pierced steel planking had been ripped up from explosions, exposing jagged edges of metal. If Fisher hit any of these, he would rip up his tires and be unable to take off.

Fisher headed down as Vazquez strafed the enemy positions. Fisher touched down on the runway but had too much speed to stop. He maneuvered his plane around the debris, hit full throttle, and took off.

Fisher climbed rapidly, chopped the throttle back, kicked in full left rudder, and made a sharp 180-degree turn back to the runway he had just left. He touched down at the beginning of the strip but needed nearly the full length of the runway to stop. He then turned the Skyraider around and taxied back along the runway while he looked for Myers.

Fisher spotted him waving like mad from a clump of bushes just off the runway. Fisher hit the brakes but still rolled one hundred feet past Myers. "I waited for just a moment, expecting Myers to be right there with me; you know, right on the side. But he wasn't.

"I figured he must be hurt more than I thought—maybe he couldn't move or something—so I set the brakes on the bird and climbed over the right seat to get on the side he was on. I looked through the mirror and saw two little red, beady eyes looking back at me. He was trying to crawl up the back of the wing."

Fisher reached out, grabbed Myers by the seat of the pants, and pulled him headfirst into the cockpit. "It was hard on his head but he didn't complain," Fisher said.

A few minutes later Fisher and Myers were airborne, on their way back to Pleiku. The ground crew later counted nineteen bullet holes in Fisher's plane.

Born in San Bernardino, California, on January 1, 1927, Fisher grew up in Utah. He served in the navy in 1945 and 1946, then moved to Kuna, Idaho, where his parents then resided. He attended college in both Idaho and Utah, took his air force commission through ROTC, and learned to fly in 1953. His Medal of Honor, the first with the new air force design, was presented to him by President Johnson on January 19, 1967.

Fisher retired from the air force as a full colonel, then returned to Idaho, where he became a farmer.

Only limited antiwar sentiment existed in the United States in 1966. To be sure, there were demonstrations, protests, and disturbances, but these were limited to hardcore antiwar activists at some of the more radical college campuses around the country. A majority of Americans supported their country's involvement in South Vietnam because they believed it to be an effort to curb an invasion by a communist nation of a peace-loving neighbor. As a result, those college students and others who marched against America's efforts were considered to be "communist inspired."

Members of the government who questioned President Johnson's war policy were decidedly in the minority. One was Arkansas Democratic senator J. William Fulbright, who presented a resolution in Congress on January 29, 1966 that called for a "full and complete investigation of all aspects" of the United States' Vietnam policy. The subsequent hearings were well publicized but had little effect on Johnson's aggressive war policy.

Many of those who did protest the war were serious, idealistic young people who were willing to go to great lengths to promote their message. On April 11, 1966, antiwar protesters marched down New York's Fifth Avenue chanting slogans and carrying signs. That same afternoon twenty-year-old Boston University student Arthur H. Zinner doused himself with gasoline in front of the White House. White House police risked injury to themselves to wrestle Zinner to the ground before he could immolate himself.

At the same time, halfway around the world, other young men of principle were demonstrating their convictions.

JAMES W. ROBINSON, JR.

Twenty-five-year-old *James W. Robinson, Jr.* did not have to be in South Vietnam. He was there by choice. He had already served a four-year hitch in the Marine Corps, enlisting after he finished high school in Cicero, Illinois, in 1959. The ruggedly handsome young man was a fiercely patriotic individual—his heroes were MacArthur and Churchill, and he read all he could on military strategy and military history—who saw the war in South Vietnam in simple black-and-white terms as a basic struggle between the forces of good and evil. Sacrifices needed to be made in order to ensure the victory of good. Robinson was willing to make those sacrifices.

On December 9, 1963, Robinson enlisted in the U.S. Army with the hope that he would be sent to South Vietnam as an adviser. Instead, the army sent him to Panama as a military policeman. Disappointed, Robinson began a yearlong letter-writing campaign for a transfer to the war zone. In August 1965 his efforts paid off—he received orders to join the famed 1st Infantry Division, the Big Red One, then in the process of relocating to South Vietnam.

Once in the war zone, Robinson remained completely dedicated to his country's goals. In one letter home he wrote, "Any American who doesn't believe in total victory in this conflict is a traitor." In another he declared, "There's a world on fire and we should do something about it." Just days before he died, Robinson wrote to his father: "The price we pay for freedom is never cheap."

On April 11, 1966, Robinson's unit, Company C, 2d Battalion, 16th Infantry, was on a sweep of a suspected Viet

Cong stronghold in coastal Phuoc Tuy Province east of Saigon. As part of Operation Abilene, the company had been hacking its way through the dense, nearly impenetrable jungle when a friendly artillery round fell short and burst above it in the treetops, showering the soldiers below with red-hot shrapnel. Two men died and twelve were wounded by the friendly fire accident. The survivors began to cut an LZ in the jungle for the incoming medevac helicopter, oblivious to the fact that they were working just yards away from the command post of the D800 Viet Cong Battalion.

Without warning, heavy automatic weapons fire raked the perimeter. Hand grenades fell from the sky. Mortar shells crashed down through the trees. Sniper fire exacted a deadly toll on the grunts.

Robinson worked with his platoon leader, 2d Lt. Kenneth Alderson, to place their men in advantageous positions. Robinson moved about under heavy fire and offered encouragement to the men. His willingness to expose himself to enemy fire inspired the infantrymen.

Robinson located the most persistent sniper and killed him with a well-placed round from an M-79 grenade launcher. He then saw a medic take a round while the man was treating a casualty. Unwilling to leave the two men at the mercy of the enemy, he dashed into the open and pulled them both to safety, then gave them medical treatment.

The desperate fight in the thick jungle raged into the afternoon. The VC were so close that some of the grunts actually wrestled with their foes. Friendly casualties mounted. The wounded along with the dead and the dying littered the tight perimeter. One soldier later said, "I've never heard such screaming in my life. Many of the wounded were calling for their mothers. I remember one guy yelling over and over for 'Gloria.'"

Several medevac helicopters were able to hover over the small LZ long enough to pull up to safety a number of the more critically wounded casualties. One of the pararescuemen from an air force helicopter voluntarily came down into the perimeter to help with the wounded. Other helicopters flew over to kick out much needed ammunition supplies. They all drew heavy enemy automatic weapons fire.

Throughout the carnage, Robinson continued to set an inspiring example of courage and fortitude to those around him. He crawled to the casualties, collected their weapons and ammunition, and redistributed the items to those still able to fight back.

When he saw a buddy cut down, Robinson sprang into action. "Hang on," he yelled. "I'm coming for ya!" He openly defied the enemy as he raced to his friend. But his luck was about to run out. Two Viet Cong rifle rounds tore into him, one in the leg and another in his shoulder. He ignored the pain, dragged his buddy to safety, and gave him lifesaving first aid.

While propped behind the protection of a thick tree so he could patch up his wounds, Robinson happened to spot the enemy machine gun that was causing the most casualties. Although he knew full well that his chances of survival were practically nil, but aware that something had to be done to save the company from destruction, Robinson grabbed two grenades and charged straight out of the perimeter at the automatic weapon.

A tracer round slammed into Robinson's leg and set his pants leg on fire. He stopped only long enough to rip the burning cloth from his body, then continued forward on his mission. As Alderson watched, the indomitable sergeant took two more enemy rounds in his chest. Yet Robinson continued. He pulled himself to his full six-foot-three-inch height, summoned his last bit of strength, and threw the grenades directly into the enemy position. He fell dead on the jungle floor as the grenades exploded, destroying the position and killing the enemy gunners.

The battle continued into the night, but never reached its previous ferocity. By the time reinforcing ground forces reached Company C the next morning, more than a third of the embattled company had been killed or wounded. That there were not more was due in part to Staff Sergeant Robinson's willingness to pay the high price of victory.

The Medal of Honor was presented to his father on July 16, 1967.

The 1st Cavalry Division (Airmobile) continued to tangle with the VC in the untamed provinces of II Corps in central South Vietnam. On May 18, 1966, twenty-three-year-old staff sergeant Jimmy G. Stewart, who had already served six years in the army, defended five wounded comrades from Company B, 2d Battalion, 12th Cavalry, against the onslaught of a Viet Cong company near An Khe in Binh Dinh Province. For over four hours this father of two small boys single-handedly fought off the enemy. When a reinforcing company finally drove off the VC, its members found Staff Sergeant Stewart's body at the bottom of his foxhole surrounded by eight enemy dead, and signs that fifteen more had been dragged away.

In early June 1966, intelligence reports reached Marine headquarters at Da Nang that a mixed force of NVA and VC were gathered in large numbers in the mountains west of Chu Lai in Quang Tin Province. To frustrate the enemy's plans to control the local population, the Marine headquarters operations staff prepared Operation Kansas. Per this plan, small teams of eight to twenty reconnaissance Marines would scout the mountains in search of signs of the enemy. When the Marines found something, they would call in air and artillery strikes. By remaining hidden, the Marines hoped to harass the enemy for days before their presence was suspected. If the Marines were discovered, they could easily be extracted by helicopter.

JIMMIE E. HOWARD

As dusk fell on the night on June 13, 1966, a flight of Korean War–vintage H-34 helicopters dropped eighteen Marines from the 1st Reconnaissance Battalion, 1st Marine Division, on top of Hill 488, twenty-five miles west of Chu Lai. At a height of fifteen hundred feet, the hill dominated the surrounding terrain for miles and provided an ideal vantage point for the spotting team.

The leader of this team, *S.Sgt. Jimmie E. Howard,* set his men in positions along the rock-strewn hilltop as best he could. The Marines settled in, some taking refuge in old VC foxholes scattered throughout the site.

For the next two days Howard called in artillery on groups of enemy soldiers that he or his men spotted near their position. And there were plenty of sightings. Hardly an hour went by that Howard did not call in a fire mission. In fact, he called in so many that his headquarters decided not to honor them all lest the enemy become suspicious of all the artillery activity, realize they were being watched, and go after Howard. Howard's CO, Capt. Timothy Geraghty, became so concerned about the security of Howard's position that he planned to pull Howard and his team out that evening.

Howard protested, however. There had been no trouble so far, and his efforts were hurting the enemy, he said. Howard asked for, and Geraghty agreed to give, one more day on station.

Geraghty could not have put a better man in charge of the mission. An epitome of the recruiting-poster Marine, the cigar-chomping Howard had enlisted in the Marines in 1950 after he left high school in Burlington, Iowa. As a young Marine corporal with the 1st Marine Division in Korea, Howard was wounded twice and earned a Silver Star for his gallantry in action. He later served as a drill instructor at the recruit depot in San Diego and was a star football player on the base's team.

While Howard checked his men's positions on the evening of June 15, a full battalion of North Vietnamese regulars began to silently swarm up the hill toward Howard and his handful of young Marines. Just past 10:00 P.M., L.Cpl. Richard Binns fired his rifle at a bush that he noticed moving closer to his position. The bush screamed, then pitched over backward. Other Marines flung grenades down the hill. More screams filled the night.

Howard reacted instantly and pulled his men into a tight

circular perimeter not more than twenty-five feet across. He personally placed each man into a firing position.

By this time the Marines were completely surrounded. Enemy grenades flew through the ink-black night to explode violently among Howard's men with sharp crashes. From positions on nearby hills, four enemy .50-caliber machine guns spat tracer rounds across the hilltop. Nearly a dozen lighter machine guns pounded away at the defenders. Mortar shells rained down on the men and added rock splinters to the deadly shrapnel already filling the air. The NVA followed the grenade barrage with a human wave assault.

Under Howard's resolute leadership, the young, mostly untried Marines fought back savagely. Howard moved among his charges to point out targets and offer words of encouragement. His calmness steadied the men. They forced the Vietnamese back down the hill.

During the temporary lull, Howard grabbed the radio. "You gotta get us out of here," Howard told Geraghty. "There are too many of them for my people."

Geraghty arranged for a reaction force, but it was inexplicably delayed. Just after midnight, the NVA came back.

Howard again rallied his men. They fired back, tossed grenades, and yelled curses at their foe. Howard fired his M-16 on semiautomatic so he could conserve ammunition, but he still hurt the enemy.

Howard seemed to be everywhere. Whenever the NVA were about to overrun a section of his perimeter, Howard moved there, strengthening the position.

By the time the enemy retreated again, several Marines lay dead and all but Howard were wounded. The Marines had thrown the last of their grenades and ammunition was low. But there was to be no evacuation. Geraghty told Howard they had to stay put.

"You know the movie, *The Longest Day*?" Howard later said. "Well, compared to our night on that hill, *The Longest Day* was just a twinkle in the eye."

Jets and gunships showed up to support Howard a short

time later. He directed the planes in strafing attacks against the enemy and brought their cannon rounds to within thirty feet of his own position. Under his excellent direction the jets also dropped napalm on the NVA; the oily black flames sent the enemy scattering back down the slope. Howard brought the gunships to within twenty feet of the hilltop. From that altitude they fired their machine guns in long sweeping bursts down the hillside.

Isolated bands of North Vietnamese still attacked the perimeter and threw grenades and fired their rifles. The Marines threw rocks at the enemy to confuse them. More often than not, it worked.

Just after 3:00 A.M., fragments of shrapnel ripped into Howard's back. His legs were immobilized from the wound. Fearful of the drowsiness effect that morphine could have, Howard refused the painkilling injection. He pulled himself from position to position, gathered ammunition from the dead, and gave it to those still able to fight.

He repeatedly told the survivors they had only to hold out until morning. "If we can hold out till dawn," he told them, "we'll be okay."

At 5:25 A.M. he shouted, "Okay, you people, reveille in thirty-five minutes." At precisely 6:00 A.M. his voice boomed out across the perimeter, "Reveille, Reveille!" They had made it through the brutal night.

The enemy fire slackened with daylight, but did not completly abate. Two of the enemy's .50-caliber machine guns were still firing their thick rounds across the perimeter. They shot down a pair of helicopters, too. The NVA seemed determined to annihilate the defenders.

But then reinforcements finally arrived. Choppers dropped them off on the protected side of the hill. The fresh Marines fought their way to Howard's position, stepping over enemy bodies all the way. The fight was not over, though. It was noon before the NVA finally retreated.

Of the eighteen men who had landed on Hill 488 three days earlier, six were dead; the surviving twelve were all wounded.

Howard recommended thirteen of his men for the Silver Star and four for the Navy Cross. He received his well-deserved Medal of Honor from President Johnson on August 21, 1967.

Howard recovered from his wounds and eventually retired from the Marine Corps as a first sergeant. He died on November 12, 1993.

On June 30, 1966, *Sgt. Donald R. Long,* a twenty-six-year-old from Blackfork, Ohio, was with a reaction force from Troop C, 1st Squadron, 4th Cavalry, on its way to rescue another 1st Infantry Division unit that had been ambushed on Route 13 near Loc Ninh in Binh Long Province, adjacent to the Cambodian border. Elements of the 271st VC Regiment had isolated four tanks from Troop B with recoilless rifle and machine gun fire from well-entrenched positions immediately beside the jungle road.

Under direct enemy fire, Long moved several wounded cavalrymen to positions of safety. He then stood completely exposed atop his armored personnel carrier (APC) to fight off enemy soldiers who were attempting to climb aboard. When the VC overran another APC, Long braved the enemy fire to run to its crew's assistance. While he reorganized the wounded, an enemy grenade landed at Long's feet. He shouted a warning, pushed aside a wounded man who had not heard him, and dived upon the deadly missile, absorbing its full blast with his own body. His deliberate self-sacrifice saved eight men.

In Quang Tri Province, just south of the Demilitarized Zone (DMZ), weeks of heavy scouting by recon Marines confirmed that large NVA formations were infiltrating across the Ben Hai River that marked the DMZ. To counter the enemy advances, the Marines set up a base at Dong Ha, which sits astride the junctions of Route 1 and Route 9, thirty-eight miles north of Hue, then used helicopters to carry infantry units into LZs just south of the DMZ. Six Marine and five ARVN battalions would combine in a sweep of the area as part of Operation Hastings. Two career Marines from the same company earned Medals of Honor during the first three days of the operation.

ROBERT J. MODRZEJEWSKI
AND JOHN J. MCGINTY, III

On the morning of July 15, 1966, CH-47 helicopters carried two battalions of the 4th Marines, 3d Marine Division, into landing zones at opposite ends of Song Ngan Valley, which sat within rifle range of the DMZ. The first wave of helicopters at the western LZ landed and took off without incident. Sniper fire harassed the second wave. Five aircraft downed in the third wave earned the LZ the sobriquet "Helicopter Valley."

The 3d Battalion swept eastward while its sister battalion, the 2d, moved west through the narrow valley. The pincers movement would clear the area of NVA. Rugged terrain, though, combined with thick vegetation and high heat restricted the Marines' progress. By late afternoon the two forces had advanced only two miles toward each other. The units set up separate defensive positions for the night, sure that the NVA would attack. At 8:00 P.M. that night they did, with the main assault coming against *Capt. Robert J. Modrzejewski*'s Company K.

Born in Milwaukee, Wisconsin, on July 3, 1934, Modrzejewski earned a B.S. from the University of Wisconsin in 1957. While in college he was a member of the Marine Corps Platoon Leader Class and received a second lieutenant's commission upon graduation. Modrzejewski arrived in South Vietnam in March 1966.

Soon after he landed at Song Ngan, Modrzejewski encountered a reinforced NVA platoon manning a well-organized defensive position. Under his skilled leadership, Company K destroyed the enemy platoon.

That night the NVA launched a series of massive frontal assaults.

Modrzejewski said, "It was so dark we couldn't see our hands in front of our faces." He had his Marines send up flares so they could see the enemy. The captain raced from hot spot to hot spot to give encouragement to his young charges. The company repulsed the NVA after a wild three-hour fight. The next morning Modrzejewski counted 28 NVA dead around his perimeter and saw evidence that 30 more had been dragged away.

That first day set the pattern for the next three. During the day snipers harassed the Marines; at night the enemy attacked the Marines' positions in strength.

Throughout each attack Modrzejewski always showed up at the site of the heaviest fighting. On the second night he was wounded, but still crawled two hundred yards to provide critically needed ammunition to a threatened sector of his perimeter. Several times he was forced to direct artillery strikes to within a few yards of his own position. It took nerves of steel and incredible self-confidence to do it, but it had to be done.

On the eighteenth, both the 2d and 3d Battalions were ordered to pull out of the valley. Although it had been hit hard the previous two days, Company K was ordered to stay behind to destroy the choppers downed at the LZ on the fifteenth. At approximately 2:30 P.M. the dense jungle around the LZ erupted with automatic weapons, mortars, and small-arms fire. Over one thousand NVA blowing whistles and bugles bore down on the isolated company. 1st Platoon, led by *Sgt. John J. McGinty, III,* was cut off.

McGinty, born in Boston, Massachusetts, on January 21, 1940, grew up in Louisville, Kentucky. He enlisted in the Marine Corps just three months past his seventeenth birthday. His nine years of service included duty as a drill instructor and as a brig guard. He had volunteered for duty in South Vietnam because he "thought it would be over before I got there. I didn't want to be earning my pay guarding a bunch of AWOL sailors."

McGinty more than earned his pay on July 18.

In the opening seconds of the attack, McGinty's radio operator and three men standing nearby were wounded. McGinty and the others hit the deck but there was little cover. The NVA seemed to be everywhere. For the next four hours McGinty and the remainder of his thirty-two-man platoon fought off wave after wave of NVA attackers.

During one savage attack the enemy cut off two of McGinty's squads. Unmindful of the shower of lead filling the air, McGinty charged forward to their position. He found twenty men wounded and the corpsman dead. McGinty reloaded magazines, shoved them into weapons, then pressed them into the hands of the wounded. "You gotta fight back," he urged them.

A few minutes later an exploding grenade drove shrapnel into McGinty's leg, back, and left eye. Despite intense pain, McGinty continued to encourage the men and directed their resistance until the NVA retreated. When a small force of enemy soldiers later tried to work their way behind him, McGinty killed five at point-blank range with his pistol and broke up the maneuver.

In the meantime, Modrzejewski had called in air strikes to fend off the NVA who were attacking the rest of his company. Bombs and napalm came in so close that one Marine had to plunge into a nearby stream to avoid being roasted to death. Those strikes stopped the NVA; they broke off their attack a short time later.

In the bloodiest fighting of Operation Hastings, Company K suffered over 50 casualties. The NVA left nearly 500 dead on the battlefield.

Modrzejewski and McGinty received their Medals of Honor together from President Johnson on March 12, 1968. Both men remained in the Marine Corps. Modrzejewski attained the rank of colonel before he retired.

McGinty was commissioned in August 1967. He reached the rank of captain before being medically discharged in 1976 after doctors had to remove the eye that never fully recovered from the 1966 wound. In 1983, as a born-again

Christian, McGinty gave away all of his medals, including the Medal of Honor. He said he considered that medal's depiction of Minerva, the Roman goddess of wisdom and war, to be blasphemous. "The medal is a form of idolatry because it has a false god on it," he told a reporter at the time. "I could never stand before God as a Christian with that thing hanging around my neck."

McGinty moved to the desolate desert east of San Diego to live the life of a hermit. After the death of his wife in the late 1990s, he moved to San Diego and went to work for the local Veterans Affairs officer.

Over the next week the Marines pursued the NVA across the rugged, mountainous terrain bordering the DMZ. A series of brief but sharp clashes resulted. That changed on the morning of July 24, 1966 when Company I, 3d Battalion, 5th Marines, was ordered to establish a radio relay station on Hill 362, just three miles south of the DMZ. The Marines had no trouble reaching the top of the hill. But when the 2d Platoon started down the hill's north face to set up defensive positions, NVA hidden in the 60-to-90-foot-high jungle growth unleashed a furious barrage of small-arms fire. More than a dozen Marines fell, dead or wounded. The North Vietnamese were on the verge of overrunning the survivors when a young lance corporal took action.

RICHARD A. PITTMAN

From a position of relative safety near the crest of Hill 362, 1st Platoon's twenty-one-year-old *Richard A. Pittman* dropped his M-14 rifle, grabbed an M-60 machine gun and several belts of ammunition, and raced downhill to the fight.

"In combat I was always aggressive," Pittman said. "I don't know if it was out of fear, but I knew I wasn't going to die without a fight. Fortunately, I was able to help."

It was more than fortunate, it was incredible because

Pittman should not have even been in the Marine Corps—he was blind in one eye. When he enlisted in September 1965, Pittman wanted so badly to be a Marine that he was able to conceal his blindness through all of his physical examinations, through boot camp, infantry training, and his first months in the combat zone. No one knew and no one would have guessed based on the way Pittman acted that day.

As Pittman ran down the trail, hidden NVA opened fire on him. Pittman dropped down and returned their fire. He could not see the enemy, but he could see the muzzle blasts of their weapons in the foliage. He aimed there. The bursts from his M-60 knocked out two enemy positions.

Pittman resumed his advance but was almost immediately pinned down again. Once more braving the enemy fire, Pittman exposed himself in order to fire back. In minutes he had destroyed a pair of enemy machine guns.

While Pittman fought his duel, other Marines and corpsmen were able to reach the wounded, patch them up, and pull them uphill to safety.

Someone yelled to Pittman that wounded members of the point squad lay fifty yards farther down the trail. Determined to provide covering fire so these men could be rescued, Pittman continued down the trail, spraying the jungle ahead of him with bursts of M-60 rounds.

Just as Pittman reached the point squad's position, several dozen NVA swarmed out of the jungle and charged him. In total disregard of his own safety and intent only on saving his comrades, Pittman took up a position in the middle of the trail and refused to move. He swung his M-60 back and forth, spraying the enemy soldiers with its deadly fire. The NVA fell, their final screams reverberating through the jungle.

When his M-60 overheated and jammed, Pittman picked up a discarded submachine gun and used that against the foe. When he had used up all that weapon's ammunition, a wounded man passed him a .45-caliber pistol. Pittman fired that at the fleeing enemy, but knew they were too far away for the inaccurate weapon to do any damage. As the few remaining NVA fled back into the jungle, Pittman tossed a grenade after them for good measure. Then he made his way back uphill.

The fight for Hill 362 continued into the night with the NVA pounding the Marines' positions with mortar shells between repeated ground assaults. Not until dawn did the enemy withdraw. They left behind the bodies of 21 of their own but had killed 18 Marines and wounded 82 more. Without Pittman's intrepid charge, Company I's casualties would have been higher.

Pittman finished out his tour, then returned to the United States. He intended to make the Marine Corps his career, but an infection he picked up in South Vietnam resulted in his disability being discovered. In April 1968 he was medically discharged.

The next month, on May 14, Pittman was presented with the Medal of Honor. Eager to fulfill his dream of being a career Marine, Pittman appealed to the commandant for a waiver. It took some time, but the request was finally granted. In January 1970, Pittman reenlisted.

In October 1988, Pittman retired as a master sergeant. It had been a successful but often difficult career. "Holding the Medal of Honor creates all kinds of jealousy, hate, and discontent," he said when he retired. "A lot of times people think Medal of Honor holders get a promotion or a job because of the medal. I've actually had to work twice as hard just to prove to people that I've earned what I have.

"I just want to be plain old Rick Pittman," said the California native.

Combat action continued to escalate throughout South Vietnam in 1966. In big operations and small, on land and on the water, American servicemen repeatedly displayed great courage when they performed incredible feats of bravery.

PFC Billy L. Lauffer of Tucson, Arizona, died on September 21, 1966 when he made a one-man assault on an enemy bunker position near Bong Son in Binh Dinh Province. Several of Lauffer's comrades in Company C, 2d Battalion, 5th

Cavalry, were badly wounded by enemy machine gun fire while they were on patrol during Operation Thayer I. When Lauffer realized that the medics could not reach the casualties under the intense enemy fire, he rose to his feet and attacked the position. Lauffer did not have to make the charge and would not have been criticized if he had not; he had been in South Vietnam for only one week and with his unit just a few days. He barely knew the other members of his platoon and they barely knew him. But it did not matter. His comrades were hurt and he was in a position to do something about it. The twenty-two-year-old headed right for the enemy position, his finger pulling the trigger on his M-16 as fast as it could. The enemy machine gunner concentrated his fire on Lauffer. The rounds cut him down before he had covered half the distance, but that was enough time for the casualties to be pulled to safety.

The U.S. Navy played a key and diverse role in South Vietnam. Navy ships anchored off the coast provided gunfire support to land-based troops. Navy fighter pilots flew bombing missions over North Vietnam as well as close air support missions for Marine and army infantry. Navy doctors manned evacuation hospitals, where they provided first-class medical treatment to the wounded, while navy corpsmen operated with Marine units as frontline medical aid men. The elite Sea, Air, Land (SEAL) commandos conducted a wide variety of behind-enemy-lines operations. And to restrict VC use and control of the vital Mekong River and its dozens of tributaries, the navy operated a fleet of river patrol boats.

Reminiscent of the glamorous PT boats of World War II fame, the river patrol boats, or PBRs (for patrol boat, river), were tasked with monitoring the heavy indigent traffic on South Vietnam's interior waterways. The VC used junks and sampans to smuggle men and supplies under the eyes of American and South Vietnamese troops. PBR crews had to develop a sixth sense about which boats to search and which to let go. The men who manned the PBRs were a unique breed who experienced none of the glamour of the World War II PT boats, but lived all the danger.

JAMES E. WILLIAMS

In March 1966, *Boatswains Mate 1st Class James E. "Elliott" Williams* had an ideal life. After more than eighteen years of naval service, he was less than two years away from retirement. His career had consisted of one routine assignment after another. Now he was stationed within three hundred miles of his hometown of Charleston, South Carolina. His wife of seventeen years and their five children were all eager for him to complete his twenty years so he could retire to their new home in Darlington, South Carolina. In just twenty months he could hang up his uniforms.

Only one thing bothered Williams about that pleasant scenario—the growing war in South Vietnam. Although he had spent nearly twenty years in the naval service, he did not feel that he had actually served his country. He wanted to do more. So he requested a transfer to the war zone. He arrived in South Vietnam in June 1966. In the following eight months he would earn every combat decoration available, some more than once, plus the navy's highest noncombat heroism award, to become one of the most decorated servicemen of all time.

Williams served as a boat commander for River Squadron 5, based at My Tho south of Saigon. He earned his first medal, a Bronze Star, on July 17, when he captured important documents from an enemy sampan he had destroyed after a brisk fight three miles south of My Tho.

A second Bronze Star was earned three weeks later when Williams's crew captured a sampan manned by nine Viet Cong. Williams's superior handling of his boat and his aggressive leadership of the other three PBRs in his squadron were cited in the award.

At dusk on August 22, Williams was in charge of a routine two-boat patrol moving down the Mekong River. Concealed in the thick foliage clogging both banks of the river, one hundred enemy gun emplacements suddenly opened fire as the two PBRs cruised between them. At the height of the battle, and after he had already knocked out a number of the enemy emplacements, Williams noticed a motorized sampan fleeing the area. Because he suspected the vessel held some high-ranking VC, Williams ignored the barrage of enemy fire and took up the pursuit. Although wounded in the subsequent firefight, Williams killed the boat's occupants and captured over one hundred important enemy documents. He also earned his first Purple Heart and a Silver Star for this action.

On October 31, Williams, in charge of PBR 105, led a two-boat patrol down the Mekong. Without warning, enemy fire erupted from two nearby sampans. Williams instantly ordered return fire that killed the crew of one sampan and drove the other off. Williams pursued the fleeing boat into a nearby inlet. AK-47 fire crackled from the vegetation-choked shoreline. As he maneuvered through the twisting waterway, Williams's patrol was suddenly confronted by two junks and two sampans. The VC had laid a neat trap.

In the savage fighting that followed, Williams, with utter disregard for his own well-being, directed the counterfire of the two PBRs against the enemy. As the battle raged and darkness neared, Williams recognized that his small force was overwhelmingly outnumbered. He called for helicopters to aid him, then pulled back.

Minutes later he stumbled onto an even larger concentration of enemy vessels blocking his route. Unwilling to wait for the choppers, Williams boldly led his boats into the fray. He plowed his way through the enemy boats, his PBR's two .50-caliber machine guns smoking out rounds. Seven junks and fifty sampans were destroyed in the hail of hot lead. A few minutes later the gunships arrived overhead. Williams personally directed by radio their attack on the remaining vessels.

Not content to let the choppers finish off the enemy, Williams ordered his boats' searchlights turned on. The double rays cut through the night's blackness. Although he was now a better target, Williams continued to press the attack.

Together, the gunships and Williams's two outnumbered boats completely routed a vastly superior enemy force. They killed and wounded scores of enemy soldiers and destroyed dozens of sampans. For this incredible display of courage during the hours-long fight, Williams would receive the Medal of Honor on May 14, 1968.

After such a harrowing experience, most men would have requested a transfer back to the States for early retirement. But not Williams. He was not done.

On January 9, 1967 he saved the lives of eight civilians from the dredge *Jamaica Bay,* which had been destroyed by a VC mine on the Mekong River. Williams earned the Navy and Marine Corps Medal, the navy's highest noncombat heroism award, for repeatedly diving into the water to rescue the victims.

Six days later, Williams took his patrol of three boats to a suspected Viet Cong passage across the Nam Thon branch of the Mekong. Intense fire from fortified enemy positions drove off the PBRs. Williams called in an air strike.

At its conclusion, Williams took his boats back into the hostile area. The aerial attack had not killed all the VC. Williams manned the .50s and knocked out several automatic weapons with his accurate fire. When he sent one of his other boats off to investigate several nearby sampans, the enemy took advantage of the moment to renew their fire on Williams's boat. He was hit in the shoulder and left arm.

According to his Navy Cross citation, "Williams led his patrol back through the heavy enemy fire, despite his painful injuries. His decisive leadership and courage succeeded in halting the crossing of four hundred enemy soldiers." He also earned his second Purple Heart.

Altogether, Williams's eight months of combat duty had earned him two dozen medals. He had served his country exceptionally well.

Williams returned to his family in March 1967. He finished his remaining year in the navy, then began a new career as a U.S. marshal. He also served two terms as president of the Congressional Medal of Honor Society, based in his hometown of Charleston, before his death in October 1999.

* * *

In Tay Ninh Province northwest of Saigon, on November 5, 1966, two members of Company A, 2d Battalion, 27th Infantry, 25th Infantry Division, earned Medals of Honor while on their way to the rescue of another company that had been pinned down by elements of the 9th VC Division. West Point graduate *Capt. Robert F. Foley,* despite several wounds, destroyed three enemy machine gun bunkers, helped several wounded members of his company to safety while exposed to enemy fire, and continued to lead his men in the fight. At one point Foley picked up a discarded M-60 machine gun and fired it from the hip as he advanced directly into enemy fire so that several wounded grunts could be rescued.

PFC John F. Baker, Jr., a twenty-one-year-old native of Moline, Illinois, destroyed several enemy bunkers in the same action, killed at least six snipers, and rescued no less than seven wounded comrades from under hostile fire. Like his CO, Captain Foley, Baker was wounded by enemy grenade fragments.

When the pair were presented their Medals of Honor at a White House ceremony on May 1, 1968, President Johnson commented on the differences in the two men's height— Foley stands six-feet-seven-inches tall and Baker five-feet-two inches. Both men remained in the army and had distinguished careers. Baker retired as a sergeant major while Foley rose to lieutenant general. When he retired in 2002, Foley was one of just two Vietnam War Medal of Honor recipients remaining on active duty.

Sgt. Ted Belcher fought as an infantryman in Germany during World War II. He returned home to raise a family, but the lure of the military continued to call. In 1960 he enlisted in the Maryland National Guard. Three years later he requested a transfer to active duty. In October 1966 he went to South Vietnam, where he joined Company C, 1st Battalion, 14th Infantry, 25th Infantry Division.

At forty-two, Belcher was old for a grunt, but he kept up with his squad members, most of whom were the same age as the daughter he had left behind in Zanesville, Ohio. On November 16, 1966 while leading his squad to the rescue of a friendly unit pinned down near Plei Djering in Pleiku Province in the Central Highlands, Belcher died when he jumped on an enemy grenade to save the lives of his squad members.

In mid-September 1966 the 1st Cavalry Division (Airmobile) returned to coastal Binh Dinh Province after it had helped the 4th Infantry Division in Pleiku Province. With the assistance of a Republic of Korea Marine Corps unit, the "First Team" launched Operation Irving to keep the heat on the 5th NVA Division, which roamed Binh Dinh Province at will. Heavy combat erupted throughout the province during the fall of 1966. Some of the bitterest fighting occurred in areas south of the provincial capital of Bong Son.

LEWIS ALBANESE

Lewis Albanese hated the army. He frequently said he was not fit for soldiering. To emphasize his point, he made a habit of avoiding any duty that required manual labor. The first sergeant of Albanese's unit, Company B, 5th Battalion, 7th Cavalry, Dayton L. Hare, called Albanese a "goof-off." He was correct, in a sense. Others, however, viewed Albanese as young, full of life, and a bit mischievous.

Born in Venice, Italy, on April 27, 1946, Albanese emigrated with his family to Seattle, Washington, as a youth. He graduated from Seattle's Franklin High School in 1964, then was drafted in October 1965. He was originally assigned to the 5th Infantry Division at Fort Carson, Colorado, but when the 5th Battalion, 7th Cavalry, was organized at the post, Albanese was transferred to the new unit. He deployed to South Vietnam with the battalion in August 1966.

Albanese saw action all over Binh Dinh Province in Operations Thayer I and Thayer II and in Operation Irving. Binh Dinh was a beautiful and dangerous place. Steep mountains covered with thick green foliage provided a striking background to the picturesque villages of thatched huts. But Binh Dinh Province also served as the home base of the 18th NVA Regiment and the 2d VC Regiment. The province would never be pacified despite a seven-year effort to do so by South Vietnamese and American forces.

On December 1, 1966, Albanese's platoon, led by 1st Lt. William E. Kail, went to the aid of a 9th Cavalry Regiment company that had been pinned down by heavy enemy fire in the hamlet of Phu Muu, about fifteen miles south of Bong Son. As Albanese's platoon entered a graveyard at the edge of the village, enemy rifle fire pinned it down, too. A sergeant killed the enemy soldier and the platoon moved forward.

S.Sgt. George Porod commanded the left flank squad, Albanese's squad. A huge man who sported a flaming red handlebar mustache, Porod maneuvered his men through the scattered huts and foliage of the village. As he brought his squad into an open area, Porod noticed a drainage ditch to his left. Suddenly, automatic weapons fire erupted from the ditch. Porod realized that he had walked into an ambush. He and his men faced certain death.

The squad members dashed for cover to the right. All except Albanese. As the left flank man in the squad, he dropped to the ground and provided covering fire for his buddies while they scurried for cover. Then he crawled into the ditch.

According to Porod and Kail, even though the slightly built Albanese was out of sight in the ditch, his progress could be followed by the sound of his rifle fire and the crash of exploding grenades. No one who survived witnessed Albanese's single-handed attack, but it was easy to reconstruct his movements.

With fixed bayonet, Albanese dropped into the ditch. He found it was actually a one-hundred-yard-long trench that connected a series of bunkers and fighting positions. "Goof-off" Albanese moved down the trench and assaulted each of the VC positions. He would take the enemy under fire, then toss a grenade. Six VC died as a result of Albanese's assault.

The action did not take long, less than fifteen minutes. Al-

CHAPTER FIVE

Westmoreland Takes the Offensive

When Gen. William C. Westmoreland looked back on 1966, he gave high marks to the major operations he had ordered to be conducted against main force enemy units. Not only had the enemy been forced to operate within easy retreating distance of his sanctuaries across the Laotian and Cambodian borders, the U.S. units had developed the battlefield tactics necessary to conduct this new type of warfare.

These lessons had been learned the hard way. Almost all of the combat in 1966 had been initiated by the VC or NVA. Besides having the upper hand in engaging American units in battle, the enemy also had the power to break contact at their discretion. When an American unit seemed on the verge of victory, whether through superior infantry tactics or superior firepower, the enemy would withdraw.

In 1967, Westmoreland wanted to go after the enemy. He would strike the enemy's base camps in border provinces and below the DMZ. Under his plan, American forces would conduct the offensive operations. ARVN units would come in behind them to secure and pacify the areas. His first big offensive campaign, the largest of the war to date, was to be Operation Cedar Falls, quickly followed by Operation Junction City.

Operation Cedar Falls (named for the hometown of 1st Lt. Robert J. Hibbs) thrust 16,000 U.S. and 14,000 ARVN soldiers into the troublesome Iron Triangle area northwest of Saigon. On January 8, 1967, two infantry divisions (the 1st and the 25th) and three full brigades (196th, 173d, and the

11th ACR) invaded the VC bastion from opposite directions in a classic hammer-and-anvil movement. Unfortunately, the VC simply pulled out rather than let themselves be hammered. The U.S. infantrymen did discover, however, a massive tunnel complex in the Iron Triangle, apparently to be used for guerrilla raids and terrorist attacks in Saigon.

Operation Junction City was to have been an immediate follow-up to Operation Cedar Falls against the VC and NVA in War Zone C in upper Tay Ninh Province, but it was delayed for a month.

Not until the morning of February 22, 1967 did paratroopers from the 2d Battalion, 503d Infantry, 173d Airborne Brigade jump out of transport aircraft above Katum, only seven miles south of the Cambodian border. The troopers landed safely in what would prove to be the only airborne operation of the Vietnam War. It was a glorious beginning to an inglorious campaign. As in Operation Cedar Falls, the enemy simply eluded the American forces by moving their supply depots and base camps into Cambodia.

Engagement rules established by President Johnson and Secretary McNamara prohibited U.S. forces from pursuing the enemy across the border. Officially, the troops' hands were tied as soon as the enemy crossed over into one of the "neutral" countries. In reality, U.S. special operations teams frequently crossed the borders in sanctioned violations of official policy.

The first U.S.-led cross-border operation occurred in October 1965, when a small team penetrated the Laotian border near the special forces camp at Kham Duc in Quang Tin Province. Their mission: find the Ho Chi Minh Trail. They found it and confirmed its existence, but the information came at the cost of five men and two helicopters lost.

Under the title Operation Shining Brass (changed to Prairie Fire in March 1967), this small incursion came under the operational control of MACV's Studies and Observation Group (SOG). SOG was a joint service high command unconventional warfare task force engaged in highly classified operations throughout Southeast Asia. Composed of nearly

2,000 Americans, mainly army Special Forces and navy SEALs, and 8,000 indigenous troops, SOG had five main responsibilities: (1) cross-border operations; (2) locating American POWs; (3) organizing resistance movements in North Vietnam; (4) psychological warfare in North and South Vietnam; and (5) kidnap and assassination teams.

Most SOG activities remained classified for years, but as the war years receded into the past, various authors have revealed many of SOG's secrets, including the fact that five of its members earned Medals of Honor. Because of the clandestine nature of their missions in Laos and Cambodia, the official citations for these awards had stated that the action occurred "deep within enemy-dominated territory" or simply "in the Republic of Vietnam." No specific locations were given.

A number of SOG operatives were denied appropriate recognition for their gallantry because of concerns that somehow the true location of their deed of valor would be revealed and future missions would be compromised. Fortunately, the outstanding valor of those SOG members recognized by the Medal of Honor outweighed the concerns of the upper echelons of the intelligence community.

GEORGE K. SISLER

1st Lt. George K. Sisler was no stranger to military secrets. He had served in air force intelligence for four years before enlisting in the U.S. Army in August 1964. In November 1965 he graduated from the army's Intelligence School at Fort Holabird, Maryland, and was commissioned a second lieutenant.

Although he had a wife and two sons back in his hometown of Dexter, Missouri, Sisler volunteered for Special Forces training. His knowledge of covert operations would be put to good use in South Vietnam.

Sisler arrived in-country in June 1966. His mail went to Headquarters Company, 5th Special Forces Group, but he was actually assigned to Command and Control–North, SOG. Soon after his arrival, Sisler began to make cross-border intelligence-gathering missions into Laos.

One of Sisler's most significant discoveries came in early January 1967 while on a mission in southern Laos, in the tri-border area not far from Dak To in South Vietnam's Kontum Province. Sisler's patrol stumbled upon a near-vertical granite formation that soared hundreds of feet into the air. From its summit, observers could see for miles. In addition, it could function as a radio-relay station that would allow the clandestine teams to penetrate even farther into Laos.

Though it took some doing, permission was finally granted for a small SOG team to man the peak, code-named Leghorn. Since he found it, Sisler was given the honor of taking the first team to the top of Leghorn on January 15.

When Sisler was relieved a week later, the value of Leghorn was unquestioned. He and his team had not only been able to observe considerable NVA activity on the nearby portion of the Ho Chi Minh Trail, but had successfully called in extraction helicopters for another SOG team under attack but unable to radio for help due to terrain blockage of its radio signals. Leghorn would remain occupied by SOG teams for five years.

Several weeks after he left Leghorn, Sisler volunteered to accompany a SOG platoon on a mission to assess damage from a B-52 strike in Laos. Helicopters inserted the team into an LZ near Laos's Highway 96 early on February 7, 1967. The team, consisting of Sisler and two other Americans and half a dozen Montagnard tribesmen, had barely stepped off the LZ when a company of NVA hit them from three sides. The ferocity of the initial attack drove the SOG team members back across the clearing used for the LZ and nearly overran them.

The heavily armed SOG members fought back so hard that the NVA fell back. About then Sisler discovered that two Montagnards from the team had been wounded and left outside the perimeter. Concerned with keeping them out of enemy hands, Sisler raced through intense enemy small-arms fire to their assistance.

He was carrying one of the casualties into the perimeter when an enemy machine gun opened up. Laying down the wounded man, Sisler went after the gun with a hand grenade. He destroyed it and killed three enemy soldiers who were sneaking up on him.

Sisler had moved the second man into the enclave when a forty-man enemy force burst out of the jungle, intent on killing the team. Without regard for his own safety, Sisler picked up some grenades and charged into the midst of the enemy force. With his rifle blazing—and throwing grenades as fast as he could pull their pins—Sisler single-handedly broke up the enemy attack.

Later, when U.S. gunships arrived on the scene, Sisler stood in the open to direct their fire onto the fleeing enemy. The fight was nearly over when an NVA sniper shot him down. The rest of the team was rescued a short time later. They brought Sisler's body out with them.

The Medal of Honor citation presented to Sisler's widow and sons on June 27, 1968 said the action happened in South Vietnam, not Laos.

Upon its arrival in South Vietnam in September 1966, the 4th "Ivy" Infantry Division was sent to the NVA-dominated Central Highlands region. In keeping with General Westmoreland's plan for aggressive offensive operations, the 4th's commander, Maj. Gen. William R. Peers, turned his men loose in the western halves of Pleiku and Kontum Provinces in January 1967.

The first month of Operation Sam Houston was relatively easy. After February 1, though, the action heated up.

Peers sent his 2d Brigade into the heavy rain forest west of the Nam Sathay River in Kontum Province. Some of the world's most hostile jungle terrain could be found there. Huge trees that reached over two hundred feet into the sky combined with dense undergrowth made movement through the rugged, mountainous terrain extremely difficult. Visibility in the jungle was restricted to a few meters at best. It was perfect country for ambushes.

On February 15, Company C, 1st Battalion, 12th Infantry, moved cautiously into the jungle from its LZ. The men had not proceeded very far when heavy automatic weapons fire ripped into their ranks. The grunts hit the dirt. One squad was caught in a ravine, unable to move its wounded to safety. Suddenly *PFC Louis E. Willett,* a twenty-two-year-old from Brooklyn, New York, rose to his feet and fired bursts from his M-60 machine gun at the enemy. Under his fire the squad began to withdraw. Urged by his buddies to pull back with them, Willett ignored their pleas and instead moved farther forward. He was hit several times but never gave up. He continued to take the enemy under fire, and that action allowed his squad to rejoin the company with all their casualties. Willett was cut down as he moved to a more advantageous position.

The next day, a few miles away, a platoon of Company C, 2d Battalion, 8th Infantry, was ambushed shortly after noon. Initially the platoon thought only a few NVA were involved. When they moved forward, however, the enemy fire intensified. The platoon faced annihilation. They called for supporting artillery fire, but the tightly woven jungle canopy made it difficult to place the rounds accurately. The NVA took the initiative and charged into the platoon. Hand-to-hand combat flared along the perimeter until the NVA were driven off. When finally rescued late that night, the survivors agreed that the actions of their platoon sergeant, *Elmelindo R. Smith,* saved their lives.

A native of Honolulu, Hawaii, the thirty-one-year-old Smith already had fourteen years of active duty behind him. He came to South Vietnam with the 4th Infantry Division from Fort Lewis, Washington, where he had left a wife and two children. Now, although he had been hit three times, Smith inspired his frightened men through his deliberate disregard of the enemy fire. He moved among the Ivy-men, directed their fire, repositioned them, and distributed badly needed ammunition.

He had moved forward to engage the enemy when a rocket propelled grenade exploded underneath him. Grievously wounded, Smith deliberately crawled into the jungle between the two forces so he could warn his platoon of any advancing enemy. The relieving company found his body there the next day.

Enemy activity also heated up in northern Quang Tri Province. On February 28 the first black Marine to earn a Medal of Honor died when he covered an exploding hand grenade with his own body. *PFC James Anderson, Jr.,* a twenty-year-old from Compton, California, was with Company F, 2d Battalion, 3d Marines, which had been sent to the relief of a heavily engaged unit northwest of Cam Lo. As the column of men proceeded down a narrow jungle trail, the NVA unleashed a vicious ambush. The battalion commander, Lt. Col. Victor Ohanesian, and the battalion sergeant major, died when the NVA showered the Marines with grenades. Anderson had hit the deck with the other members of his squad. As they lay together, a grenade rolled into their position. Anderson pulled it underneath him a split second before it detonated.

One of the more dangerous jobs in the air force belonged to the forward air controller. The FAC flew low and slow over a battlefield and spotted targets for army ground troops or air force attack planes. In their unarmed, light, single-engine aircraft, the FACs were particularly vulnerable to ground fire. In spite of this inherent danger, the FACs knew they were often the only contact between the ground forces and their desperately needed support—so they stayed above the battleground and relayed vital information long after it was unsafe to be there.

The aircraft most frequently flown by FACs was the Cessna-built O-1E Bird Dog. Closely resembling the popular Piper Cub, the O-1E offered no armor protection. The only weapons the pilot carried were an M-16 rifle and a .45-caliber pistol. These were supposed to be defensive weapons in case the plane went down. They were not designed to be offensive weapons.

HILLIARD A. WILBANKS

Hilliard A. Wilbanks earned his wings in 1954 after spending four years as an enlisted air force security guard. He served one year as an instructor before joining a squadron flying F-86 Sabre jets. In 1965, Wilbanks was tapped for training as a FAC. He reported to Hurlburt Field, Florida, then went to the 21st Tactical Air Support Squadron operating out of the South Vietnamese coastal city of Nha Trang.

In February 1967, Captain Wilbanks had completed the tenth month of his tour. Most of it had been spent in the area around Dalat, fifty miles west of Cam Ranh Bay, where he flew missions for an assortment of ARVN units. Late on the afternoon of February 24, Wilbanks took off on his 488th mission.

Earlier that day a local VC force had attacked three companies of ARVN from well-constructed positions hidden on two hills that overlooked a tea plantation. From their advantageous positions, the Viet Cong had let the friendly units walk deep into a trap before springing their ambush. The loss of vital radio gear kept them from warning a relieving column from the 23d Vietnamese Ranger Battalion about the deadly trap that awaited them.

Wilbanks was in contact with the Rangers' U.S. adviser, Capt. R. J. Wooten, and two nearby helicopter gunships. The Rangers had entered the tea plantation when Wilbanks spotted the enemy's camouflaged positions. He grabbed his microphone to warn Wooten.

When the VC realized their ambush had been compromised, they immediately opened fire on the Rangers, dropping them easily in a barrage of rifle fire.

Overhead, Wilbanks brought his Bird Dog directly over the enemy's positions. He marked their location with a smoke rocket, then called for the gunships. They roared in with machine guns blazing. Return fire hit one; the other chopper escorted it out of the area. In the lull that followed, the Viet Cong spilled out of their bunkers. With knives and bayonets bared, they advanced down the hill toward the badly disorganized and outnumbered Rangers.

Suddenly a smoke rocket exploded among the VC, diverting their attention. Wilbanks had brought his little Bird Dog down in a daring attack. When he came buzzing in for another pass, the VC let loose at him with .30- and .50-caliber machine gun fire. It did not stop Wilbanks. He fired off another smoke rocket, then came back again and let go his fourth, and last, rocket.

Captain Wooten said, "On each pass he was so close we could hear his plane being hit."

This would have been a good time for Wilbanks to retreat from the fight and let jet aircraft strafe the Viet Cong, but he did not think so. He still had one weapon at his disposal.

Wilbanks poked his M-16 out the side window of his Bird Dog and blazed away at the startled enemy. His audacious attack confused the VC. Some broke and ran, others ducked for cover. Wilbanks made three low passes over the enemy. Another adviser, Capt. Gary Vote, recalled that, "He was no more than one hundred feet off the ground."

On the last pass disaster struck. Vote watched in stunned silence as VC rifle fire brought the little plane down between the opposing forces. Vote gathered up a handful of Rangers to go to Wilbanks's aid. They protected the unconscious pilot until a medevac helicopter arrived. It took two attempts, under heavy fire, before the chopper could land. Vote helped put Wilbanks aboard, but it was too late. He died on the helicopter before it arrived at Nha Trang.

For his unsurpassed courage in disrupting the VC attack, Wilbanks was posthumously awarded the Medal of Honor on January 24, 1968.

* * *

The quick action of a young sailor saved five lives on March 6, 1967. *Seaman David G. Ouellet* served as a gunner on Patrol Boat 124. While the PBR slowly cruised the Cua Dai tributary of the Mekong River eighteen miles south of My Tho, the twenty-two-year-old from Wellesley, Massachusetts, saw a grenade being tossed at the boat from shore. He pulled himself from his protected gun position and ran aft down the narrow gunwale, shouting, "Duck!"

Ouellet bounded onto the engine compartment cover and pushed the boat's commander, Seaman James W. Van Zandt, to safety. A split second later the grenade landed in the boat. Ouellet threw himself between it and the rest of the crew as the grenade exploded. His body absorbed the lethal fragments and saved his shipmates from injury or death.

In the Central Highlands, the 4th Infantry Division was maintaining pressure on the NVA along the Cambodian border. The North Vietnamese regulars responded by going on the offensive. On March 12, 1967 one of its attached units, the 2d Battalion, 35th Infantry, was attacked in Kontum Province. In the opening minutes of the fight, *1st Lt. Stephen E. Karopczyc,* a platoon leader in Company A, took an enemy round in his chest just above his heart. Rather than accept medical evacuation, he plugged the bleeding hole with his finger. For over two hours the twenty-three-year-old from Bethpage, New York, led his platoon in a spirited defense of their isolated position. When a grenade landed by him and two wounded soldiers, Karopczyc attempted to cover the deadly missile with a steel helmet. The explosion drove more shrapnel into his body. Two hours later, still at the head of his men, the gallant officer died from loss of blood.

The average Viet Cong soldier was a tenacious fighter whose willingness to die for his cause was reminiscent of the fanatical Japanese soldiers of World War II. Some VC went to great lengths to kill their enemy. Forty-two-year-old Special Forces master sergeant *Charles E. Hosking* was escorting a VC suspect back to his base camp in Phuoc Long

Province on March 12, 1967 when the enemy soldier suddenly grabbed a grenade off of Hosking's web belt and ran toward a group of four Americans standing nearby. Hosking took off after him. When he reached the VC, he leaped on the man's back, forced him to the ground, and held him there in a bear hug. Hosking, an original member of the Special Forces who had been wounded during World War II's Battle of the Bulge, died in the explosion that followed but saved his command group from certain death.

Meanwhile, in Hau Nghia and Tay Ninh Provinces west of Saigon, the units participating in Operation Junction City continued to push their offensive against the wily foe.

RUPPERT L. SARGENT

During a sweep of a hamlet in Hau Nghia Province on March 15, 1967, a former VC led *1st Lt. Ruppert L. Sargent* and three members of his platoon to a Viet Cong meetinghouse and weapons cache. Sargent, twenty-nine years old, saw that the tunnel entrance was booby-trapped. He called for a demolition man to place a charge that would detonate the booby trap. The resulting explosion did not work, but it did flush a VC from hiding. One of Sargent's men cut the man down.

Sargent and two others stepped toward the tunnel entrance. Suddenly another VC broke from cover, tossed two grenades at the Americans, then fled. Sargent fired three shots from his rifle at the man, then turned and threw himself over the grenades.

Sargent was killed in the explosion, but his gallant efforts saved the lives of his two comrades.

In July 1968 the recommendation for Sargent's posthumous Medal of Honor was approved. He would be the first black officer so recognized. Pentagon officials who contacted Sargent's widow to arrange for the presentation ceremony were stunned when she refused to accept the award. Her refusal stemmed from her strong religious convictions.

A Jehovah's Witness, she professed allegiance to God alone and not to any organized government. Sargent's mother, also a Jehovah's Witness, supported her daughter-in-law. She had, in fact, opposed her son's entrance into the army.

Born January 9, 1938 in Hampton, Virginia, Sargent had enlisted in the army in January 1959 after finishing two years of college. Although he was raised as a Jehovah's Witness, the attraction of a military career overcame his religious beliefs. After six years as an enlisted man, Sargent was accepted for officer's training. He received his gold bars on October 15, 1965. He went to Company B, 4th Battalion, 9th Infantry, 25th Infantry Division, in September 1966. Six months later he was killed in action.

For several months after Mrs. Sargent's refusal, senior army officers continued their efforts to persuade her to accept the award. She continued to decline. At last, when the army agreed to make the presentation in private, with no publicity, she consented.

On March 10, 1969, Brig. Gen. Donly P. Bolton drove from Washington to Hampton. In the presence of Sargent's two children, Bolton solemnly handed the widow the medal and citation.

One Pentagon official, after reading Sargent's citation, said he felt sure Mrs. Sargent had no right to keep her husband's award a secret. "He belongs to the country now," he said.

DAVID H. MCNERNEY

David H. McNerney typified what many of the young, conscripted soldiers and Marines who served during the Vietnam War derisively referred to as a "lifer." Born July 2, 1931 in Lowell, Massachusetts, McNerney grew up in Houston, Texas. McNerney's father Edward instilled a great sense of patriotism and responsibility in all of his children. As a genuine hero of the First World War, Edward McNerney knew what he was talking about.

The first sergeant of Company K, 104th Infantry Regiment, 26th Infantry Division, Edward McNerney earned a Distinguished Service Cross on July 22, 1918 when he rescued a wounded man under heavy enemy machine gun fire near Epieds, France. In addition to that prestigious medal, he came home with a Silver Star, two Purple Hearts, and the French Croix de Guerre.

Because of their father, the McNerney children understood better than many others that life in a free country often carries a hefty price tag. Two of Edward McNerney's children served in World War II. Another flew combat missions in Southeast Asia as a navy pilot.

David McNerney first served a four-year hitch in the navy, then enlisted in the army in 1954. When he arrived in South Vietnam in September 1966 he had already served two one-year tours there as an adviser. Now, like his father before him, McNerney was the first sergeant of a rifle company.

In the final days of the 4th Infantry Division's Operation Sam Houston, radio contact was lost with a recon platoon that had been operating near Polei Doc in Kontum Province. McNerney's Company A, 1st Battalion, 8th Infantry, got the mission to go in after them.

At 7:30 A.M. on March 22, enemy machine gun fire hit Company A hard. McNerney assisted his CO in establishing a perimeter and putting out a strong base of fire. As he led a squad into position, he noticed several NVA slinking through the thick jungle. He killed them all, but was blown off his feet by an exploding enemy grenade. Badly injured in the right side of his chest, McNerney ignored the pain and assaulted an enemy machine gun bunker and destroyed it. A few minutes later, McNerney learned that his CO and the artillery forward observer had been blown to bits by a direct hit from an enemy B-40 rocket. As a result, the company panicked. Men threw away equipment and fought without coordination.

McNerney did what any good "first shirt" would do under similar circumstances: He took charge.

The brave NCO ran among his men and yelled, cursed, and cajoled the grunts into maintaining discipline under fire. "Pick your targets," he yelled. He had a radio operator bring him the forward observer's radio, then called for artillery fire to within fifty feet of his company's position. The rounds crashed into the ground, weakening the NVAs' grip on the unit.

McNerney called for air strikes, too, but the company had run out of the colored smoke grenades used to identify their position to friendly aircraft. Without them the jets would not know where the infantry was located.

McNerney solved that problem when he dashed into a nearby clearing and held aloft an identification panel. He remained in the open, oblivious to the enemy fire, until he was sure that the aircraft had spotted him. Then he climbed a tree and tied the panel to its highest branches.

Because of McNerney's actions, the supporting aircraft were able to properly drop their ordnance and reduce the enemy's fire. In order to clear an LZ for the medevac choppers so they could carry away the wounded and dead, McNerney crawled outside the company's perimeter to recover explosive charges from abandoned rucksacks.

Although his injuries would have allowed him a place on an outbound helicopter, McNerney refused to go. The company, his company, needed him. He stayed with Company A until a new commander flew out the next day.

President Johnson presented McNerney with the Medal of Honor in White House ceremonies on September 19, 1968. McNerney finished twenty years' service to his country in 1969, retired, then took a job with the U.S. Customs. Today he is completely retired.

In Quang Tri Province, Company I, 3d Battalion, 9th Marines, 3d Marine Division, spent March 30, 1967 on a routine patrol between Con Thien and Cam Lo. After the CO, Capt. Michael P. Getlin, selected a night defensive position atop Hill 70 about seven miles northwest of Cam Lo, he dispatched his rifle platoons on ambush duty. They had not been gone long when NVA mortar shells dropped out of the sky and pounded the Marines on the hill. A short time later a company of North Vietnamese regulars swarmed out of the surrounding jungle. Captain Getlin called for artillery fire. From their base at Camp Carroll, west of Cam Lo, the howitzers barked and their shells flew through the night. They landed with remarkable accuracy among the NVA and drove them back into the jungle.

In the meantime, Company I's platoons abandoned their ambush mission and headed back to Hill 70. The NVA ambushed them and blunted their movement.

Back at the CP, the NVA attacked out of the jungle a second time. *2d Lt. John P. Bobo,* a twenty-four-year-old from Niagara Falls, New York, who commanded the Weapons Platoon, helped organize a defense. He moved from position to position and offered encouragement to the outnumbered Marines. After he recovered a rocket launcher from a disabled man and put it back into action, an NVA mortar round exploded at his feet and blew off his right leg below the knee.

The intrepid Bobo never faltered. He refused evacuation. Instead, he wrapped a belt around his leg, then, with his bloody stump jammed into the dirt, stayed on the firing line to cover the withdrawal of the command group to safety.

"I saw him kill at least five North Vietnamese soldiers although he had been seriously wounded," said the company's first sergeant, Raymond G. Rogers. "He killed the NVA who had wounded me in the leg and who was standing over me."

Bobo's heavy firing made him a target for the NVA. He was still kneeling there, rifle blazing, when he was cut down. In addition to Bobo, Getlin and fifteen other Marines were killed and forty-seven were wounded. Bobo's Medal of Honor was presented to his family on August 27, 1968.

MICHAEL J. ESTOCIN

On April 20, 1967, navy lieutenant commander *Michael J. Estocin* led three jet fighters from the carrier *Ticonderoga* in a raid on surface-to-air missile (SAM) sites near Haiphong, North Vietnam. His A-4 Skyhawk was struck early in the assault, but Estocin, a graduate of Slippery Rock University in Pennsylvania, continued on his mission. He repeatedly ignored the enemy antiaircraft fire directed at his plane to press home his attack. Several times he flew through the intense firing and destroyed three SAM sites. As a result of his intrepid actions, his plane was leaking fuel so badly that it was necessary for Estocin to fly the last one hundred miles back to his carrier sucking fuel from an airborne tanker. Despite the damage to his aircraft, he coaxed his plane down to a perfect landing.

Six days later, and one day before his thirty-sixth birthday, Estocin was again over Haiphong. A SAM exploded with violent fury abeam the port intake of Estocin's Skyhawk and ripped huge holes all along its nose and the cockpit area. The plane was thrown into a violent half barrel roll to the right, went inverted, and headed down. Flames burned the aircraft's belly and wing roots. Estocin's wingman, Lt. John B. Nichols, pulled up alongside the crippled plane as it rolled upright. Nichols repeatedly and frantically radioed Estocin, but had no response. He could see Estocin slumped forward in the cockpit, motionless.

From their original altitude of 21,000 feet, the two planes descended earthward. Nichols stayed right beside Estocin the entire time, ever watchful for some sign of life, some evidence that Estocin was alive, but he never observed the slightest movement. Through a cloud layer hanging 1,500 feet above the ground, the two planes continued their descent. At about 600 feet, Estocin's crippled jet rolled left, its nose pointed downward, then crashed.

Nichols circled, searching for any sign of life or a parachute. But there was nothing. He called off any rescue attempt. Back aboard the *Ticonderoga,* Nichols related the day's events at his debriefing.

Amazingly, despite Nichols's eyewitness account of Estocin's crash, rumors began to circulate one year later that Estocin was a POW in Hanoi. Although these rumors later proved false, they allowed Estocin's family a glimmer of hope that he might be alive. As a result, when a posthumous Medal of Honor for his heroic actions on April 20, 1967 was approved a few years later, Estocin's widow refused to accept it. By accepting it she would have allowed the navy to finalize their declaration of her husband as killed in action rather than missing in action, and this action would have drastically changed the benefits she had been receiving as an MIA's wife.

By 1978, though, the inevitable could no longer be denied. The navy officially declared Estocin killed in action. His widow accepted his posthumous Medal of Honor on February 27, 1978.

When three men from Company C, 1st Battalion, 35th Infantry, 25th Infantry Division, were critically wounded by an enemy machine gun near the hamlet of Duc Pho (on the coast in southern Quang Ngai Province) on April 25, 1967 *Sp4. Kenneth E. Stumpf* made three trips through a barrage of exploding enemy mortar rounds to carry the casualties to safety. He then armed himself with grenades and used them to wipe out three enemy bunkers.

Discharged after his two years of conscripted service ended in September 1967, Stumpf returned to his hometown of Menasha, Wisconsin. After receiving his Medal of Honor on September 19, 1968, the twenty-three-year-old reenlisted. He served two more tours in South Vietnam and earned several more valor decorations and a Purple Heart. He remained in the army and eventually retired as a sergeant major.

On April 28, 1967, General Westmoreland made an unprecedented appearance before a joint session of Congress. Never before had a military commander addressed Congress while he was directing an ongoing war. Westmoreland had come at the express invitation of President Johnson, who was seeking a way to silence the increasingly vocal opponents of his war policy.

Westmoreland told the assemblage that no previous military man "could have more pride than is mine in representing the gallant men fighting in Vietnam today." But Westmoreland was not very optimistic. "In the months ahead," he said, U.S. soldiers would see "some of the bitterest fighting of the war, with no end in sight."

The general's concerns over the progress of the war were reflected in his new demands for additional troops. Westmoreland submitted two plans: one he dubbed a "minimum essential" force of 80,500 more men for a total of 550,500. His optimum plan, though, called for 200,000 more men, a number that would raise the total to 670,000.

When questioned by President Johnson and his advisers, Westmoreland exhibited the same frustration experienced by a growing number of Americans. Pressed for an answer on when the war might end, Westmoreland could only say "three or more years" with the minimum number of troops, perhaps "two years" with the higher level.

In a war where progress was based on specificity of numbers and systems analysis, it was not a very good estimate.

The 9th Infantry Division was the first unit specifically organized for service in South Vietnam. Earmarked for the swamps and rice paddies of the Mekong River Delta south of Saigon, the deployment of the division had been expedited by chopping three months off of its training cycle. When the division arrived in-country in December 1966, its mission was to clear the Viet Cong from Long An and Dinh Tuong Provinces south of Saigon. Accustomed to operating unmolested in this area, the VC fought back hard. Even after several months of tough combat, the VC still controlled the countryside.

LEONARD B. KELLER
AND RAYMOND R. WRIGHT

For most of the morning of May 2, 1967, Company A, 3d Battalion, 60th Infantry, 9th Infantry Division, had slogged through the rice paddies around Ap Bac in Long An Province. Throughout the hot, sticky day intermittent sniper fire had harassed the men. Capt. Joseph Mazuta sent out small patrols to locate and destroy the snipers but had no luck. Now, as his company approached a tree line at the end of a rice paddy, he planned to break for lunch, then head back to his base camp.

Mazuta had finished giving instructions to his first sergeant when enemy automatic weapons fire erupted from the tree line. A dozen grunts fell. The rest of the company scrambled to find cover. Mortar rounds crashed into the paddy, spewing water and spreading death.

In response to Mazuta's call for help, three air force jets strafed the tree line. When they finished, the captain prepared two platoons for an attack. But as the men rose, a new burst of heavy fire drove them down. The VC were so well entrenched that the aerial attack had caused them little damage.

Mazuta was ready to take his entire company in after the enemy when movement at the end of the line caught his eye. Two of his men were going into the tree line alone.

Two draftees, twenty-year-old sergeant *Leonard B. Keller* from Rockford, Illinois, and twenty-one-year-old Sp4 *Raymond R. Wright* from Mineville, New York, raced forward. The pair entered the tree line and leapfrogged through the bunkers. Together the two gallant youths destroyed one position after another.

Armed with an M-60 machine gun, Keller would take a bunker under fire and pin down the occupants. Then Wright would sneak up to drop in a grenade. For over thirty minutes the two fought the VC. They repeatedly ignored the enemy fire directed at them to knock out seven enemy bunkers and kill no less than a dozen VC. Their heroic actions forced the other enemy soldiers to withdraw from the battlefield. When their self-appointed mission was completed, the pair returned to the company perimeter, where they helped treat and evacuate the wounded.

As soon as it became apparent that the men were going to be recommended for the Medal of Honor, they were pulled out of the field; the commanding general of the 9th Infantry Division did not want to run the risk of them being killed in a subsequent action. They spent the balance of their tour as aides to the general, essentially digging his foxhole for him whenever he visited the field. But it was safe duty and ensured that the intrepid duo would live to wear their medals.

And they did. In a ceremony at the White House on September 19, 1968, long after each man had been discharged, President Johnson presented them their well-deserved awards.

After the ceremony, the two went their separate ways and never spoke again. Wright returned to his home in the isolated mountains of upstate New York. He married, raised a family, and went to work on a state highway department road repair crew. He held that job until he retired a few months before his death on September 23, 1999. He seldom spoke of his war experiences and rarely participated in any veterans functions. The newspaper that serves Mineville did not know that he was a Medal of Honor recipient and thus did not carry his obituary.

Keller also avoided the limelight. He left his family in Rockford and moved to Florida soon after he received his medal. He found employment with the navy at their base in Pensacola. He participated in some veterans activities but never was comfortable in the role of war hero.

The war in the Central Highlands heated up in early May for the 4th Infantry Division. For over a week, dubbed the "Seven Days in May" by the Ivy-men, the NVA attacked the division's units whenever and wherever they chose. The fighting was brutal and vicious and resulted in a number of Medals of Honor.

On May 18, 1967 the commander of Company B, 1st Battalion, 8th Infantry, sent one of his platoons to investigate the sighting of a lone enemy soldier on a nearby well-used trail. Unfortunately, it was a favorite tactic of the NVA to lure an American unit into an ambush.

The K4 Battalion, 32d NVA Regiment, attacked the platoon and isolated it from the rest of the company. Survivors of that desperate fight told how their leader, *Platoon Sgt. Bruce A. Grandstaff,* of Spokane, Washington, organized the platoon in its fight against the NVA. He seemed to be everywhere as he threw grenades, fired his rifle, and cared for the injured. Even after he was wounded twice, he still destroyed one enemy machine gun. Hit a third time, he called down artillery fire directly on his location when he realized the NVA were on the verge of overrunning his position.

Only seven of the thirty-five platoon members lived through that fight. They told of how the NVA walked over the battlefield and systematically shot any American who showed any sign of life. The enemy looted and mutilated the bodies before melting back into the jungle. The survivors also reported that it took a direct hit from an enemy rocket to put thirty-two-year-old Grandstaff out of action.

Two nights later and just a few miles away, the entire 1st Battalion, 8th Infantry, was savagely attacked by three human-wave assaults by soldiers from the K5 Battalion, 32d NVA Regiment. The grunts fought off the enemy, but at heavy cost. Two men earned Medals of Honor in the bitter fight. Twenty-five-year-old private first class *Leslie A. Bellrichard,* a rifleman in Company C who had grown up in Madison, Wisconsin, and who had a wife in San Jose, California, was ready to throw a hand grenade when an exploding mortar round knocked it from his hand. Realizing the danger to the four men sharing his bunker, Bellrichard dropped down and covered the grenade with his own body. Although mortally wounded by the explosion, Bellrichard nonetheless struggled to an upright position and defiantly fired his M-16 into the charging enemy. He remained in that position until he succumbed to his massive wounds.

S.Sgt. Frankie Z. Molnar, a squad leader in Company B, had been among the first to spot the enemy when he cut down five NVA who were sneaking up on his position. He fought bravely throughout the attack and several times left the relative safety of his spider hole to bring badly needed ammunition to his men. As the battle waned, Molnar moved among the many casualties and administered first aid. He and several other soldiers were moving a severely injured man to an evacuation point when an enemy grenade landed at their feet. Rather than dive for cover, Molnar dropped on the grenade, shielding the others from the explosion. The twenty-four-year-old native of Logan, West Virginia, died instantly in the blast, but the casualty and Molnar's four buddies survived.

MELVIN E. NEWLIN

Just before midnight on July 3, 1967, one of Marine 1st Lt. James B. Scuras's outposts reported movement out in front of their position. Scuras's unit, Company F, 2d Battalion, 5th Marines, 1st Marine Division, provided security for South Vietnam's only producing coal mine, at Nong Son in Quang Nam Province. Before the officer could respond, the radio crackled with the desperate message "We're being overrun," then went silent.

Seconds later, enemy mortar rounds fell out of the sky; one destroyed the 4.2-inch mortars' supply of ammunition. Immediately thereafter, Viet Cong sappers appeared at the company's perimeter, where they threw satchel charges into the Marines' bunkers. The attack would have overwhelmed the company if it had not been for the valor of one eighteen-year-old Marine.

One month after graduating from high school in the Ohio River town of Wellsville, Ohio, in June 1966, *Melvin E. Newlin* enlisted in the Marine Corps. He completed boot camp at Parris Island, South Carolina, then attended infantry training at Camp Lejeune, North Carolina. He arrived in South Vietnam in March 1967.

Newlin fought with his company throughout Quang Nam Province in Operations New Castle, Union, and Calhoun. When his company was assigned guard duty at the coal mine, it looked like it would be two months of easy duty, or "skating" as the troops called it. Until the night of July 3.

An explosive charge thrown during the initial moments of the attack killed Newlin's four foxhole buddies and seriously wounded him. Ignoring the pain, Newlin kept his M-60 machine gun in action and halted two determined attempts by the VC to silence him. Then an exploding VC grenade knocked him unconscious.

With the main threat to their attack thus silenced, the VC moved into the center of the perimeter. There they destroyed the company's two 4.2-inch mortars and killed the weapons' crews. The Viet Cong were on the verge of wiping out the Marine positions on the opposite side of the perimeter when Newlin came to.

Instead of seeking treatment for his grievous wounds, Newlin remanned his machine gun. Burst after burst of hot lead from his weapon cut holes in the enemy's ranks. At one point Newlin temporarily shifted his fire to kill some VC who had taken over the Marines' 106mm recoilless rifle.

Even though he became the main target of a renewed enemy assault, Newlin never faltered. He continued to fire his machine gun until an enemy soldier sneaked up and killed him. Newlin's actions completely disrupted the enemy attack, though, and allowed the Company F Marines a chance to reorganize and time for a relief unit to arrive.

The posthumous Medal of Honor earned by Private First Class Newlin was presented to his parents on March 18, 1969 by newly inaugurated president Richard M. Nixon. During the ceremony Newlin's mother broke down and sobbed heavily. Nixon put his arm around her in a comforting gesture while he grimaced at her obvious pain. When a UPI wire photo of the moment appeared in newspapers across the country the next day, the president was furious. Nixon, who never believed the press treated him fairly, thought the photograph made him appear to be grinning at the grieving mother. He immediately banned the media from all future Medal of Honor presentations at which he presided. Thereafter only official government photographers enjoyed access to the ceremonies.

* * *

The most versatile weapon in the Vietnam War was undoubtedly the helicopter. The choppers not only provided the infantryman with a previously unknown mobility, but the rotor-winged machines lifted him into and out of battle, evacuated the dead and wounded, brought in supplies, and helped overcome many of the advantages held by the NVA and VC. Flown by courageous, and mostly young, pilots, the choppers flew so many hazardous missions that extraordinary valor became an everyday occurrence. It took a truly outstanding display of heroism for a chopper pilot to earn a Medal of Honor.

STEPHEN W. PLESS

The UH-1E helicopter (the famed "Huey") piloted by Marine captain *Stephen W. Pless* on August 19, 1967 was the "chase," or backup, helicopter for an emergency medevac mission. Pless was airborne over southern Quang Ngai Province when he picked up an emergency call over his radio. Four soldiers were stranded on the beach north of Duc Pho and were about to be overrun by a large Viet Cong force. Unless they were rescued soon, they would not live.

With a quick glance at his copilot, Capt. Rupert E. Fairchild, Jr., Pless broke off from his mission and turned his Huey toward Duc Pho.

Born in Newnan, Georgia, on September 6, 1937, Pless enlisted in the Marine Corps in 1956 while a student at Georgia Military Academy at College Park, Georgia. Three years later he was accepted for flight training, and he earned his wings on April 20, 1960.

Over the next several years Pless participated in a number of peacekeeping missions, including service in Africa and a tour in South Vietnam in 1962. In 1966 he returned to that country to serve as air adviser to the Republic of Korea Marine Brigade based at Chu Lai. In March 1967 he transferred to Marine Observation Squadron 6, Marine Air Group 36, as assistant operations officer.

When Pless brought his chopper over the battleground north of Duc Pho on August 19, he saw about fifty Viet Cong in the open; some were bayoneting and beating the trapped grunts. Pless flew in low while his door gunners fired at the enemy. He came in again and unleashed a pair of rockets into the swirling mass of enemy soldiers. Pless then came back around for several more passes. He came in so low that the Huey repeatedly flew through the debris thrown up by his rocket's explosions. But the rockets and machine gun rounds killed and wounded a score of VC and sent the others scurrying for cover.

Pless ignored the small-arms fire ripping through his thin-skinned Huey and deliberately set the machine down between the wounded men and the enemy. The two crewmen, G.Sgt. Leroy N. Paulson and L.Cpl. John G. Phelps, leaped from the chopper and raced through the enemy fire to the casualties.

Pless then hovered his Huey and used the Huey's pilot-operated weapons to send streams of machine gun fire into the nearby tree line. That kept most of the VC pinned down. A few did sneak through, though. Copilot Fairchild shot three of them within ten feet of the chopper before he too left the ship to help load the wounded.

While Pless skillfully maneuvered the Huey and kept a steady hail of fire directed at the enemy, the three crewmen piled the wounded soldiers aboard. Pless then headed the dangerously overloaded Huey out to sea, away from the murderous enemy fire. Four times the chopper settled on the water. Four times Pless nursed the machine back into the air while the crew tossed out all unnecessary equipment. At last the Huey became airborne and limped off to Chu Lai.

Besides being credited with the rescue of his countrymen, Pless was credited with killing 20 VC with another 40 as probables. The three crew members each received a Navy Cross for their heroism. Pless received the Medal of Honor from President Johnson on January 16, 1969.

Promoted to major in November 1967, Pless was considered a sharp, up-and-coming young Marine officer with general's stars in his future when tragedy struck. Early on the morning of July 20, 1969, after a night of heavy drinking, Pless raced his motorcycle up an opening drawbridge that spanned Santa Rosa Sound between Pensacola and Pensacola Beach, Florida. Whether he thought he could safely jump the widening gap or planned to stop before his bike reached the barricade will never be known. He and his motorcycle flew into the night air and disappeared. Pless's body was fished from the murky waters of the sound the next day.

Pless was buried at Barrancas National Cemetery in Pensacola at the naval air station. He left a widow and three children.

Marine Corps combat photographer *Cpl. William T. Perkins, Jr.* was covering the action of Company C, 1st Battalion, 1st Marines, 1st Marine Division, during Operation Medina in the rugged Hai Lang National Forest in southern Quang Tri Province on October 12, 1967. While he waited at the company command post for a medevac chopper to carry out the wounded from a just-concluded engagement, the twenty-year-old Californian saw an enemy hand grenade land behind the company commander. Perkins yelled "Grenade!" then threw himself on the deadly missile. The explosion killed him but the officer lived. Perkins is the only combat photographer to earn the Medal of Honor in any war.

JEDH C. BARKER

Devotion to the Marine Corps and a high commitment to military service characterized the George C. Barker family of Franklin, New Hampshire. George had served in the Marines in World War II and saw action on Bougainville. He instilled patriotic values in his children. His oldest son, Warren C., was commissioned a second lieutenant in the Marine Corps when he graduated from college, earned a Purple

Heart in Korea, and decided to make the Marines his career. The second son, Jedh C.—named for George's four best buddies from World War II: John, Ezekial, Donald, and Herbert—quit college in May 1966 to enlist in the Marines. Jedh told his father, "You guys did your job, now it's my turn."

Maj. Warren Barker saw his brother for the last time in June 1967. "It was probably the only time many of the other Marines there saw a lance corporal hug a major," Warren said. Jedh had arrived in South Vietnam in March 1967. Assigned to Marine Air Group 12 at Da Nang, he was a machine gunner on security duty at the air base. Jedh asked Warren to pull some strings. But Jedh was not trying to avoid combat; indeed, he wanted a transfer to a line company.

"I said, 'Stay where you are,'" Warren said. "But he insisted and was transferred."

Jedh Barker arrived in Company F, 2d Battalion, 4th Marines, in June 1967. On September 2, 1967 the company was pulling duty at Con Thien, a Marine strong point just a few miles south of the DMZ. Barker's platoon was sent on a reconnaissance patrol that day. As the Marines moved through the scrub brush, an enemy automatic weapon opened fire.

Barker dropped. He had been hit along with several others. Despite intense pain, Barker set up his M-60 machine gun and returned the enemy's fire.

Almost immediately Barker became a target. The NVA focused their fire on his weapon. A flurry of enemy rounds ripped into the position. Several men were hit, including Barker for the second time. An enemy round nearly destroyed his right hand. Before the severity of that injury had fully registered on Barker, an enemy hand grenade dropped among the cluster of wounded Marines.

Barker reached out with his good hand and pulled the grenade underneath him. The subsequent blast horribly wounded Barker and several other Marines. Thinking only of others, Barker spent the last moments of his life trying to put a battle dressing on the wound of a buddy.

When George Barker accepted his son's posthumous Medal of Honor, he said simply, "Jedh was a real God-and-country man."

In the spring of 1967 the elite 1st Brigade of the 101st Airborne Division was assigned to Task Force Oregon. Organized around three separate army brigades (the others were the 196th Infantry Brigade and the 3d Brigade, 25th Infantry Division), TF Oregon was sent into enemy-dominated Quang Ngai Province so the Marine units there could move north to battle the NVA along the DMZ.

Throughout the summer and fall of 1967, TF Oregon searched for the 2d VC Regiment, the primary opponent in the province. A typical day for troops of the task force involved light combat action against an elusive foe. On occasion, though, the VC went on the offensive.

WEBSTER ANDERSON

At 3:00 A.M., October 15, 1967, the Viet Cong hit Battery A, 2d Battalion, 320th Artillery (Airborne), at its fire support base near Tam Ky in Quang Tin Province. The intensity of the attack stunned the cannoneers. That the battery did not suffer more was due to the valor of a thirty-four-year-old staff sergeant from Winnsboro, South Carolina.

Webster Anderson reacted to the furious attack by mounting the exposed parapet of his howitzer position to direct point-blank cannon fire on the VC hordes. The blasts from two enemy grenades destroyed both his legs, but Anderson never faltered. Despite his crippling injuries and in excruciating pain, Anderson remained in position to direct the fire of his crew. When an enemy grenade landed near a wounded comrade, Anderson picked it up and attempted to throw it back. It exploded before he could toss it away, carrying away his right hand. Although only partly conscious, Anderson continued to inspire his men until the attack ended. Only then would he consider evacuation.

The fourteen-year veteran spent nearly a year recuperating from his grievous injuries. On November 24, 1969 he stood proudly on his two artificial legs while President Nixon draped the blue ribbon of the Medal of Honor around his neck. Anderson died on August 30, 2003.

The American (23d Infantry) Division was formed on September 25, 1967 from the remnants of Task Force Oregon after the 1st Brigade, 101st Airborne Division, was released to its parent unit and the 3d Brigade of the 25th Infantry Division was redesignated the 3d Brigade, 4th Infantry Division (the 4th's 3d Brigade went to the 25th in the swap). The American had its roots in World War II, when it was originally activated on New Caledonia by Gen. Douglas MacArthur for use alongside the 1st Marine Division on Guadalcanal. During its fifteen-hundred-plus days in South Vietnam, the American operated in the I Corps area, primarily in Quang Nam and Quang Tin Provinces.

The first Medal of Honor recipient from the division was *1st Lt. James Taylor,* a twenty-nine-year-old Californian. When enemy forces struck his column of armored personnel carriers from Troop B, 1st Cavalry, on November 9, 1967 near Que Son in Quang Tin Province, Taylor braved heavy enemy fire to rescue fifteen trapped crew members from three burning vehicles. He then attacked and killed three NVA who were manning a machine gun that had been pouring deadly fire on his position.

The 25th Infantry Division continued to aggressively pursue the VC in the jungles and rubber tree plantations northwest of Saigon throughout 1967. Although the combat never reached the intensity experienced by the division during Operation Junction City, the action was often sharp.

RILEY L. PITTS

Born in Fallis, Oklahoma, on October 15, 1937, *Riley L. Pitts* grew up in Oklahoma City. He was commissioned through the ROTC program when he graduated from the University of Wichita in June 1960. Before being assigned to the 25th Infantry Division's 2d Battalion, 27th Infantry, in December 1966, Pitts had served two years in France.

Like most officers in South Vietnam, Pitts's combat command time was limited to six months. He spent his first six months in-country as a public information officer working with civilian reporters who wanted to visit the division's field units. During that time he repeatedly asked for reassignment to a rifle company, but there were more infantry captains than there were infantry companies.

When Pitts finally took over Company C, he proved himself to be a tough, capable, and fair commander. Never one to ask his men to do something he would not do himself, Pitts earned a Silver Star and a Bronze Star in his first three months of combat. His heroism peaked on October 31, 1967 following an air assault near Ap Dong in Tay Ninh Province.

The LZ was cold when the unarmed Hueys dropped Company C off. But no sooner had the "slicks" left than the VC opened up with heavy automatic weapons fire from a position in the nearby jungle. This was a favorite ambush technique of the VC.

Pitts hastily organized his men and overran the enemy position, personally killing the gun's crew. Ordered to head north to aid another company that had come under attack by a strong enemy force, Pitts led his company into the jungle. The grunts had not proceeded very far when they were hit from three sides by enemy fire. Pitts dived for cover. Two of the four enemy positions were less than fifteen yards away. He could not maneuver his company due to the heavy volume of fire; instead, he took it upon himself to wipe out the bunkers.

While his small command group provided covering fire, Pitts tried to knock out one bunker with shots from his M-16. When that did not work, Pitts grabbed a Chinese grenade carried by one of his men and stood up to toss it at the enemy bunker.

To the horror of those watching, the grenade rebounded off a tree branch and fell back into the command group. Without hesitation Pitts dropped on it, intent only on saving his men.

As Pitts lay there on the jungle floor, bullets snapping overhead, his men diving for cover, the seconds passed like hours. After what seemed to be forever, Pitts realized the grenade was a dud. With a weak laugh he rolled aside, picked the bomb up, and tossed it away.

Unable to spare any time to reflect on his release from sure death, Pitts ordered his company to fall back so that he could bring in artillery support. When the barrage ended, the determined officer led his company back into the battle. He died at the head of his men, urging them on even as he collapsed from multiple gunshot wounds.

Pitts's recommendation for the Medal of Honor slowly worked its way up through the chain of command over the next year, but some reviewers recommended against making the award. After all, the grenade had not detonated, they said. In the end, Pitts's supporters won. The fact that the grenade was a dud, they favorably argued, lessened not one bit Pitts's deliberate willingness to sacrifice his own life to save his men.

When President Johnson presented Pitts's widow and two children with his posthumous Medal of Honor on October 10, 1968, it was the first ever awarded under such circumstances. It would not be the last.

Beginning in the fall of 1967, the North Vietnamese army general Nguyen Giap launched a series of offensive operations that were designed to pull American forces away from South Vietnam's cities and population centers and bog them down in the remote interior regions. Known as the "border battles" to the Americans, this initiative resulted in increased fighting in and around Con Thien below the DMZ, in the Central Highlands near Dak To, and at Loc Ninh northwest of Saigon near the Cambodian border.

On October 27, Viet Cong main force units launched what proved to be a futile attempt to capture Loc Ninh, a district capital. To blunt the attack, the commander of the U.S. 1st Infantry Division, who had tactical responsibility for that region, sent several rifle companies to the area. The grunts began what was called a reconnaissance-in-force; essentially they patrolled through the nearby rubber plantation until they made contact with the enemy. Contact was made on November 7, 1967.

ROBERT F. STRYKER

As a young man growing up in the town of Throop, New York, near Auburn, *Robert F. Stryker* was quiet and kept to himself. Rather than hang around with a group of buddies, Stryker preferred to catch crabs and minnows by himself in one of several creeks that ran near his rural home. He liked to ride his bike along the paths in Pine Hill Cemetery, just a few miles up the road from the house his widower father had built by hand.

Harold Stryker had raised his two sons and daughter alone after his wife died in 1950. Harold was a strict single parent who kept a tight rein on his children because he wanted the best for them. That is why he balked when Robert wanted to quit school after the ninth grade. Harold wanted his children to have the education he lacked so they could have a better life. But Robert persisted. He did not like school and saw no reason to continue. When he announced one day that he had found a job in Auburn with a tire company, Harold relented.

Robert enjoyed working around cars; it was a perfect job for the quiet young man. His brother John once described Robert as "so quiet you didn't even know he was around. And he never got mad at anybody."

After five years at the tire shop, Robert Stryker realized he would soon be drafted. Because he wanted a chance to pick his job and travel, Stryker enlisted in the army on January 22, 1963. He ended up in Germany. He wrote home every few weeks but seldom mentioned himself, his travels, or any buddies. Mostly he just asked how everyone was.

When his enlistment was up, Stryker could have taken his discharge, returned home, and gone back to the tire shop. But the war in South Vietnam had erupted. Stryker felt an obligation to go. He reenlisted in January 1967. His sister Leola said, "He knew he had to be there, defending his country."

Robert Stryker left for the war zone in April 1967. Upon his arrival, he was assigned to Company C, 1st Battalion, 26th Infantry, 1st Infantry Division.

Stryker's letters home mentioned little of the war, any buddies, or the combat he experienced. Whether he wanted to spare his family worry or was just being his normal quiet self, no one will ever know.

On November 7, 1967, Company C was part of the multi-company reconnaissance sent to search for the VC near Loc Ninh. Stryker carried an M-79 grenade launcher. As his company moved through the dense underbrush, the VC opened fire. Rocket-propelled grenades, automatic weapons, and small-arms fire tore into the Americans.

Stryker pumped rounds out of his grenade launcher as fast as he could reload. He detected an element of VC who were working their way through the foliage to outflank his company. Without hesitation Stryker moved to the threatened area and took the enemy soldiers under fire. His grenades stopped their advance.

As Stryker moved back to his original position, he noticed an enemy claymore mine near a group of wounded grunts. He yelled a warning and flung himself on the mine. The device erupted. Stryker died, but six Americans lived as a result of his action.

Word of Robert Stryker's death reached his family on November 9, his twenty-third birthday. They buried him in the cemetery he used to play in as a youth. Over the next few months a number of medals were delivered to the family. Among them were a Bronze Star, a Purple Heart, and several South Vietnamese awards. But they were not told how Stryker met his death—until the Medal of Honor was presented to Harold on November 4, 1969. His sister Leola said, "We had wondered how he had died, and it had bothered us. We knew it must have been something great because all these medals kept coming."

Some of the heaviest fighting that fall occurred around the small Central Highlands town of Dak To in Kontum Province along the Cambodian border. The sparring between the two forces actually began in June when the 24th NVA Regiment chewed up Company A, 2d Battalion, 503d Infantry, 173d Airborne Brigade. Seventy-six paratroopers died in a vicious ambush on a mountainside south of Dak To.

The paratroopers spent the rest of the summer searching the region for the NVA, but to no avail. There were a few contacts, but the enemy would not come back across the border in any strength. The 173d was pulled out of the region in the early fall and sent to coastal Tuy Hoa.

In late October, in accordance with Giap's master plan, the NVA threatened the Special Forces camp at Ben Het, west of Dak To. The 173d was called back to the area. The Sky Soldiers began intense patrol activity in the rugged, jungle-clad mountains that dominated the region.

Almost immediately the paratroopers as well as units of the 4th Infantry Division and the ARVN units assigned to the Central Highlands ran into the NVA. The fights were hard, bitter contests that caused many casualties on both sides and once again demonstrated the heroism of the individual American fighting man.

JOHN A. BARNES

On November 10, Company C, 1st Battalion, 503d Infantry, under Capt. Thomas McElwain, was on patrol southwest of Dak To. The presence of the enemy was sensed throughout the day, but none were seen. That night the company along with half of Company D, together designated Task Force Black, dug deep foxholes in a bamboo grove on a hilltop. Beneath them the red and green lights the NVA used to move troops at night were visible all around them.

The following morning, 1st Lt. Gerald Cecil led his platoon out of the perimeter. After traveling less than two hundred yards, Cecil sensed that he was in the midst of the enemy. He ordered his men to open fire. The return barrage from the NVA drove the paratroopers into a tight perimeter. The rest of TF Black raced down the hillside to join the fight, but the enemy proved too strong. In a few minutes the Airborne troopers were completely surrounded. With little cover and no time to dig holes, dozens of men were cut down. The enemy fire slashed across their hillside position like a well-honed scythe.

When the two men manning a forward machine gun were shot down, the enemy might have breached the perimeter were it not for the actions of twenty-two-year-old private first class *John A. Barnes* of Dedham, Massachusetts. In his seventeenth month in South Vietnam, Barnes dashed across the bullet-swept ground, dropped behind the M-60, and opened fire. He killed nine NVA before concentrated enemy fire cut him down. During a subsequent lull, Barnes, nicknamed "Combat" because he had voluntarily left a safe rear area job to serve with a rifle company, made his way back to where the medics had gathered the wounded. After receiving treatment, Barnes settled in near several other casualties.

Suddenly an enemy hand grenade plopped down between Barnes and another man. "Combat" Barnes could have turned the other way and saved himself, but he did not. He never hesitated. He just yelled "I got it," and rolled over on the projectile. He used his own body to shield his comrades from the blast. Barnes died, but six of his fellow Sky Soldiers lived.

Later that afternoon TF Black was rescued when a sister company broke through the enemy lines and reached the unit. The NVA melted back into the jungle. Twenty men from Company C died and 154 were wounded in the fight.

Barnes's family in Massachusetts received his Medal of Honor on November 4, 1969.

* * *

On November 18 the 173d's commander, Brig. Gen. Leo Schweiter, learned that the 174th NVA Regiment had occupied Hill 875, about twenty miles southwest of Dak To and less than two miles from the Cambodian border. Schweiter ordered his 2d Battalion, 503d Infantry, to dislodge them.

The next day Companies C and D moved up Hill 875 following artillery and air strikes. Company A protected their rear. At 10:30 A.M., as the two lead companies gingerly picked their way through the vegetation and thick tree trunks mangled by the bombardment, the enemy cut loose. From dozens of concealed bunkers the NVA felled the young American soldiers. Air strikes were called in, but they had little effect. The enemy was too well dug in.

In the meantime, Company A to the rear also came under attack.

CARLOS J. LOZADA

A three-man squad commanded by Sp4. James Kelley set up thirty-five yards downhill from Company A's position. From there they could alert the company to any movement in that area. Almost immediately the men could hear the NVA moving uphill toward them, but the thick jungle prevented any visual contact.

Suddenly twenty-one-year-old private first class *Carlos J. Lozada* yelled, "Here they come, Kelley!" He started firing long bursts from his M-60 machine gun downhill. His bullets killed some of the NVA and alerted the rest of the company to the threat behind them.

Kelley joined Lozada and Sp4. John Steer in firing down the hill, but the enemy kept coming.

"Fall back, fall back," Kelley ordered. The enemy attack was quickly overwhelming his small force. Kelley headed up the hill.

Lozada ignored the order. With the NVA moving in on three sides, he kept up a steady and accurate fire. Then

Lozada picked up his M-60, moved a few yards uphill, and joined Steer behind a fallen tree. From that position he again took the enemy under fire.

Lozada, born in Puerto Rico but raised in New York City, must have realized that if he gave up his position, the rest of the company would be jeopardized. He elected to stay behind.

"Get out of here," he yelled to Steer. "I can handle them." He fired quick bursts at the approaching NVA.

To get a better shot at the enemy and cover Steer's withdrawal, Lozada arose from behind the log. He fired his red-hot M-60 in long, sweeping bursts into the dense foliage he knew concealed his foe. When he paused to reload, an NVA sniper got him. An AK-47 round hit him in the head. He slumped over on top of Steer. Steer knew instantly that Lozada was dead. He pulled himself free from the corpse and headed up the hill.

Lozada's widow accepted his posthumous Medal of Honor on November 18, 1969. With her was her thirty-month-old daughter, who had never seen her father.

The battle for Hill 875 raged for four more days. That first evening, while the beleaguered defenders hid in hastily dug holes, a Marine jet accidentally dropped a five-hundred-pound bomb directly on the command group. The tremendous explosion killed more than thirty paratroopers and wounded dozens more, including Spec Four Steer.

It took two more days before the 503d's 4th Battalion fought through the NVA to reach their buddies. Later that night, two more Airborne companies made it into the lines and brought in critically needed supplies. At last, on Thanksgiving Day, the Americans were able to go on the offensive. They attacked outward from their small perimeter and reached the summit of Hill 875 five days after they had started up. The NVA were gone.

In all, the two assault battalions sustained more than 550 casualties, including 158 dead. Enemy fatalities were estimated at 500.

* * *

Even while the battle of Dak To raged, General Westmoreland felt optimistic enough about the progress of the war to pay another visit to Washington, DC. When he addressed the assembled reporters who had met his jet at Washington's National Airport, Westmoreland described the situation in South Vietnam as "very, very encouraging. I have never been more encouraged in my four years in Vietnam."

President Johnson had asked Westmoreland back to Washington in response to the massive antiwar rally held at the Pentagon on October 21–23. More than fifty thousand people participated in the "Stop the Draft" program. The demonstrators peacefully marched to the Pentagon, where they held a rally protesting the war. To protect the military bastion, the Defense Department flew in ten thousand 82d Airborne Division troopers from Fort Bragg, North Carolina. Considering the potential for trouble, it turned out to be a peaceful gathering.

General Westmoreland exuded confidence in all his meetings with the press. Appearing on the TV program *Meet the Press,* Westmoreland told the audience, "The United States may be able to start withdrawing its troops from South Vietnam in two years or less."

On November 21, Westmoreland told the National Press Club, "We are making progress . . . we have reached an important point where the end begins to come into view."

The situation in South Vietnam, as far as President Johnson and his advisers were concerned, was very positive. Even though U.S. forces had been hit hard at Dak To, the administration declared the contest a victory.

While General Westmoreland was meeting with members of the press in the United States, the 1st Cavalry Division (Airmobile) was pursuing the enemy in Binh Dinh Province. Throughout late 1967 a number of brief but violent firefights erupted on the Bong Son Plain. In early December elements of the 9th Cavalry Regiment engaged NVA forces near the coastal village of Tam Quan. For several days the fighting raged around Tam Quan and Dai Dong. When the mechanized infantry of the 1st Battalion, 50th Infantry, found the fight too tough, reinforcements from the 12th Cavalry Regiment's 1st Battalion were called in.

ALLEN J. LYNCH

A year after he joined the army in November 1964, *Allen J. Lynch* was transferred to Berlin, Germany. It was a cushy assignment with regular hours and plenty of activities to fill his free time. He could have remained in Germany, safe from the horrors of the growing war in Southeast Asia, but that was not Lynch's style. It was important to him to be involved in the war. And he wanted to see if he could handle combat.

After a forty-five-day leave at home in the south Chicago suburb of Dolton, Spec Four Lynch reported to Company D, 1st Battalion, 12th Cavalry, in June 1967 for duty as a radiotelephone operator (RTO).

By the time Lynch had spent six months in combat with the 12th Cavalry, few doubts remained in his mind about his ability to stand up under combat conditions. Any that did were erased forever on December 15, 1967 when Lynch's battalion was sent to Dai Dong to reinforce the worn 50th Infantry.

Company D conducted a sweep near the small village of My An 2. Bordered by rice paddies, bamboo thickets, sugarcane fields, and thick hedgerows, this area of the Bong Son River lowlands was crawling with Viet Cong soldiers from the 9th VC Regiment. The two point men for the company had just entered a bamboo grove when enemy rifle fire brought down both of them. Seconds later, machine gun fire pinned down the rest of the company, leaving the casualties about fifty meters away across an open field.

Unwilling to leave his wounded buddies at the mercy of the enemy, Lynch dashed out across the open ground, unmindful of the heavy enemy fire. When he reached the casualties, he found one man hit in the shoulder, the other in the leg and arm. He patched them up the best he could, then pulled them to cover in a shallow ditch.

While the three men returned the enemy fire, another grunt tried to reach their isolated position. The enemy cut him down halfway to his destination. Lynch rushed out and brought him into the ditch.

In pain but still able to fight, the fourth man aided Lynch in holding off several enemy probes.

Then someone from his company called over to Lynch, "Who's over there?"

Lynch shouted back, "There's four of us. Three are wounded." He repeated the words several times but could not seem to make his situation understood. Silently, he watched his company pull out of the village. He was left alone with his three wounded comrades.

For the next two hours Lynch, helped by the three casualties, repulsed several determined enemy movements on his position. A short while later, members of Company D returned to the village and called for Lynch to run to them while they provided covering fire. He refused. Without him the others would be at the mercy of the enemy.

A few minutes later, jets roared in from the east and sprayed the VC-held tree line with machine gun bullets, bombs, and napalm. From his position just meters from the carnage, Lynch prayed that the pilots were accurate.

When the jets pulled away, an eerie quiet descended on the battlefield. No sound, friendly or hostile, could be heard. Lynch whispered to his comrades, "You guys stay here. I'll go see what's happening."

Alone, Lynch reconnoitered the area around him but found no sign of the enemy. He moved to the small cluster of hootches that comprised My An 2, checked each one and the surrounding brush, but still found no sign of the VC. Confident that the enemy had left the field, Lynch hastened back to the casualties. One at a time he helped them to the village. He left them well armed under a wide tree while he went in search of a friendly unit.

Lynch followed the tracks of an APC for a few hundred yards, then came upon his company; no one in his unit had expected to see him alive again. Under his direction, the three wounded men were recovered, treated, and evacuated. Lynch never saw any of them again.

Lynch was discharged in April 1969. One year later he put his uniform back on to receive the Medal of Honor from President Nixon in White House ceremonies.

Because of his deep concern over the problems faced by many Vietnam War veterans, Lynch dedicated his civilian career to working as a counselor and adviser with a number of veterans' assistance organizations.

CHAPTER SIX

Tet: The Turning Point

MACV started 1968 in a very optimistic mood. General Westmoreland had over four hundred thousand soldiers, sailors, and Marines in his command to carry out his war of attrition. The multibattalion operations that he directed against enemy strongholds seemed to be working effectively. The body counts faithfully reported every week clearly showed that the United States was winning.

In nearly every corner of South Vietnam, U.S. troops aggressively went after the NVA/VC. Among the major efforts: the 25th Infantry Division's Operation Yellowstone in Tay Ninh Province; the 9th Infantry Division's combination with Navy Task Force 117 to beat back the VC in the northern half of the Delta region; and the 1st Infantry Division's successful efforts to finally reopen Route 13 through War Zone D to Quan Loi.

There were threats against the strategic Khe Sanh Combat Base in western Quang Tri Province, held by the 26th Marines, but Westmoreland was prepared for that. He shifted the 1st Cavalry Division (Airmobile) to Phu Bai early in January. If the NVA did attack Khe Sanh, Westmoreland now had over one-half of his maneuver battalions in I Corps ready to repulse them.

However, despite all the offensive operations launched by U.S. troops, the enemy still initiated most of the ground action.

On January 6, 1968 a heavy barrage of rocket and small-arms fire hit Troop F of the 11th Armored Cavalry Regiment's 2d Squadron while it patrolled south of Loc Ninh in Binh Long Province. At the first sign of trouble, twenty-five-year-old corporal *Jerry W. Wickam* of Leaf River, Illinois, left his armored vehicle to attack two enemy bunkers. He killed three VC and captured another in his vicious one-man assault. After an air strike pummeled the enemy positions, Wickam voluntarily led a patrol back into the area. Attacked by the surviving enemy soldiers, he destroyed a third bunker and killed two more VC before he fell, mortally wounded.

That same day, up north at Chu Lai, a helicopter pilot earned a Medal of Honor for a series of daring rescue operations.

PATRICK H. BRADY

If it had not been for a university requirement mandating ROTC participation, *Patrick H. Brady* might not have pursued a military career. Brady was born October 1, 1936 in Philip, South Dakota; his parents brought him to Seattle, Washington, when he was three years old. When he enrolled at Seattle University in 1955 to be near his girlfriend, he was quite upset to find out he had to join the ROTC.

"I couldn't believe it," he later said. "Boy, how I hated it. I said, 'This is communistic!' but they forced me to join."

Brady started out as a poor student. He would have flunked out if he had not married his sweetheart, Nancy Parsek. Brady's attitude changed overnight. He graduated with top honors and was voted into the students' "Who's Who."

After being commissioned an army lieutenant in 1959, Brady spent three years as a medical service officer before volunteering for flight training. He earned his wings in 1963. The next year he served his first tour as a medical evacuation pilot in South Vietnam, then went to the Dominican Republic during the uprising there in 1965. In July 1967 he returned to the war zone and joined the 54th Medical Detachment, 67th Medical Group, 44th Medical Brigade. When he left

South Vietnam one year later, he had flown over 3,000 combat missions and received credit for rescuing over 5,000 people. More than 50 of those were saved on one memorable January day.

In a fogbound valley outside Chu Lai, two seriously wounded South Vietnamese soldiers desperately needed evacuation. Seven rescue attempts had already been made on January 5, but the fog kept forcing the helicopters back. The next day Brady volunteered to bring the men out.

Brady descended into the gray fog, then flew slowly along a trail, using the chopper's rotor wash to blow away the fog. The flight took incredible flying skill and nerves of steel, and Brady had them both. He soon found the Allied position. Seconds later the casualties were aboard, and Brady lifted his Huey straight up through the fog.

Soon after Brady delivered those men to an evacuation hospital, he learned of more casualties. A rifle company of the 198th Light Infantry Brigade had suffered sixty wounded during a firefight with the NVA in a fog-shrouded section of nearby Hiep Duc Valley. One "dustoff" (medevac) chopper had already been shot down. Brady ignored the danger to race to the scene.

Brady found a hole in the fog layer, then dropped down through it to treetop level, where he followed a stream that led to the battleground. Oblivious to the heavy enemy fire coming from as close as fifty yards, Brady brought his chopper in for a load of wounded. As enemy rounds slammed into his aircraft, he made the perilous journey back upstream.

Three more times Brady made the hazardous trip to this battleground. Altogether, his fearlessness saved thirty-nine men.

Later, on his third separate rescue mission that day, enemy fire hit Brady's helicopter so badly he could barely keep it under control. Lesser men might have called it a day right then, but not Brady. He continued his mission and pulled out six casualties. He flew them to the evac hospital, then picked up another helicopter.

Before the day ended, Brady had rescued wounded soldiers from two more locations and acquired a third aircraft.

Ground crews later counted over four hundred bullet holes in the three Hueys Brady flew that memorable day.

Brady's actions on January 6 were remarkable by anyone's standards but his own. "I had a lot worse days," he said. The army was sufficiently impressed to recommend him for the Medal of Honor. President Nixon presented it to Brady on October 9, 1969 while Brady's wife and their four children watched with pride. Brady remained in the army and rose to the rank of major general before retiring.

WILLIAM D. PORT

A divorce sent *William D. Port* of Petersburg, Pennsylvania, to South Vietnam. The draft would not take a man if he was married and had children. As it was, Port's ex-wife got their two children and the army got Bill Port. He was inducted in March 1967, six months short of his twenty-sixth birthday.

Soon after Port finished his basic training at Fort Benning, Georgia, he went overseas and reported in to Company C, 5th Battalion, 7th Cavalry, 1st Cavalry Division (Airmobile). On January 12, 1968, Port's company battled superior enemy forces in the Que Son Valley of Quang Tin Province, west of Tam Ky. His platoon gave ground under heavy enemy fire. Although he had been wounded in the hand during this movement, Port still helped a more seriously wounded soldier to safety. Later, while huddled with three other casualties, Port saved their lives when he covered an enemy grenade with his own body. The tremendous blast caused severe wounds to his head, chest, arms, and legs.

For two and one-half hours the platoon medic worked on Port, but then the VC forced the platoon to retreat. Port, whom the medic had reported as dead, was left behind. When the platoon retook the area a few hours later, Port's body could not be found. The army carried him as missing in action for four months before it changed his status to presumed dead.

But Bill Port was not dead. Grievously wounded but still alive, Port had been taken prisoner by the VC. They treated him at their field hospital in the nearby mountains before sending him to a POW camp deep in the jungle.

Port never recovered from his shattering injuries. He languished in the primitive camp for ten months before he died on November 27, 1968. In December 1969 the army listed Port as dead and notified his family for the first time that he had been held prisoner by the VC. Not until the POWs returned in 1973 were the full details of Port's death and burial in the jungle reported to his family.

In the meantime, Port's posthumous Medal of Honor recommendation was approved and the award was presented to his son and daughter by President Nixon on August 6, 1970.

As the years passed, the family abandoned hope that Port's remains would be found. Then, in August 1985, a team of American investigators, working with a more liberal Vietnamese government, was led to a common grave site that held the remains of nine American POWs. In October of that year Port's remains were positively identified as one of the nine.

After funeral services in his hometown, William D. Port was interred at Arlington National Cemetery.

For several months beginning in November 1967, the U.S. intelligence network had uncovered information regarding a pending major North Vietnamese offensive. The evidence led General Westmoreland to conclude that the enemy intended to overrun the combat base at Khe Sanh. Accordingly, he shifted his forces northward. This was precisely what North Vietnamese general Nguyen Giap wanted Westmoreland to do.

On January 31, 1968, in what became known as the Tet Offensive, Giap unleashed his forces. Viet Cong and North Vietnamese Army units struck nearly every major city, thirty provincial capitals, and scores of other towns and villages throughout South Vietnam. Coming as it did on the heels of General Westmoreland's earlier pronouncement of imminent victory, the intensity and ferocity of the attacks stunned the American high command and the American public. The Tet Offensive would prove to be the watershed of American involvement in South Vietnam, but first the enemy had to be thrown back.

Two heavily armed VC battalions attacked Chau Phu, the capital of Chau Doc Province southwest of Saigon and bordering Cambodia, and completely broke down the defenses of the city. Special Forces staff sergeant *Drew D. Dix,* on the MACV advisory staff for IV Corps, received credit for single-handedly driving out the Viet Cong.

For two days, January 31 and February 1, Dix led repeated attacks against enemy strong points in the city. He led by personal example and continually inspired his ARVN troops to new heights of heroism. In fierce street fighting, Dix knocked out one enemy position after another. The Pueblo, Colorado, resident captured over 20 enemy soldiers, killed another 40, and rescued no less than 20 U.S. and free world civilians from imprisonment.

Although more than thirty thousand North Vietnamese regulars did surround the Marine base at Khe Sanh, the expected major ground attack never materialized. A heavily armed NVA force did move against the Special Forces camp at Lang Vei, on Route 9 between Khe Sanh and the Laotian border. In their first use of armor in the war, the NVA overran the small camp and sent the Americans and their Civilian Irregular Defense Group (CIDG) troops reeling.

SFC (Sergeant First Class) *Eugene Ashley* rallied a group of CIDG survivors and four times led them in assaults on the enemy-held camp. Four times the gallant Green Beret and his small band were repulsed. Ashley, a thirty-six-year-old from New York City, gathered up the few remaining soldiers for a final attack. Halfway to the objective, he died in a hail of enemy fire at the head of his men. When he fell, the counterattack collapsed. The remaining CIDG fled in terror to the Marine base at Khe Sanh.

Despite the fact that over one hundred cities were attacked on January 31, for America the epitome of the Tet Offensive was the enemy capture of Hue and the battle for its freedom. The third-largest city in South Vietnam and the capital of Thua Thien Province, Hue had great cultural and religious symbolism for the struggling nation. Holding it for even a short period of time would give the enemy a tremendous propaganda victory. They held Hue for nearly six weeks. It took twenty-one American and ARVN battalions to pry out the eight enemy battalions entrenched in the city. Four Americans earned the Medal of Honor during the bitter fighting.

On the first day of the attack, Huey pilot *Frederick E. Ferguson,* a chief warrant officer from Phoenix, Arizona, with Company C, 227th Aviation Battalion, 1st Cavalry Division (Airmobile), flew low over the city's Perfume River while under enemy antiaircraft fire to rescue some Special Forces soldiers trapped behind enemy lines. Ferguson landed in the small courtyard that held the troops—barely missing a flagpole that no one had told him about—loaded the five men aboard, and lifted off to depart the area via a different route. At that instant an enemy mortar round exploded directly beneath his Huey. The blast turned the aircraft around 180 degrees. Ferguson now had to make a split-second decision. Should he take the time to turn around and go out the way he was expected to and where his escorting gunships waited, or should he just keep going the way he was headed, back down the Perfume River and through the gauntlet of enemy fire?

Ferguson never hesitated. He pushed the control stick forward and his Huey roared toward the river. Miraculously the helicopter sustained no serious hits as he flew above the water. Ferguson delivered his rescued charges to safety and resumed his routine flights.

Twenty-one-year-old sergeant *Alfredo Gonzalez,* from Edinburg, Texas, served with the first reaction force sent by the Marines to battle the enemy in Hue. The Marine command had no idea of the magnitude of the enemy involvement in the city. Gonzalez's unit, Company A, 1st Battalion, 1st Marines, was nearly overwhelmed by the superior enemy forces.

From the morning of January 31 until he was killed on

February 4, Gonzalez repeatedly exposed himself to danger to rescue wounded comrades and assault enemy positions. Even after he was seriously wounded on February 3, Gonzalez remained in the forefront of the attack. The next day he single-handedly assaulted a series of NVA bunkers. At one point Gonzalez fearlessly stood in an open window of a Marine-occupied building to fire a rocket into an enemy position in the next building. His well-aimed round destroyed the position. He stepped up to the window again to fire at another NVA position, but it was one time too many. He fell in a blaze of enemy fire.

With the Marines locked in bitter house-to-house fighting inside Hue, elements of the 501st Infantry Regiment of the army's 101st Airborne Division were moved into positions outside the city to block the movement of any NVA reinforcements into the city. On February 21, Company D, 2d Battalion, was pinned down by an enemy force hidden in a tree line. *S.Sgt. Clifford C. Sims,* a twenty-five-year-old career soldier from Port St. Joe, Florida, led his squad into the wood line when it became apparent the other company units could not move. Sims repeatedly displayed tremendous courage in his daring assaults on enemy strong points. When he spotted an enemy booby trap that threatened his squad members, Sims flung himself on the explosive. His self-sacrifice saved his buddies from certain death.

During the same fight, another career soldier from Sims's company also earned a Medal of Honor.

JOE R. HOOPER

After a three-year tour in the navy, *Joe R. Hooper* enlisted in the army in 1960. Born in South Carolina in 1939 and raised in rural Moses Lake, Washington, Hooper volunteered for Airborne training upon completion of his basic training. He spent the next six years in a variety of Airborne units, where he earned a reputation as a tough-as-nails noncommissioned officer. Several times he requested a transfer to South

Vietnam, but it was not until he joined the 501st Infantry, 101st Airborne Division, at Fort Campbell, Kentucky, that he knew for sure he was going overseas. Deployment of the 501st was completed just before Christmas 1967.

The enemy unit that pinned down Company D on the morning of February 21, occupied a series of well-protected bunkers along a riverbank a few miles outside of Hue. The company commander requested an air strike. It was denied; the planes were too busy in Hue.

As rockets, machine guns, and small-arms fire exploded along the company's line, Hooper suddenly turned to his squad. "Follow me!" he commanded.

With several men running close behind him, Hooper splashed through the water and took a bunker under fire. In a few seconds he silenced it. While the rest of his company fanned out through the densely wooded area, Hooper used the time to pull several wounded men out of the line of fire. He had turned the last of them over to the company medics when he was shot by an enemy sniper. Instead of seeking treatment, Hooper returned to his squad.

At the vanguard of the battle again, Hooper knocked out three more enemy bunkers. Seconds later he killed two NVA who had attacked and wounded the battalion chaplain while the priest was tending to the American wounded.

Hooper continued his attack and blew up three hootches that concealed several enemy snipers. He was on his way back to his men when a North Vietnamese officer charged him from behind a tree. Hooper killed him with his bayonet.

Later, accurate fire from an enemy machine gun pinned down Hooper's squad. He flanked the weapon and killed the three gunners with a well-tossed hand grenade. Suddenly enemy fire erupted from four previously unseen bunkers. Though wounded again, Hooper refused to stay down. He gathered up an armful of grenades, raced down a small trench that passed behind the bunkers, and tossed grenades into each one as he ran past it. All four of the bunkers were silenced by his furious attack. A few minutes later he destroyed three more enemy emplacements.

When Hooper learned that one of his men was lying wounded and trapped in a ditch, he braved sniper fire to go to the man's aid. Just as he reached the position, he came face-to-face with an enemy soldier. Before the NVA could raise his rifle, Hooper pulled out his .45 and shot his foe. He then found the wounded man and carried him in to safety.

Throughout the rest of the day Hooper continued to set an inspiring example for his men and the rest of Company D. After the enemy had been driven from the area, Hooper insisted on setting his squad into position before finally consenting to have his wounds treated. Even then he refused evacuation. Not until the following day did he leave his squad.

Hooper spent six weeks in the hospital, then returned to the field. In the summer of 1968 he was honorably discharged, but spent only nine months as a civilian before reenlisting. On March 7, 1969, President Nixon presented Hooper with the Medal of Honor for his outstanding actions near Hue.

The gallant NCO went back to South Vietnam in 1970 and served with a reconnaissance unit. A year later, after he had finished his second tour, Hooper received a direct commission to second lieutenant.

Disappointed with the opportunities available to him in the postwar army, Hooper resigned his commission in February 1974. He was employed by the Veterans Administration for several years before he left to follow an ambition to breed racehorses. He was working on his degree in animal husbandry when he died of natural causes on May 6, 1979 while attending the Kentucky Derby.

In the Mekong River Delta provinces, the U.S. 9th Infantry Division worked with the ARVN 9th Infantry Division to expel the NVA and VC from contested villages. As they did in all ARVN units, the American advisers worked directly alongside their South Vietnamese counterparts. Because the ARVN 9th Infantry Division was ranked as a weak division, its American advisers often had to go to great lengths to motivate its members. That was the situation *1st Lt. Jack H. Jacobs* found himself in on March 9 in Kien Phong Province.

Jacobs assumed command of an ARVN rifle company in the 9th's 2d Battalion, 16th Infantry, after its commander was wounded and the men began to panic. With blood flowing into his eyes from a serious head wound, the twenty-two-year-old Rutgers University graduate reorganized the company, rescued several wounded men from exposed positions, and single-handedly drove off repeated attempts by the enemy to overrun his company. His forceful leadership helped stabilize the ARVN and allowed them to defeat the determined enemy.

Although the 1st Brigade of the 101st Airborne Division had been in South Vietnam since July 1965, the division's two Stateside brigades did not receive notice to prepare for movement to the war zone until August 2, 1967. At that time the brigades were barely more than training units for men who were moving on to South Vietnam. So depleted were the ranks of the brigades that just to fill the rifle companies to a 75 percent level would require over forty-five hundred men. Units throughout the army were ordered to provide personnel to the 101st. As is usual in such a situation, the affected commanders used the edict as an excuse to get rid of their weakest and most troublesome soldiers. Some of the rifle company commanders in the 101st resented it when these problem soldiers arrived in their units, but at least one man sought them out.

PAUL W. BUCHA

When twenty-three-year-old army captain *Paul W. Bucha* arrived at Fort Campbell, Kentucky, in June 1967 to take command of a rifle company in the 3d Battalion, 187th Infantry, he had already served six years in the army but had never commanded troops. The son of an army colonel, Bucha had entered West Point after finishing high school in

Hinsdale, Illinois, in 1961. Before graduating in 1965, Bucha would serve as regimental commander (the No. 2 position in the cadet chain of command), be captain of the swimming team, a member of the water polo team, an all-American swimmer, and the first recipient of the Association of Graduates Award for overall excellence.

Upon graduation from West Point, Bucha was selected to attend Stanford University's Graduate School of Business in Palo Alto, California, to earn his MBA. Two weeks after earning that degree, he reported to Fort Campbell. He arrived there to find his unit, Company D, a company in name only. He was going to have to build it from scratch.

While other company commanders searched through personnel files to weed out men who had disciplinary problems, Bucha welcomed such soldiers with open arms. He said later, "I wanted people no one else wanted. I wanted to build a team; to be able to give my men a sense of belonging. I felt I could do that best by working with people who had no experience or who had had bad experiences."

Said Bucha, "I promised my people I'd do everything I could to bring them all back from Vietnam alive. But we had to work and work hard to do that. While other companies in the 187th took weekend liberty, my 'clerks and jerks,' as some called us, went on extra night maneuvers. I'm sure that that cohesiveness, that teamwork, that extra training, helped us tremendously in Vietnam."

Bucha's brigade went to South Vietnam just before Christmas 1967. Sent to War Zone C northwest of Saigon, Bucha's company was the first in the brigade to contact the enemy. "From then on," Bucha said, "we had nearly daily contact with the VC or NVA. Unlike other outfits, we were always in the field. Day after day we hunted the VC. And we found him."

Bucha's emphasis on teamwork paid off. For the first three months of its tour, despite frequent firefights with the enemy, Company D suffered no killed in action and no serious wounded. Then came March 18.

As part of a post-Tet U.S. offensive operation in Binh

Duong Province, Company D was helicoptered into landing zones near Phuoc Vinh on March 16. Over the next two days the company battled the NVA and destroyed bunkers, supply caches, and an enemy base camp area. At the end of the third day, the hot, tired infantrymen prepared to settle in for the night.

"It was just getting dark," Bucha remembered. "We were moving to a night position when we surprised an NVA battalion preparing themselves for the night. They hit us with everything they had. We tried to hold on until daylight."

Subjected to a veritable hail of heavy automatic weapons fire, rocket-propelled grenades (RPGs), claymore mines, and small-arms fire, Bucha functioned throughout the night with one thought uppermost in his mind: to keep his promise to his men.

Even though most of his company was pinned down, Bucha moved to the most threatened portions of his perimeter to direct his men's fire against the NVA. When he realized that one particular machine gun was doing most of the damage to his men, Bucha low-crawled through heavy foliage to destroy it with a well-placed grenade. Bucha was wounded while returning to his company's perimeter, but he pulled his men into a tighter circle when he saw that the outlying squads could not repel the human-wave assaults being sent by the enemy.

As the battle wore on through the night, Bucha began to doubt his company's chances of survival. It seemed that at any minute the enemy would overwhelm his beloved men. Before his feelings of despair could take over, Bucha's radio operator, a new man who was experiencing his first combat action, turned to him and said excitedly, "Sir, we're really kicking the hell out of them, aren't we!"

The youngster's naïve confidence inspired Bucha. "Yes," he answered, "I guess we are."

When enemy sappers probed his perimeter to learn its exact location, Bucha radioed his platoon leaders. "Knock off the noise. I'll do the firing from here," he told them. He reasoned that his single weapon, firing from a central location, would keep the NVA from learning his unit's boundaries. That would prevent them from rushing a weak spot. It would also keep his men from taking more casualties.

Bucha's brigade commander, who was in constant radio contact with him, told him that he was sending in reinforcements. Bucha declined the help. Since the nearest units were more than one-half mile away, their movement would unnecessarily endanger more lives. Company D would be on its own.

During a lull in the fighting, Bucha sent a squad out to retrieve some casualties. Almost immediately the NVA cut the squad off. Unwilling to risk even more wounded, Bucha radioed the squad members to hug the dirt. He was going to call friendly artillery down around their position. It was risky, but it had to be done.

A few hours before daybreak, Bucha called in medevac choppers to carry out his wounded. Unwilling to risk the lives of any of his men, Bucha completely ignored the fire from enemy snipers to move into a clearing, where he used flashlights to direct the choppers into the LZ. Three helicopters were needed to carry away the wounded.

At daybreak the enemy broke contact, allowing Bucha to recover the dead and wounded members of his cut-off squad. His company had suffered its first killed in action, 11 in total; 54 more were wounded. Without the spirit of teamwork instilled in the company members by Bucha, it would have been worse.

Bucha spent two more months in the field before being rotated to a staff position in brigade headquarters. In November 1968 he returned home. Following a six-month course at Fort Knox, Kentucky, he was assigned to West Point as an instructor in the social services department. He was still serving in that capacity when he received word that he had been awarded the Medal of Honor.

"I thought a mistake had been made and I wanted to straighten it out," he recalled. "I just didn't think there was anything unusual about my actions that night."

Bucha tried to reach an officer in the Pentagon, but a senior

NCO in his office cut him off. "Sir, with all due respect, your men put you in for that medal. It's the highest symbol of respect they could give you. Don't disappoint them."

Bucha did not. He accepted his award from President Nixon on May 14, 1970. In his view he holds the medal on behalf of his company. "I am as proud of them as I am of the medal," he said. "I feel I accepted the award more for them than myself."

Further honors awaited Bucha. In recognition of his military accomplishments and his efforts to establish a job placement program at West Point for civilian ex–drug addicts, Bucha joined such notables as entertainer Elvis Presley and presidential press secretary Ronald Zeigler as one of the Jaycee's Ten Outstanding Young Men of 1971. He was the youngest so honored and the only military man on the list.

A desire to attend law school so that he could aid returning Vietnam War veterans led Bucha to resign his commission in August 1972. He was prepared to enter Harvard University when he met Texas businessman H. Ross Perot.

Perot offered Bucha a job running his fledgling computer programming business in Europe. Bucha jumped at the chance. For the next six years he lived abroad and developed and oversaw the growth of Perot's business from nothing to one producing millions of dollars in annual revenue.

In 1980, Bucha launched his own international marketing consulting firm, which he continues to run. Today a millionaire several times over, he frequently reflects on the events that brought him his country's highest award for valor: "I think medals are often awarded for actions one gets involved in which, if he had done a better job to begin with, wouldn't have resulted in anyone being called a hero or anyone being hurt."

The U.S. military considered the Tet Offensive a resounding defeat for the enemy. In some ways they were correct. The Viet Cong suffered such severe losses they never again posed a serious threat to South Vietnam. And none of the attacking forces was able to hold even one military objective.

Regardless of the military losses, though, Tet was a definite political victory for North Vietnam. Even the most diehard supporters of the United States' war policy began to express doubts about the country's ability to win the war.

The administration's advocates themselves expressed shock when General Westmoreland asked on March 10 for 206,000 more troops. Just four months previously he had all but announced a victory.

America's efforts in South Vietnam stood at a crossroads.

On March 31, President Johnson announced a halt to the bombing of North Vietnam. He would give General Westmoreland some of his requested reinforcements, but nowhere near the number of men he was asking for. President Johnson then startled the nation by announcing he would not seek another term as president.

The Joint Chiefs of Staff cabled Westmoreland on April 16 and ordered him to shift more of the burden of the war to South Vietnam's military forces. The term "Vietnamization" would not be coined by Defense Secretary Melvin Laird for nearly a year, but the process had begun.

The presidential decision to halt the bombing of North Vietnam led to the commencement of peace talks in Paris on May 10, 1968. Unfortunately, five more years of tough combat faced American troops before the negotiations finally brought peace to the war-torn country.

Despite political assassinations, student riots, a bitter presidential campaign, and dwindling support for their sacrifices, young men continued to battle the enemy in South Vietnam.

As part of General Westmoreland's post-Tet counteroffensive, the 1st Cavalry Division (Airmobile) went into the rugged A Shau Valley in western Thua Thien Province. Literally untouched by U.S. troops since 1966 except for a few Special Forces operations, this remote area not only harbored NVA units but was also liberally sprinkled with antiaircraft guns. Two battalions of the 7th Cavalry Regiment were air-assaulted into the northern A Shau Valley on April 19, 1968. For the next five days, under dense fog and intermittent thundershowers, the cavalrymen sparred with the

NVA. A brisk firefight occurred on April 25, when Company D of the 7th's 5th Battalion bumped into a retreating NVA battalion. It was an indecisive part of the overall fight, but it brought a Medal of Honor to a young first lieutenant.

JAMES M. SPRAYBERRY

Aboard the slicks (Huey gunships) bearing the men of the 7th Cavalry's 5th Battalion into the LZ near the Chaine Annamitique mountains along the Laotian border was twenty-year-old first lieutenant *James M. Sprayberry*. He had been wounded in the fighting in Binh Dinh Province in January and had only recently rejoined his company to serve as its executive officer.

A native of Sylacauga, Alabama, Sprayberry enlisted in April 1966 after spending a year at the local junior college. "I was bored with school," Sprayberry explained. "I was looking for some excitement. And I was tired of being a pacifist."

Sprayberry completed basic training at Fort Benning, Georgia, then advanced infantry training at Fort Jackson, South Carolina, before entering armor officer candidate school at Fort Knox, Kentucky. He was commissioned in January 1967. He then spent ten months at Fort Benning before joining the 7th Cavalry in South Vietnam in November 1967.

Even though Sprayberry was as young as or younger than most members of the company, he quickly earned their respect. He was a tough but fair officer who never needlessly risked a life.

Company D spent the first four days of Operation Delaware marching through monsoon rainstorms in pursuit of an elusive foe. Signs of the NVA were everywhere, though. The cavalrymen destroyed tons of equipment and supplies they found in the many caves dotting the craggy hillsides.

One surprising discovery in one cave was hundreds of pounds of heroin found neatly stacked on pallets. "That explained why many of the NVA we encountered would keep

on coming after they'd been shot repeatedly," Sprayberry
said.

On April 24, Sprayberry celebrated his twenty-first birthday. After a brief party and congratulations from his men, he
went back to the war. Late the next day, the company commander, Capt. Frank Lambert, took his command group and
the 1st Platoon on a patrol down a finger of a steep mountain.
He was seeking the main supply road used by the enemy.

What Lambert did not know was that an NVA unit was retreating from other 7th Cavalry units located farther down
the road. Lambert ran right into them and a brisk firefight developed. The stronger NVA force pinned down the cavalrymen with their superior fire. Within minutes Lambert's little
force suffered 50 percent casualties.

At the company perimeter about three hundred yards to the
east, Sprayberry sprang into action as soon as he received the
distress call from Lambert. He led his platoon down the finger, hoping to rescue the others. Vicious enemy automatic
weapons fire, though, drove the soldiers back. Sprayberry
had only one option left.

"I figured the only way to save the men was to go for them
after dark," Sprayberry recalled. "I asked for volunteers to
go with me."

Every man in his platoon offered to go. Sprayberry picked
ten. Around 10:00 P.M. he loaded himself with grenades and
led his small rescue party down the finger.

"It was pitch dark," Sprayberry said, "We moved slowly
down the trail. Cover was scarce because of all the recent
bombings. I knew the enemy was out there, I just didn't
know where."

Sprayberry did not have to worry—the NVA found him.
Tongues of fire spat from an enemy machine gun as it fired
on the Americans. Sprayberry moved his men to cover, then
crawled forward toward the enemy bunker. From forty feet
away he tossed a grenade. It landed in the bunker. The firing
stopped.

The rescue party continued forward. The men soon found
themselves in the middle of a cluster of one-man spider

holes. Sprayberry single-handedly destroyed each of them with grenades.

As Sprayberry neared the site of the surrounded platoon, he sent some of his men out to bring in scattered U.S. soldiers. "The soldiers were hiding all through the area. In the dark they didn't know if we were friend or foe, so it took a good deal of courage for my troopers to move off into the dark."

Some groups of wounded soldiers were led to Sprayberry's position by radio directions. Those without radios had to be rounded up by hand. When Sprayberry had gathered up six or seven men, he sent them back up the trail to the company perimeter. Those too badly wounded to walk were placed on litters.

Several times, when he ventured out from his position, Sprayberry happened upon an enemy fortification. He destroyed no less than ten bunkers, killed a dozen NVA, and eliminated two machine gun positions in his quest to save his comrades.

When he was convinced that he had found all the beleaguered soldiers, Sprayberry formed up a column and then led it back through the night to safety. During the seven-hour foray, the young lieutenant rescued forty men, including Captain Lambert.

Sprayberry finished his tour in October 1968. He returned to the United States and was stationed at Fort Polk, Louisiana, when his Medal of Honor was awarded on October 9, 1969. He was the youngest officer to earn the medal since World War II.

Sprayberry remained in the army even though he never felt completely at home there. "I was even more uncomfortable with the outside environment," he explained. "So that's why I stayed in." He retired as a lieutenant colonel.

Although the NVA had suffered terrible casualties during their offensive, that did not mean they were defeated. Indeed, throughout South Vietnam, U.S. forces continued to battle their foe. The city of Hue fell to the Marines at the end of

February, but the enemy still lurked in the region. Elements of battle-hardened NVA divisions roamed the Hue–Phu Bai area, spoiling for a fight.

MILTON A. LEE

If there was ever an unlikely candidate to be a hero, it was *Milton A. Lee*. Born February 26, 1949 in Louisiana, Lee and a brother were abandoned by their parents at an early age. Grandparents in San Antonio, Texas, took the two boys in and raised them.

Even though Lee's grandparents were not overly religious people, as a youngster he embraced Christianity with a fervor that eluded many adults. An extremely shy youth, Lee played clarinet in his high school band and spent nearly all of his free time studying his Bible. Charles Nelson, a high school friend, said of Lee, "Milton was not an athlete. He was not a person you would imagine being a hero, or much of a military man for that matter."

The few friends Lee had were surprised when he enlisted in the army in June 1967 right after he graduated from high school. Throughout his high school years he had talked of little else except becoming a minister. Why he enlisted remains a mystery.

Basic training was physically difficult for Lee, but he persevered and successfully completed it. He must have had an inkling of his fate, for he wrote Nelson, "The sergeant told us that every man or nearly all would be in Vietnam by January or earlier.

"I am not worried about death because for a Christian there is no such thing as death. Only the freedom from the bondage of this flesh. The only thing that will keep me from serving the Lord in this life is going over to the 'other side.' If anything does happen, I'll meet you on resurrection day."

Lee arrived in South Vietnam in late December 1967. In January 1968 he joined Company B, 2d Battalion, 502d Infantry, 101st Airborne Division (Airmobile), then operating near the coastal city of Phan Rang south of Cam Ranh Bay. When the Tet Offensive erupted a few weeks later, Lee's battalion was rushed to the Cambodian border to blunt the enemy's advances there. Employed as a reaction force, the unit was next sent to the Da Nang area at the end of February. Two months later they moved to Phu Bai.

Lee experienced an incredible amount of combat in his four months in the war. He wrote Nelson, "Children are being killed, women become widows, villages are burned and anything that moves is shot." For a youngster who had just turned nineteen on February 26, Lee had seen a lot.

On April 26, 1968, Company B was on a sweep near Phu Bai. Lee was serving as the radiotelephone operator (RTO) for 3d Platoon, the point platoon. A surprise attack by well-emplaced NVA dropped half of the platoon, including its commander. The platoon pulled back to a position of relative safety where the wounded could be treated. Lee not only demonstrated great presence of mind by calmly radioing details of the platoon's situation to the company commander, he also moved boldly across the battlefield to gather up the wounded and help them to the aid station.

When the advance was resumed, Lee was in the front ranks. He spotted four NVA setting up a machine gun and grenade launcher. Lee recognized that he was in the best position to take on the enemy. He passed his radio to another soldier, said, "Cover me," and set out alone.

Other enemy soldiers spotted Lee and opened fire. The shy Christian ignored the bullets zinging by him and continued his one-man assault. He boldly charged the machine gun nest, firing his M-16 from the hip. All four NVA died under his onslaught.

Lee could have stopped there, but he saw another enemy position. Once again he single-handedly charged the enemy. This time the enemy's rounds hit him. Greviously wounded, Lee crawled forward, determined to finish his self-appointed mission. He emptied several magazines of ammunition into the enemy position. Under this fire, other members of Lee's platoon were able to maneuver forward and destroy the position.

By the time the medics reached Lee, he had died.

Because of his background, few people besides family members knew that Lee had been posthumously awarded the Medal of Honor for his actions that day. Lee's younger brother, Ronald Collins, born after Lee was abandoned and later abandoned himself, did not know of Lee's heroism until 1993. Since then Collins has devoted a considerable amount of his time to finding out what he can about Milton. "It (has) made me feel very proud of him because not only had he done something for all of his fellow men in Vietnam, but it proved he was just a good person . . . the kind of person you could trust."

After the brutal battles in Hue, Khe Sanh, and other northern cities, the Marines continued their mission to stymie NVA movement across the DMZ. The 3d Marine Division was prepared to go on the offensive near Dong Ha when the NVA brought the battle to them. On April 29, 1968, the 320th NVA Division chewed up an ARVN regiment near the village of Dai Do, two miles down the Cua Viet River from Dong Ha. From that position they threatened to cut off the Marine base at Dong Ha. The NVA ambushed the first Marine battalion sent against them. Another Marine battalion, 2d Battalion, 4th Marines, was fed into the foray. In the five-day battle that developed, two company commanders earned Medals of Honor.

Capt. Jay Vargas, a twenty-seven-year-old career officer from Winslow, Arizona, ignored painful wounds to stay at the helm of Company G through three days of tough fighting. Isolated for a day and a night in Dai Do, Vargas rallied his Marines to drive off three determined NVA counterattacks. At one point he raced through enemy fire to rescue his wounded battalion commander and carry him to a place of safety.

The next morning, Company E, led by twenty-eight-year-old captain *James E. Livingston,* reinforced Vargas. The two officers combined their forces to drive the enemy from Dai Do. The pair then consolidated their positions and allowed a third company to pursue the NVA into the adjacent village of Dinh To. When the NVA hit that unit with a furious counterattack, Livingston gathered up the effective men of his company and led them back into battle. Even though he was immobilized by a third wound during this bold maneuver, Livingston continued to direct the advance. Only when the NVA had been repulsed did Livingston agree to evacuation.

Both men remained in the Marine Corps after the war, Vargas retiring as a colonel and Livingston as a major general.

In Phuoc Long Province north of Saigon, along the Cambodian border, *Sp4. Robert M. Patterson* of the 101st Airborne Division's 2d Squadron, 17th Cavalry, earned a Medal of Honor on May 6 near the hamlet of La Chu. B Troop's 3d Platoon had been attacking enemy bunkers when interlocking machine gun fire pinned down the lead squad. Unwilling to wait for someone else to do something, Patterson sprang into action. Covered by rifle fire from two buddies, Patterson raced into the open to destroy two bunkers with M-16 rifle fire and grenades. When he spotted another bunker, Patterson went after it and did not stop until he had wiped out all enemy resistance. By official count the twenty-year-old North Carolinian knocked out five enemy strong points and killed no less than eight enemy soldiers.

In mid-May 1968, a strong enemy force besieged the Special Forces camp at Kham Duc on the Laotian border, forty-five miles southwest of Da Nang. After three days of intense battle, the high command elected to air evacuate the one thousand friendly troops holding the camp. C-123 and C-130 cargo aircraft landed at the remote camp's airstrip to board and fly out the men while fighters circled overhead to provide protective fire. By the afternoon of May 12 the evacuation was complete. Or was it? Somehow, three men had been left behind.

JOE M. JACKSON

On Mother's Day, May 12, 1968, *Lt. Col. Joe M. Jackson* was taking his semi-annual check ride in a C-123 cargo plane. No matter how long a pilot had been flying, the air force demanded that he take a proficiency test twice each year. After twenty years of service, Jackson was used to the requirement. This check ride was to be an easy trip. He would fly north from Da Nang to a strip near the DMZ to deliver some supplies, then return to Da Nang. Everything seemed routine.

By 3:00 P.M. that Sunday, Jackson had satisfactorily completed the check ride. He was on his way back to Da Nang when his radio crackled with frantic voices from Kham Duc. They needed help. Another C-123 had tried to land to bring out the three remaining ground personnel. Under heavy enemy fire, the pilot had aborted the approach. Now he was low on fuel. He pleaded for someone else to try and get the soldiers out.

Jackson turned to the flight examiner in the right seat, Maj. Jesse Campbell, and said, "We're going in."

Twenty years and thousands of hours as a fighter pilot had prepared the forty-five-year-old Jackson for this moment. When he reached the vicinity of Kham Duc, he was at nine thousand feet. Reasoning that the enemy gunners would expect him to make the same approach as the first C-123, Jackson resorted to an unorthodox approach.

Jackson banked his plane over to line up with the six-thousand-foot-long runway, then chopped power, dropped full flaps, and pushed the nose down. The rate of descent rapidly reached a terrifying four thousand feet per minute. It was the stomach-churning roller-coaster ride of a lifetime.

The book says you do not fly a C-123 that way—and Jackson knew it. He said later, "I was afraid I'd reach the 'blow-up' speed, where the flaps, which were in the full-down position for this dive, would be blown back up to the neutral position. If that happened, we'd pick up additional speed and not be able to stop the descent."

As it was, Jackson barely had enough time to bleed off the extra speed he was carrying. One-quarter mile from the runway, he brought the huge cargo plane out of its dive—just inches above the treetops. He had only a few seconds to set up for touchdown when he crossed the runway's threshold. He was down! Jackson jammed his feet on the brakes, hoping to stop the big bird before it collided with a wrecked helicopter twenty-two hundred feet down the runway. With screaming tires, the heavy plane skidded to a halt just short of the debris.

Before Jackson or his crew could even look for the stranded men, the three raced from a ditch alongside the runway. A crewman, S.Sgt. Manson L. Grubbs, pulled them aboard. Amidst hugs and backslapping, Grubbs radioed Jackson that the men were safely aboard. He could take off.

But Jackson had a problem. He and Campbell watched helplessly while an enemy soldier fired a 122mm rocket directly at them. Down the runway it flew, its deadly tip packed with high explosives. Halfway to the airplane the rocket hit the asphalt and broke in two, the pieces skidding to a halt just twenty-five feet away. They did not explode.

"Let's get out of here," Jackson said. With the plane's throttle jammed full forward and dodging debris as they picked up speed, Jackson lifted the aircraft off the ground through a cross fire of enemy tracer rounds. "We were scared to death," he remembered.

Jackson climbed at maximum power until beyond the range of the enemy's weapons, then set a course for Da Nang. He had been on the ground less than one minute. Miraculously, not one enemy round hit a crew member or the plane.

Jackson was born on March 14, 1923 in Newnan, Georgia, where his family was friendly with the family of Marine helicopter pilot hero Stephen Pless. Jackson left home in 1941 to enter the army air force. He served throughout World War II as a crew chief on a B-25 bomber. After the war, he took flight training and earned his wings. In Korea he flew 107 fighter sorties and earned a Distinguished Flying Cross in the process. In the late 1950s he was among the first air force pilots to fly the U-2 spy plane. He received his well-earned Medal of Honor on January 16, 1969. Two years later he retired as a full colonel.

Reinforcements for the war in South Vietnam were in the pipeline even before the enemy launched his Tet Offensive. The 5th Battalion, 12th Infantry, was formed at Fort Lewis, Washington, in November 1967 expressly for service in the war zone. Though it seemed unrealistic to train soldiers destined for hot, tropical South Vietnam in icy, snowy, pine tree forests, nonetheless the men spent five months there before orders came assigning the battalion to the 199th Light Infantry Brigade. The majority of the troops in the battalion were freshly drafted with no combat experience. Among them was a twenty-two-year-old graduate of the University of Minnesota.

KENNETH L. OLSON

When *Kenneth L. Olson* graduated from college in June 1967, his plan was to complete his graduate studies in agricultural economics on a full scholarship at Purdue University. By then, though, the Selective Service System had eliminated deferments for graduate students. Olson, who had been his high school's class president and was a member of the National Honor Society, decided to volunteer for the draft. That way, he figured, he would get his military obligation out of the way and be able to continue his studies and return to the family farm. Plus, with his education he thought he could get a desk job.

The army assigned him to the infantry.

In November 1967, Olson went to Fort Lewis and Company A of the 5th Battalion. He had no illusions about the war. In fact, while home on leave after his basic training, he told his father, "We'll never win that war." But like so many young men of his generation, he accepted his fate to fight in that war.

The battalion sailed for South Vietnam in late March; it arrived there on April 1, 1968 and set up a base camp near the sprawling army depot at Long Binh, outside Saigon. The 199th Light Infantry Brigade badly needed a fifth maneuver battalion to fulfill its mission of protecting Saigon. It had suffered heavy casualties in weeks of street fighting in the capital and its suburbs.

Olson's natural leadership skills brought him an early promotion to specialist fourth class and command of a rifle squad soon after he arrived in-country. In their first few weeks of combat the men of the 5th Battalion began to learn the hard lessons of war.

Although he was in a war zone, Olson did not forget his family. He arranged for a corsage to be delivered to his mother for Mother's Day. A few days earlier he had penned a note to her. Dated May 11, 1968, it read, "I know that you got the flowers and they probably made you smile. Well, someone's mother in our unit is not going to have a nice Mother's Day for her son was shot." (He was the first man in Olson's company to die.)

The corsage arrived at the Olson farmhouse in Paynesville on Saturday. The next day a green army sedan started up the long driveway.

Halfway around the world, Company A had been on a routine mission southwest of Saigon. One of its platoons came under fire. Olson's platoon was sent to reinforce it. After overrunning the first trench line, Olson and a buddy, PFC Gary Lindley, moved forward. An enemy machine gun opened fire from just thirty feet away. The two grunts dropped to the ground.

While Lindley provided covering fire, Olson popped up and threw a hand grenade at the enemy. He missed. Olson pulled the pin on a second grenade and jumped up again. The enemy was waiting. A burst of machine gun fire stitched up Olson's right arm. He fell backward, the armed grenade slipping from his grasp.

Fully aware that he had only a few seconds to act, Olson rolled over, grabbed the grenade, and pulled it under him.

The blast killed Olson instantly. Lindley suffered minor injuries. The rest of the platoon swarmed forward and killed the Viet Cong manning the machine gun.

On April 7, 1970, Olson's parents accepted their son's posthumous Medal of Honor.

In 1993, after serving twenty-one years in the army and a second tour in South Vietnam, Gary Lindley finally overcame his fear and contacted Ken Olson's parents. "Through all those years I was afraid. I didn't know how they'd react because I was the one who was still alive."

He need not have worried. Lindley's initial cautious correspondence developed into a warm personal relationship. The letters culminated in a personal meeting in June 1998 at a ceremony that dedicated a bronze bas-relief portrait of Olson in the University of Minnesota/St. Paul's student center.

Valor is not the province of battle-hardened veterans only. Even the most inexperienced rookie can perform a great deed of heroism.

Company E, 4th Battalion, 47th Infantry Regiment, 9th Infantry Division, had spent most of May 14, 1968 chasing Viet Cong through the vast Mekong River Delta's swampland six miles south of Dong Tam. As evening approached, the company set up a perimeter on some dry land. A resupply helicopter was called in.

Sp4. Hollis Franks was at the LZ when the chopper arrived. Besides needed supplies, two new men jumped off of the Huey. "They were brand-new," Franks said. "You could tell because they were clean and so were their uniforms."

The two men were PFCs Larry Reid and *James W. Fous.* Fous, a University of Omaha dropout who had been drafted in October 1967, and Reid were assigned to join two veterans in a bunker on the perimeter.

Less than three hours later, someone called out that some VC were sneaking up on the perimeter. From his hole a few meters away, Franks heard several quick rifle shots. Then came a yell followed by a muffled explosion. At dawn he found out what had happened.

A pair of VC had crawled up close to the perimeter. When a grunt spotted them, he called out a warning. Another man fired at the intruders. The enemy got away but not before throwing a grenade at the Americans.

The missile landed in the hole occupied by Fous and the other three. Fous instantly fell on the grenade. It exploded and killed him. The other three escaped injury. The next day Reid said, "Words are just too shallow to explain how I feel. We were both on our first mission. He is dead. I am alive. He saved us."

One of the first reinforcing units to arrive in South Vietnam after the Tet Offensive was the 27th Marine Regiment. On February 17 the unit landed at Da Nang, where it provided security to the air base and other installations until it was sent home in September 1968. Even though they were in-country for only six months, the 27th Marines clashed with the VC several times. A particularly fierce fight occurred on May 17 at Le Nam hamlet south of Da Nang and west of Highway 1 in an area known to the Marines as Go Noi Island.

As Company I approached a dry riverbed that fronted a tree line, it came under heavy fire from a well-concealed Viet Cong force. Half a dozen Marines were hit and fell in the open. The others scrambled for cover.

Then an eighteen-year-old private first class from Monticello, Illinois, picked up his M-60 and began a one-man assault against the enemy. *Robert C. Burke* never hesitated. He raced to the waist-high bank and sent burst after burst of machine gun fire into the VC positions. While he kept the enemy pinned down, other Marines moved the wounded men to safety. When his own weapon jammed, Burke picked one up from a casualty and moved deeper into the VC-held tree line, where he killed five VC. In the meantime, another Marine fixed the jammed M-60. Burke took it back. He stepped into the open and fired deadly bursts into the VC bunkers until he was killed.

Burke was the youngest recipient of the Medal of Honor for service in the Vietnam War.

PHILL G. MCDONALD

Phill G. McDonald's draft notice ordered him to report for induction on September 12, 1967, one day before he turned twenty-six and would become ineligible for conscription. He took the news courageously, but several members of the Sunday school class he taught broke into tears when he gave them the news.

McDonald and his twin sister Phyllis were born in Avondale, West Virginia. One of twelve children, he and Phyllis did their best to raise their siblings after their parents died, but it was too much for the teenagers. The younger children were placed in foster homes. McDonald dropped out of high school at age sixteen and moved to Greensboro, North Carolina. No one ever knew what brought him there. He just showed up one day, found a room, and then a job at a local cedar plant. He also became a member of the local Assembly of God church.

A devout Christian, McDonald devoted nearly all of his free time to the church. He took an active role in a wide variety of church-related activities. He was a popular Sunday school instructor and played gospel songs on his guitar at the weekly services.

A brief marriage protected McDonald from the draft for some time, but the growing American commitment in Southeast Asia eventually led to the induction notice. Six months after that McDonald was in South Vietnam, assigned as an infantryman to Company A, 1st Battalion, 14th Infantry Regiment, 4th Infantry Division, in the Central Highlands.

Almost immediately McDonald's Bible-reading earned him the nickname "Preacher." But he was well regarded. Older than almost everyone else in his company, McDonald brought the maturity of his years to the unit. Younger enlisted men sought his counsel. It was easy for him. Many of these men were just a few years older than his Sunday school students.

When Company A was attacked near Kontum City on June 7, 1968 by well-concealed NVA regulars, McDonald risked his own life to escort two wounded buddies to an evacuation site. Later, when an enemy machine gun threatened the evacuation route, McDonald crawled alone into the jungle and killed the enemy soldier.

McDonald returned to his platoon and learned that it had been ordered to withdraw. He volunteered to cover the movement. He set up an M-60 machine gun in a forward position and raked the jungle in front of him with its heavy rounds.

The NVA turned their fire on McDonald. He was seriously wounded in the barrage. Refusing to relinquish control of his position, McDonald seized another M-60 and put it into action. Behind him, other soldiers were able to gather up the wounded and get them to safety.

Before the withdrawal was completed, another NVA machine gun opened fire. Still suffering terrible pain from his wounds, McDonald went after the weapon. He crawled into the jungle, and when he was within range he threw a hand grenade at the enemy position. It landed on target and killed the NVA. Seconds after that an enemy sniper shot and killed McDonald. His gallant conduct had saved his platoon.

News of McDonald's death was slow to reach Greensboro because his next-of-kin, Phyllis, lived in West Virginia. Not until his body showed up at a local funeral home for burial in Greensboro did his friends learn the sad news.

Few people in Greensboro were aware that Phyllis had accepted a posthumous Medal of Honor for her brother on April 7, 1970. Eventually, time faded the memories of Phill McDonald and his battlefield heroism from those who did know, until he was all but forgotten. Then in 1988, Barry Cohen, a local Vietnam War veteran, learned of McDonald's self-sacrifice. He was startled to find out that there were no memorials to Greensboro's only Medal of Honor recipient. He started a campaign to change that. His efforts led to a permanent display about McDonald at the Greensboro Historical Museum and the naming of a plaza at the local county government complex in his honor.

Air crewmen shot down over enemy territory had a good chance of avoiding capture if a search-and-rescue team could reach them. Highly professional and extremely dedicated, SAR crewmen were a special breed. Called on to fly over enemy-held territory, SAR crews were frequently the targets of enemy fire themselves. The North Vietnamese and Viet Cong often used a downed aircrew as bait to lure in slow-moving SAR aircraft. When the rescue chopper came within range, enemy gunners would shoot it down, sometimes using that crew as additional bait. Unmindful of the hazard, SAR crews exhibited tremendous courage in their daily struggle to save American lives.

CLYDE E. LASSEN

Clyde E. Lassen always demonstrated energy, tenacity, and zeal. Born on March 14, 1942 in Fort Myers, Florida, Lassen enlisted in the navy in 1961 after graduating from high school in Venice, Florida. Although he had enlisted as an aviation mechanic, Lassen had his sights set on becoming a naval aviator. Through four years of enlisted service he worked hard, took courses at junior colleges near his duty stations in San Diego, California, and Pensacola, Florida, and proved to the navy that he had the skills to be a pilot.

After Lassen successfully completed flight school, he received his wings and an ensign's commission. Two years later he was an SAR helicopter pilot aboard the USS *Preble* (DLG-15), a guided missile destroyer assigned to SAR duty off the coast of North Vietnam.

On the evening of June 19, 1968, Lassen hovered his UH-2 Seasprite helicopter over the water a few miles offshore as he patiently awaited word of two downed naval aviators. There had been no contact with the pair since they had jumped from their disabled plane about twenty miles south of Hanoi over an hour earlier. Just when it seemed the pilots would be given up as captured or dead, Lassen's copilot, Lt. Clarence L. Cook, got their map coordinates over his radio. The downed airmen were on the side of a steep, heavily wooded hill surrounded by tall trees and enemy soldiers. The NVA were closing in on them. The pilots had to be rescued—and fast.

Lassen set a course for the site. An overcast sky cut visibility. When he arrived at the coordinates, there was no sign of the pilots. Lassen thought he had missed the location, but suddenly a flare flashed through the inky sky.

As he moved toward the illumination, Lassen looked for a pickup spot. A rice paddy at the bottom of the hill looked promising. Lassen radioed his plan to the downed airmen, then hovered a few feet over the muddy water. This maneuver drew the fire of several nearby NVA. A shower of small-arms fire flew at the chopper. Lassen's door gunners, Aviation Machinist Mates Bruce B. Dallas and Donald N. West, returned the fire. Lassen made up his mind to sit out the enemy fire, but then he was advised that the stranded pilots could not get down the hill. The brush was just too thick and the enemy too close.

After gaining some altitude, Lassen decided that if the trapped aviators could not get to him, he would go to them.

Cautiously, mindful of the tall trees and the enemy fire, Lassen nursed his craft up the hill. After he called for an overhead plane to drop some flares to illuminate the area, Lassen found a good pickup spot between two trees. Dallas and West dropped the rescue hoist into the darkness below.

Just as rescue seemed likely, the last of the overhead flares died out. Lassen immediately lost his depth perception and suffered a bout of vertigo. "Look out for the trees!" one of the gunners screamed into the intercom. A severe jolt shot through the chopper as its rotor blades hacked into the branches.

Lassen fought for control of his ship with every ounce of strength and all of his skill. The helicopter vibrated heavily, but somehow the intrepid pilot was able to regain control.

As if the damage to his helicopter was not bad enough, Lassen now realized that he was running low on fuel. And the overhead plane reported that it had run out of flares.

It would have been acceptable for Lassen to abandon his mission at this point—no one would have criticized him if he had; the odds were really stacked against him—but he did not. He had not completed the rescue and he was determined to do so.

Lassen radioed for another flare ship, then contacted the downed aviators to tell them they had to make their way downhill. Lassen's door gunners could keep the enemy marksmen at bay, but he wanted nothing more to do with those tall trees.

Lassen hovered out of range until the replacement flare ship arrived. Then he went back to the rice paddy. The volume of enemy fire increased dramatically as he neared the pickup site. Numerous rounds riddled the chopper's thin skin. Amazingly, none hit the crew.

With only thirty minutes of fuel remaining, Lassen began his descent toward the anxious pilots. He was fifty feet above the paddy when the flares burned out. Once again it seemed as if his luck had ended.

With no time left for the flare ship to circle back to drop another flare, and absolutely determined to save the two men, Lassen turned on his landing light. The high-powered beam cut a bright swath through the night and made the helicopter a perfect target for the enemy gunners. Lassen ignored the withering fire. His door gunners sent streams of bullets into the night as he set the chopper down. Seconds later the two pilots, having homed in on the landing light, burst out of the night. Eager hands pulled them aboard the Seasprite. Once he was satisfied that the two pilots were safely on board, Lassen flew his injured helicopter higher into the night sky, turned, and headed for the sea.

Dangerously low on fuel, Lassen landed on the first friendly vessel he saw. Crewmen aboard the USS *Jouett,* another guided missile destroyer, measured less than five minutes of fuel left in the Seasprite's tanks.

Each member of the crew was decorated for his role in the daring rescue: Lassen received the Medal of Honor, Cook earned the Navy Cross, and Dallas and West each received the Silver Star. Lassen continued his career in the navy and eventually attained the rank of commander. He died on April 1, 1994.

On June 3, 1968, General Westmoreland, reassigned as army chief of staff, turned over command of Military Assistance Command, Vietnam, to his deputy, Gen. Creighton W. Abrams. Under Abrams, the strategy of large-scale search-and-destroy operations shifted to one of smaller, company-size maneuvers. Already the United States was attempting to reduce its losses. Any battalion-size or larger operations would be left mainly to the ARVN.

Even with the reduction in offensive operations, service in South Vietnam was replete with danger, for those in traditional noncombat roles as well as for combat troops. Truck convoys were particularly vulnerable to enemy ambush. Crisscrossing South Vietnam in a never-ending round of deliveries, the convoys presented enticing targets to the VC and NVA. This was the case when a convoy traveling from the massive American supply base at Long Binh outside Saigon was ambushed near Ap Nhi, sixty miles northwest of the capital.

Rockets, grenades, automatic weapons, and small-arms fire wracked the deuce-and-a-half trucks from the 62d Transportation Company. One of the truck drivers, nineteen-year-old sergeant *William Seay,* sprang from his cab to take up a fighting position behind the big wheels of the vehicle in front of him. From there, he blazed away with an M-16 and dropped two enemy soldiers a scant thirty feet away. Twice he left his position of relative safety to scoop up enemy grenades and throw them back at the advancing NVA. On his second try, an enemy rifle round tore into his right wrist.

Seay rolled into a ditch to wait for a medic. Then he spotted three enemy soldiers preparing to fire at the other casualties huddled around him. Seay shouted a warning and stood up. With his right hand limp at his side, he fired his rifle with his left. He killed the three soldiers, but an enemy sniper mortally wounded the Brewton, Alabama, native.

On August 26, 1968, the 1st Platoon, Company B, 4th Battalion, 21st Infantry, Americal Division, ran into trouble while on a routine patrol with an armored unit west of Tam Ky in Quang Tin Province. A twenty-two-year-old squad leader from Phoenix, Arizona, *Sgt. Nicky D. Bacon,* took his men forward in an assault on the enemy bunker line. Minutes later the platoon leader fell with a severe wound. Bacon, who had served a previous Vietnam tour with the 1st Infantry Division in 1966, took charge of the platoon. Under his expert leadership the men surged forward to attack the enemy.

When the nearby 3d Platoon lost its leader, Bacon assumed command of it, too. The intrepid soldier led both units against the reinforced bunkers. When he was unable to destroy a particularly well-defended bunker, Bacon climbed aboard the rear deck of a tank. From that completely exposed position, he poured a hail of bullets into the enemy ranks and drove them off.

In the Fishhook area of War Zone C, northwest of Saigon, the 1st Infantry Division spent the fall of 1968 searching for the 1st NVA Division. During the last week of October, members of the Big Red One clashed repeatedly with the enemy. 1st Division artillery units supported all of these actions. From their fire support bases spread throughout the region, the division's massive firepower poured down on the enemy.

On one memorable night the division's 5th Artillery Regiment severely damaged an NVA unit that was crossing the nearby Cambodian border. One of its shells struck an enemy ammunition depot and caused 128 secondary explosions. It was probably this action that resulted in the enemy's attempt to destroy the responsible fire support base (FSB).

CHARLES C. ROGERS

Fire Support Base Rita was manned by the 1st Battalion, 5th Artillery, commanded by *Lt. Col. Charles C. Rogers*. Almost one thousand yards in diameter, FSB Rita had been painstakingly carved out of the jungle adjacent to the Cambodian border by sweating soldiers a few months earlier. Night after night the artillerymen sent H&I (harassing and interdiction) fire missions from their 155mm howitzers into target areas where NVA units were believed to be sneaking across the border. As long as FSB Rita remained operational, the NVA were not safe.

Lieutenant Colonel Rogers was in his twelfth month incountry. He had originally volunteered for duty in South Vietnam because service there was critical to his well-thought-out career plans. "I wanted the combat experience, and I felt it was imperative to my career to get a combat command," he said.

The son of a coal miner, Rogers was born in Claremont, West Virginia, on September 6, 1929. After his 1951 graduation from West Virginia State College Institute, where he took two degrees, in chemistry and mathematics, Rogers was commissioned a second lieutenant through the school's ROTC program. Fifteen years of routine assignments preceded Rogers's arrival in South Vietnam in the fall of 1967.

Rogers had been scheduled to depart the war zone in mid-November, but extended his tour so he could take a staff position with MACV. It was an excellent opportunity to add more experience to his already brilliant career. Now, on Halloween, he had just two weeks to go before he gave up his command.

For the previous three nights, FSB Rita had been heavily mortared. Halloween night was no different. As soon as the sun dropped below the horizon, enemy rockets and mortar shells fell from the darkening sky.

All of this enemy activity had kept Rogers from getting much rest over the past few nights. This night he was determined to get some sleep. At 12:30 A.M., November 1, 1968,

Rogers crawled into his sleeping bag under the radio complex in his tactical operations center. Fifteen minutes later the base erupted in a "mad minute" (at irregular intervals, every weapon on a base fired outward in an attempt to catch an attacking enemy unaware).

The noise awakened the colonel. When the mad minute did not stop, Rogers radioed one of his battery commanders. "Captain Dan Settle told me the enemy had broken through the wire and was all over his position. So I grabbed my steel pot and flak jacket and headed over there," Rogers recalled.

What Rogers saw outside the TOC astonished him. "All of the infantry's armored personnel carriers on the west flank had been hit by rocket-propelled grenades. I instantly realized there was nothing there to stop the enemy but my batteries."

Rogers raced through the carnage toward his guns' positions. On the way there, he shot at several NVA soldiers running through the base. When he reached the howitzer position, Rogers found most of the crewmen huddled in their bunkers so they could avoid the murderous fire. He went from bunker to bunker and ordered the men to their weapons, then issued fire commands to the crews.

While so occupied, Rogers was hit in the face by a ricocheting round. The slug struck the left side of his nose and lodged in his palate. Choking on the swell of blood filling his throat, Rogers reached into his mouth. "I pulled the bullet from the roof of my mouth and threw it on the ground; the wound continued to bleed profusely."

Still full of fight, Rogers advanced on several NVA hiding behind a log pile. Before he reached them, an RPG went off at his feet. A nearby enlisted man died in the blast and Rogers took shrapnel in both legs, but he did not give up. He crawled forward and killed the enemy soldier with hand grenades.

Over the next several hours, using a rifle as a crutch, Rogers moved throughout FSB Rita and directed his men in repulsing the fanatical enemy. Wherever the fighting seemed the hardest, that was where Rogers went.

On one of his visits to a howitzer position, he found the cannoneers again hiding in their bunkers. Rogers ordered them back to their guns. "Sir, we can't come out. We'll all be killed out there," one man answered.

Rogers shouted back, "Dammit! Don't you see me standing here? I'm not getting killed. Now get your butts out of that bunker."

Sheepishly, embarrassed by the colonel's bravery, the crew crawled out. A few minutes later their howitzer was back in action.

On through the night the NVA came. No matter what the Americans threw at them, the enemy kept coming. "I was amazed," said Rogers. "I just couldn't understand it. As fast as we cut them down, why here comes another row of them."

All of Rogers's batteries were firing, knocking down enemy soldiers by the score. The colonel stood in a howitzer emplacement and helped the crew fire the weapon into the screaming horde of onrushing enemy soldiers. Enemy mortar shells still crashed down around the base. "They were hitting all around," he said, "and then I saw a series of rounds being walked in my direction. One hit seventy yards east of me, the next thirty. I thought, 'I bet the next one is coming right into this parapet . . .'"

Rogers came to in an upside-down position against a bunker. His mind was filled with a vague image of flying through the air and the howitzer keeling over. Both his legs were badly injured; he could not walk. Then a medic appeared. "The Old Man's been hit again," the youngster called out. "We need a litter." Seconds later strong hands lifted him onto the litter and carried him back to the TOC.

Still fully conscious, Rogers barked orders to those around him. He called in air strikes and directed their fire to within one hundred yards of the perimeter wire. "I'd never seen the guys lay it on so close and so effective," Rogers said later.

Helicopter gunships arrived at daybreak. Their massed firepower finally broke up the enemy attack. The NVA retreated into the jungle, pulling along their wounded as they fled. At least 328 enemy dead were counted around FSB Rita.

Medevac choppers flew in to take out the dozens of American casualties. Rogers refused to leave. He stayed on, evaluating reports from the gunships. He wanted to be sure the enemy was gone. Only when he was convinced the fight was over did he let the medics place him on a chopper.

After medical treatment and three months of recuperation in Japan, Rogers asked to be allowed to take his job at MACV. The doctors refused, but Rogers persisted. He won. Three days after he was released from the hospital, Rogers flew back to South Vietnam. "I still had a job to do," he explained. He finally returned to the United States in July 1969.

On May 14, 1970, Rogers received his Medal of Honor from President Nixon. Rogers continued his army career and graduated from the prestigious Command and General Staff College as well as the Army War College. He also earned a master's degree along the way. The highest-ranking black to ever earn a Medal of Honor, Rogers received the second star of a major general in 1980. After his retirement in 1985, Rogers was ordained and ministered to army troops in Germany. He died on September 21, 1990.

To support the Studies and Observation Group's clandestine operations in Cambodia, MACV assigned a unique unit to the stealthy organization. The U.S. Air Force's 20th Special Operations Squadron (SOS) was officially based at Cam Ranh Bay. In reality, every ten days its Hueys and crew members rotated to Ban Me Thuot. From there the "Green Hornets," a nickname they had picked up because their helicopters were unmarked except for a stenciled green hornet on the tail, flew to SOG's various bases.

The Green Hornets and the men of SOG developed a close relationship. The SOG teams depended on the Green Hornets to get them into an LZ, for gunship support, and for extraction. A Green Hornet pilot considered a SOG team that he had inserted to be "his." He would not rotate back to Ban Me Thuot as long as "his" team was across the line.

That devotion led to the circumstances that resulted in a Medal of Honor for a young helicopter pilot.

JAMES P. FLEMING

It took *1st Lt. James P. Fleming* five months of combat flying to be elevated to aircraft commander (AC) in the 20th SOS. Not that he was not qualified. He was, in fact, a highly skilled pilot. It was just that there were so many senior officer pilots in the squadron that it took that long for a slot to open for a lowly lieutenant.

On the morning of November 26, 1968, Fleming, a twenty-five-year-old native of Sedalia, Missouri, was on his second day as an AC. His mission was to fly a SOG recon team, RT Chisel, into Cambodia. He would then return to the forward operating base at Duc Co to fly other missions.

The insertion was completed without incident. Fleming flew back to Duc Co, refueled, ate, and flew another recon team into another LZ in Cambodia.

In the meantime, RT Chisel had reached its objective, a position along a wide river from which they could observe enemy boat traffic. The six-man team, three Americans and three Montagnards, hunkered down in the thick brush. They had barely settled in when a force of NVA attacked. The team leader, S.Sgt. Ancil Franks, realized he was trapped. The NVA were on three sides and the river was on the fourth. He called for an emergency extraction.

Thirty miles to the south, Lieutenant Fleming was in a formation of five Hueys, two gunships and three troopships, on their way back to Duc Co from the second insertion. When they got word that RT Chisel was in trouble, they immediately set course for the team. Once on station, the two gunships strafed the enemy positions while Fleming and the other two troopships hovered nearby.

Almost immediately one of the gunships was hit. It went down in a nearby clearing. One of the troopships peeled off to pick up that crew and fly them back to Duc Co. A few minutes later the other troopship pilot announced that he was low on fuel and had to depart. That left Fleming and one gunship on station.

The gunship rolled in and put rockets all around RT Chisel's position, but the aircraft was hit as it pulled up. Fleming noticed smoke trailing the Huey, but it kept on flying. Fleming now had to make a life-altering decision. His Huey was low on fuel and his gunners were low on ammunition. He could have called and announced his low fuel situation. No one would have said a word. But he could not leave. RT Chisel was his team, his responsibility. He would bring them out.

Fleming banked around a low hill to hide his approach from the enemy. Then he dropped down low to just above the water and flew along the river to Chisel's position. His two gunners blazed away with their M-60s at enemy soldiers lining the river.

Just as Fleming reached the riverbank where the SOG team was supposed to be, the NVA hit Chisel with so much strength that every member of the team was too busy firing back to run to the Huey. Franks frantically radioed Fleming, "They've got us. Get out!"

Fleming pulled pitch and climbed away. From a safe altitude he could see the battle below him. It was obvious that the team could not hold out much longer. Unless he picked them up soon, the members of RT Chisel were goners. Fleming radioed the pilot of the gunship to make one more pass. Then he would take his troopship back to the pickup zone.

Fleming followed the gunship down the river. At the pickup zone, the river seemed alive with the geysers of bullets smacking into the water.

Fleming hovered over the water while his crew frantically searched the densely foliaged bank for any sign of RT Chisel. After what seemed an eternity one of the door gunners shouted, "There they are!"

Franks and four men came racing through the jungle. When they reached the bank, they turned and fired back into the trees. Then they splashed into the river.

Fleming backed his Huey up until he was nearly over the five desperate men. With bullets filling the air all around them, the crew struggled to pull the team members from the water.

In the cockpit Fleming saw individual NVA burst out of the jungle to take up firing positions. He could not do anything but hover in position.

Bullets shattered the Huey's windshield and damaged some instruments, but Fleming held his aircraft level. More bullets ricocheted off the water and tore into the Huey. Fleming had to get out soon or the NVA would shoot down his aircraft and they would all die.

But there was one man missing.

Fleming would not leave a man behind. He waited until a big, burly figure crashed through the underbrush about fifty yards away. The man turned, fired into the jungle, then dived into the water. He stroked his way toward the Huey. Fleming maneuvered toward the figure. Once the helicopter was over him, the last RT Chisel member grabbed a rope ladder hanging outside the machine. Assured that the man was secure, Fleming flew off, the SOG commando hanging below the chopper. NVA bullets and rockets followed the Huey down the river. Once out of range, Fleming stopped and his crew pulled the man aboard. Then Fleming climbed and flew toward Duc Co.

When they landed there, the fuel gauges of Fleming's helicopter read EMPTY. It was one of the most dramatic rescues of the entire Vietnam War.

Fleming completed his tour of duty and returned to the United States. On May 14, 1970 he was presented his well-deserved Medal of Honor. He remained in the air force and retired as a colonel.

The 1st Cavalry Division (Airmobile) left northern I Corps in November 1968 to take up positions along the Cambodian border in Binh Long Province north of Saigon. Almost from the moment they arrived in the area, the First Team was in contact with the enemy. The firefights were frequently brief—but always bitter.

JOHN N. HOLCOMB

The men of Company D, 2d Battalion, 7th Cavalry, 1st Cavalry Division, were anxious for December 3 to end. This was to be their last air assault before Christmas. After sixty straight days in the field, they were all looking forward to a much-needed break. In honor of the approaching holiday, some of the grunts sported tiny Santas on their rucksacks. Others carried Christmas wreaths.

It was supposed to be a routine assault, if any combat action can be termed "routine." Out on the choppers, a ground sweep of the area around the LZ, then a flight back to the base camp.

Among the men waiting to board the choppers was twenty-two-year-old sergeant *John N. Holcomb*. A native of Richland, Oregon, he had enlisted in October 1966. His first duty station after basic training was Germany. In March 1968, with MACV screaming for replacements, Holcomb was transferred to South Vietnam.

On December 3 he was a short-timer with less than ninety days left to serve on his twelve-month tour.

As the troop-laden Hueys approached the LZ, Holcomb saw friendly artillery rounds hitting around the open meadows. Helicopter gunships crisscrossed overhead and zipped rockets and machine gun bullets into the surrounding jungle. The first slicks touched down. The grunts spilled onto the ground. They raced to set up positions on the LZ's perimeter in anticipation of the crack of enemy rounds. They did not come. The LZ was cold.

Holcomb set up his squad in defensive positions. The last helicopter rose from the meadows. Then it happened. An RPG flew from the jungle toward the chopper and exploded against the aircraft with a deadly roar. An enemy force estimated to be battalion-size opened fire on Company D. Holcomb's squad lay directly in the path of the main enemy attack.

In the first few minutes of the fight, an exploding RPG wounded Holcomb's M-60 machine gunner. Fully aware that the enemy was concentrating their fire on that position, Holcomb nonetheless picked up the weapon, moved it forward, and sent belt after belt of ammunition into the enemy's ranks, forcing them to pull back.

During the lull that followed, Holcomb reestablished his men into a tighter defensive position. Concerned only for their welfare, he carried the wounded to safety and gave them what first aid he could.

When the enemy returned for a second attack, Holcomb was ready. Supported by one rifleman, he took up the most exposed position. Again his accurate fire forced the charging enemy back. Just as he was ready to go for more ammunition, an RPG hit his machine gun, destroyed it, and grievously wounded him.

Undaunted by the pain, Holcomb crawled back to his men through grass set on fire by mortar round explosions. As the last surviving leader of the decimated platoon, Holcomb radioed the enemy's location to the overhead gunships. Then he went forward a third time.

A survivor of that fight, Stephen Benko, remembered Holcomb's last minutes. "We didn't know each other very well and didn't like each other very much, but he died keeping me alive. John died in my arms after sprinting across twenty-five yards of open ground to bring a new machine gun to my position. Before that, he'd been racing around the LZ with ammo and bandages for the score of wounded and dying. Together, we'd succeeded in stopping an all-out ground attack by the North Vietnamese, who had us outnumbered and surrounded."

Benko recalled "being very angry at Holcomb for charging across that clearing. I was mad because I needed him alive; because he was a good soldier and I was scared. He must have known he couldn't make that run. All the enemy fire was being focused on us because we were among the few firing back.

"His big body must have made a huge target for the NVA," Benko said. "John was a brave man. But he was more than that. He was a man who made others brave."

Holcomb's posthumous Medal of Honor was presented to his parents on February 16, 1971.

On December 8, 1968 near the Central Highland hamlet of Song Mao, twenty-three-year-old sergeant *Ray McKibben* of Felton, Georgia, led the point element of a recon patrol from Troop B, 7th Squadron (Airmobile), 17th Cavalry, 1st Aviation Brigade, through the triple-canopy jungle. A veteran of an earlier tour in South Vietnam, McKibben's mission today was to make contact with the enemy. He did not fail.

Enemy fire erupted from a bunker set along a trail. McKibben boldly charged the position, killed the enemy gunner, and captured his weapon. A short distance later, the patrol again came under fire. McKibben braved the buzzing bullets to rescue a wounded grunt and pull him to safety behind a large boulder. After administering first aid, McKibben again single-handedly assaulted the enemy positions. He plunged right through the thick underbrush toward the first enemy bunker. There he killed one NVA and captured his weapon. He continued on to the next bunker, but his M-16 ran out of ammunition. McKibben then used the captured AK-47 to keep the enemy at bay while he moved close enough to destroy the position with a well-placed grenade.

After he reloaded his M-16, McKibben used it to provide covering fire so the rest of the patrol could move toward him. As they advanced, NVA in a third bunker opened fire. McKibben, for the fourth time that day, charged alone toward the enemy. This time his luck ran out. He was hit and mortally wounded. He dropped to his knees. Focused on taking out the enemy, he fired a final burst from his M-16 and killed two enemy soldiers. The rest of the recon patrol rushed forward, but there were no enemy-occupied bunkers left. McKibben had destroyed them all.

While the soldiers and Marines fought their ground actions in late 1968 throughout South Vietnam, the Studies and Observation Group continued its clandestine operations in Laos and Cambodia. On one of these, a remarkable Green Beret added the Medal of Honor to his long list of decorations.

ROBERT L. HOWARD

When choppers dropped *SFC Robert L. Howard,* an officer, and a small force of Chinese Nungs (mercenaries who worked with the Special Forces) into a small clearing in Laos on December 30, 1968, the twenty-nine-year-old NCO was in the middle of his third tour of duty in South Vietnam. A deeply religious man, Howard was also extraordinarily devoted to his men—that trait had earned him a well-deserved reputation as one of the most courageous men to serve in the war.

"When things really got bad," he said later, "I'd try to think about my men. Thinking about what I could do to help them kept me from giving up or getting scared."

Wounded fourteen times during fifty-four months in South Vietnam with the Special Forces, Howard earned every possible combat decoration, including eight Purple Hearts.

Howard had left his Opelika, Alabama, home twelve years earlier to enlist. He first went to South Vietnam with a brigade of the 101st Airborne Division in July 1965. During that tour he was accepted for Special Forces training, completed it, and returned to the war zone.

One and one-half years later, on his second tour, Howard earned a Distinguished Service Cross. On November 21, 1967, during a furious battle with North Vietnamese soldiers guarding a large supply dump, Howard personally destroyed two heavily defended bunkers. When he went to inspect one of them, a survivor opened fire. Pinned down directly in front of the automatic weapon with its barrel just six inches above his head, Howard calmly threw a grenade through the opening and killed the gunner.

Now in late December 1968, Howard was on a mission to find a missing American soldier. And the enemy was waiting. No sooner had the helicopters headed back across the bor-

der than the NVA opened up. In a blaze of small-arms fire
and grenades, the officer fell, badly wounded. The Nungs
fled into the jungle, firing wildly. A grenade exploded near
Howard and drove shrapnel deep into his legs, nearly tore off
several of his fingers, and ruined his rifle.

Unable to stand and in excruciating pain, Howard thought
only of his lieutenant. He ignored the bullets snapping overhead to crawl through the underbrush, dragging his bleeding
legs behind him.

Somehow Howard reached the officer. As he started to ad-
minister first aid, an enemy round hit one of the lieutenant's
ammunition pouches. Howard ducked for cover as the
rounds exploded, then returned to the unconscious officer.

Summoning up a reserve of superhuman strength, Howard
stuffed one of the lieutenant's feet in his armpit and, slowly
and painfully inching backward, pulled the man to safety. He
then set about reorganizing his small remaining force.

The indomitable NCO crawled from position to position,
moving his men into a better defensive arrangement. Over
the next three and one-half hours, Howard led the Nungs in
holding off the enemy. He called in air strikes, directing them
to within fifty yards of his position. Finally Howard felt secure enough to call in helicopters for an evacuation attempt.

He had been wounded in the legs, foot, hand, stomach, and
buttocks, but Howard refused to board the chopper until all
of his men were safely aboard. Only then would he allow
himself to be pulled up.

After he recuperated from his injuries, Howard spent eight
more months in Southeast Asia before being rotated back to
an instructor's position at Fort Bragg, North Carolina. In August 1970 he went back to South Vietnam for his fourth tour.

Howard was still there when word came that he was to receive the Medal of Honor. "At first, I wasn't sure what the
medal was being awarded for," he recalled. "I'd been told I
was put in for a decoration for a fight in November 1968, but
that wasn't it."

Actually, Howard had been recommended three times for
the Medal of Honor. The first was downgraded to the Distin-

guished Service Cross. When the decorations board reviewed the second and third recommendations, they elected to award a Silver Star for the second and the Medal of Honor for the third.

Some board members felt that Howard should have had three Medals of Honor, but military custom would not allow that to happen.

When the blue ribbon and its Medal of Honor was placed around Howard's neck on March 2, 1971, he was wearing lieutenant's bars; he had received a direct commission in December 1969.

After the war in South Vietnam ended, Howard spent most of his time as an instructor at the Special Forces School at Fort Bragg, teaching the way of war to a new generation of Green Berets. He continued his own training, too. He completed his undergraduate degree, then in 1980 received a master's degree from Central Michigan University. He retired from the army as a colonel in 1992 after thirty-six years of service.

CHAPTER SEVEN

Medics and Chaplains at War

A man wounded in the Vietnam War had an excellent chance for survival—better than 90 percent. In most cases a casualty was in an evacuation hospital within thirty minutes of being hit. Once there, the survival rate soared to nearly 100 percent. Never in the history of warfare had combatants received such excellent care.

The first and most important link in this chain of care was the medic or corpsman attached to an army or Marine field unit. These youngsters, many of whom had never given a career in medicine much thought before they started their military service, often found themselves the sole source of medical treatment in hostile territory.

Charged with making daily life-and-death decisions at a young age, many medics assumed an overly protective attitude toward the men in their unit. They frequently became so involved with their "patients" that they went to extraordinary lengths to save them.

Twenty medics earned Medals of Honor during the course of U.S. involvement in Vietnam. Only nine survived to wear their decoration.

In addition to the medics, three Roman Catholic chaplains earned Medals of Honor in the Vietnam War, two posthumously. Although considered noncombatants, chaplains accompanied combat units into the field, where they not only provided spiritual support but also assisted the medics in treating the wounded. Armed only with their courage, the chaplains often faced the same dangers as the grunts.

A twenty-three-year-old medic from Covina, California,

earned a posthumous Medal of Honor in Kontum Province on January 27, 1967 when he saved the lives of men from his platoon and several from another nearby platoon. *Sp4. Donald W. Evans*'s platoon of Company A, 2d Battalion, 12th Infantry, 4th Infantry Division, had not yet been committed to the battle near the hamlet of Tri Tam when he heard that an adjacent platoon had taken casualties.

Without hesitation, Evans charged forward through one hundred yards of open ground, mercifully untouched by exploding mortars and small-arms fire. After treating a half dozen casualties, two of whom he carried back to his platoon's position, Evans was hit by grenade fragments. He ignored his wounds to rejoin his platoon as it entered the fray. Twice more he carried wounded out of the line of fire. He was running toward another when the enemy shot him down.

CHARLES C. HAGEMEISTER

After a year at the University of Nebraska, nineteen-year-old *Charles C. Hagemeister* decided that the war raging halfway around the world demanded his attention. It did not seem right for him to be enjoying college life while other people his age were dying in rice paddies. He enlisted in the army on May 19, 1966.

Following basic training at Fort Polk, Louisiana, where he qualified as an Expert on the rifle range, Hagemeister went to Fort Sam Houston, Texas, where army medics received their training at the Brooke Army Medical Center. Courses in anatomy, biology, chemistry, and physiology coupled with hands-on training in the hospital's wards prepared the fledgling doctors for their work in South Vietnam.

Hagemeister went overseas to the 1st Battalion, 5th Cavalry, 1st Cavalry Division (Airmobile), in November 1966. He saw action in scores of fights during which he received credit for saving dozens of lives. His toughest fight, though, came on March 20, 1967 as part of Operation Pershing in northern Binh Dinh Province.

On March 19 the 1st Battalion, 8th Cavalry, ran into a tough force from the 18th NVA Regiment. Two battalions of the 5th Cavalry, including Hagemeister's 1st, were sent in as reinforcements. The next day the NVA attacked his company.

Fire from enemy small-arms and machine guns ripped into the walking troopers from three sides. Hagemeister raced to treat two casualties from the lead squad. A few minutes later word reached him that his platoon leader had been hit.

Hagemeister crawled rapidly through the blistering enemy fire. He reached the officer, treated him and several others, then prepared to evacuate them. At that moment the crack of a sniper's rifle sent a round zinging past Hagemeister's ear. He jumped for cover, his eyes frantically searching the tree-tops for the deadly foe. He spotted him.

Nearby soldiers were unable to bring their weapons to bear on the sniper, so Hagemeister picked up an M-16. His Expert rating with the weapon back at Fort Polk paid off. Hagemeister killed the enemy with one shot.

Seconds later Hagemeister killed three enemy soldiers who were trying to outflank his position, then he exchanged rounds with an NVA machine gunner. Hagemeister won that duel, too.

His private battle over, Hagemeister raced through the enemy fire to contact a nearby platoon. He brought them into his perimeter, where he personally placed riflemen in defensive positions. Under their covering fire, the gallant medic moved the casualties to a position of safety.

For his conspicuous gallantry Hagemeister was recommended for the Medal of Honor. Amazingly, the award was nearly denied because someone higher in the chain of command questioned the intensity of the combat action, since Hagemeister was not wounded performing his deed. Fortunately, the more experienced reviewers prevailed and the heroic medic received his award from President Nixon on May 14, 1968.

Hagemeister remained in the army, received a direct commission, and in 1985 entered the army's prestigious Command and General Staff College at Fort Leavenworth,

Kansas. Upon graduation he was asked to join the school's staff as a tactics instructor. He held that position until he retired in June 1990 as a lieutenant colonel.

In addition to tending to the religious needs of the men in the field, chaplains were cross-trained in medicine. Although they were not expected to function as medics in battle, they could help the medics tend the wounded. The three chaplains who earned Medals of Honor in South Vietnam all received their decorations for rescuing wounded men under fire. All three earned their medals during one sixty-day period in the fall of 1967. The first was a navy chaplain from Staten Island, New York.

VINCENT R. CAPODANNO

One of nine children, *Vincent R. Capodanno* was ordained a Maryknoll priest in June 1957. He devoted the next seven years of his life to missionary work in the Far East. Compelled by a desire to serve his God and his country where he was most needed, he applied for service with the Navy Chaplain Corps in July 1965. He specifically requested duty with the Marines in South Vietnam. Father Capodanno joined the 1st Marine Division as a navy lieutenant at Da Nang in April 1966.

Chaplain Capodanno's first eight months in-country were spent with the 1st Battalion, 7th Marines. He quickly became known as a field chaplain, a man who would rather spend time with the grunts on a combat operation than in the rear. He earned a Bronze Star for his heroism in rescuing the wounded and recovering the dead during an operation near Chu Lai in November 1966.

In December 1966, Chaplain Capodanno was transferred to the 1st Medical Battalion at Da Nang. The priest found the work with the patients gratifying, but he longed to return to the field. Though it was no longer his responsibility, the 1st Battalion, 7th Marines, received frequent visits from Capodanno. He would fly in on a resupply helicopter, stay a few days to say Mass and hear confessions, then return to the hospital.

As Chaplain Capodanno's one-year tour neared completion, he volunteered to serve an additional six months. The request was granted. The priest took a thirty-day leave during which he visited family members in New Jersey. Upon his return to South Vietnam, he received an assignment to the 5th Marines, then operating in the Hiep Duc Valley (also known as the Que Son Valley) west of Tam Ky in Quang Tin Province.

The Marines of his new regiment soon learned that Father Capodanno was one of them. The priest lived and worked alongside the men, sharing the hardships and the dangers.

Early on the morning of September 4, 1967, Company D, 1st Battalion, 5th Marines, was badly mauled by a strong force of Viet Cong near Dong Son in the Hiep Duc Valley. Reinforcements were rushed to the scene of the action. Two companies from the 3d Battalion, 5th Marines, were sent into the fray. Chaplain Capodanno asked to accompany Company M. He knew the men and had operated with them recently. Initially his request was denied. But the priest persisted and the battalion commander gave his okay.

Helicopters carried the Marines of Company M to an LZ four miles from the battlefield. From there they advanced in a double column across small hills and through rice paddies. As the lead platoon descended the crest of a hill, the enemy struck with a sudden fury. A second platoon moved around the base of the hill to outflank the enemy, but it too was soon engulfed by intense enemy fire.

From the relative safety of the company CP on the back side of the hill, Chaplain Capodanno heard the screams and cries of the wounded. He voluntarily left the command group to help. Completely ignoring the heavy volume of enemy fire tearing across the hillside, the intrepid chaplain moved throughout the battlefield, gave aid to the wounded, and administered his church's Last Rites to the dying.

One of the men Capodanno tended was *Sgt. Lawrence D.*

Peters, a squad leader. Peters had distinguished himself by ignoring the enemy fire to point out targets to his men. Even after Peters was severely wounded, he continued to aggressively lead them against the enemy. Although Peters lay in an open area, Father Capodanno ran toward him through the scrub brush. An enemy mortar round exploded behind him and a large chunk of shrapnel ripped into Capodanno's right shoulder. A stream of blood poured from the jagged hole, but that did not halt the chaplain. He made it to Peters. The priest lay by the young Marine's side and prayed with him until Peters died (Peters was posthumously awarded a Medal of Honor on April 20, 1970).

Throughout the long fight Chaplain Capodanno persisted in seeking out those in need despite the gunfire sweeping the hillside. Time after time the fearless Maryknoll priest risked his own life to give medical aid to the wounded and comfort to the dying. His total disregard for his own safety greatly inspired the Marines who saw him that day.

When a mortar round severely wounded the priest in the arms and legs and nearly severed his right hand, he pushed aside the corpsman who tried to treat him. "Take care of the others," Capodanno said.

At 6:30 P.M. that day, Chaplain Capodanno spotted a Marine trying to pull a wounded corpsman to safety. At the same time he saw an enemy machine gunner aiming at the pair. Father Capodanno dashed forward. His movement drew the enemy's fire. His bullet-riddled body was recovered later that night. He had been shot twenty-seven times.

On January 7, 1969, Father Capodanno's brother, James, accepted his posthumous Medal of Honor. Four years later the navy named a destroyer escort in honor of the heroic chaplain.

CHARLES J. WATTERS

In an interview given a few months before he was killed in action, army chaplain *Charles J. Watters* told a reporter that he volunteered to go on combat patrols "just to get a little exercise. You haven't lived until you've crawled on your hands and knees through thick overgrowths of bamboo."

A tall, lean man, Father Watters had wanted to be a priest ever since he was in the fourth grade in Jersey City, New Jersey. After high school he entered Seton Hall University, then attended the Immaculate Conception Seminary in Darlington, New Jersey.

Watters's first parish assignment after his ordination in 1953 was to St. Mary's Church in Rutherford, New Jersey. He later spent seven years at a parish in nearby Paramus. There, he learned to fly and eventually earned a commercial pilot's license and an instrument rating.

In the early 1960s, Father Watters decided he wanted to serve his country as well as his God. He enlisted as a chaplain with the New Jersey National Guard. In 1965 he requested a transfer to the army and active duty.

Never a man to shrink from danger, Father Watters—at age thirty-eight—volunteered for Airborne training. He spent some time with the 101st Airborne Division at Fort Campbell, Kentucky, before being sent to the 173d Airborne Brigade in South Vietnam.

Father Watters loved the camaraderie among his paratroopers. "They may be a bit crazy in many ways, but you have never seen more spirit and drive than from these boys. And, most important, in combat, they never leave a man behind," he noted.

Asked by the reporter if he carried a weapon in combat, Father Watters smiled and answered, "I'm the peaceful kind. All I shoot is my camera, and if they start to shoot at me I'll yell, 'Tourist!' Seriously, a weapon weighs too much and, after all, a priest's job is taking care of the boys. But if we ever get overrun, I guess there'll be plenty of weapons lying around."

Father Watters estimated he had been in at least fifty engagements with the enemy. He was one of just three chaplains to make the war's only combat jump, which occurred near Katum during Operation Junction City in January 1967.

He said it was the only one of his seventeen jumps on which he had "no uneasy feelings. There was too much else to think of."

Father Watters's one-year tour of duty ended in June 1967, but he was not ready to go home. His "boys" needed him. He extended for another year of service in the war zone.

Watters never completed it. He died on November 19, 1967, during the battle of Dak To.

Father Watters was in the forefront when the paratroopers of the 2d Battalion, 503d Infantry, became embroiled with the NVA on Hill 875. He moved among the battling paratroopers and gave encouragement and first aid to the wounded. When he noticed a wounded soldier wandering in shock and confusion between the two forces, Father Watters ran into the open, hoisted the man onto his shoulders, and carried him to safety.

During that brutal afternoon the Airborne chaplain left the safety of the perimeter at least five times to retrieve casualties. When he was satisfied that all of the wounded were recovered, Father Watters busied himself helping the medics, applying bandages, gathering up and serving rations, and providing spiritual and mental strength and comfort.

According to reports later filed by survivors of that grim battle, Father Watters was on his knees giving the Last Rites to a dying paratrooper when, at dusk, an American plane accidentally dropped a five-hundred-pound bomb in the center of the paratroopers. Father Watters died in the blast. His two brothers accepted his posthumous Medal of Honor on November 4, 1969.

CHARLES LITEKY

On December 6, 1967 a small force of Company A, 4th Battalion, 12th Infantry, 199th Light Infantry Brigade, was scouring the jungle thirty miles north of Saigon in Bien Hoa Province. The Viet Cong had dropped mortars on the company's position the night before. If the grunts found the mortar site, maybe they could also find evidence of the men who operated it.

In the middle of the column, walking with the company commander, Capt. Bruce Drees, was the battalion chaplain, *Capt. Angelo Liteky* (Angelo was his ordination name). Father Liteky had been in South Vietnam for eight months. In that time he had been in a number of brushes with the enemy, but nothing too serious. He was glad for that.

The infantrymen snaked their way cautiously through the dense jungle. Suddenly three VC briefly appeared on the trail ahead. A deadly pall of silence covered the jungle—then a cacophony of weapons fire erupted. Rocket-propelled grenades (RPGs) streaked out of the trees. Claymore mines filled the air with deadly steel balls. Machine guns chattered. The grunts hugged the ground for cover.

Liteky made his way to two wounded men. The first was a young medic who had told Father Liteky the night before that he was going to start a rock 'n' roll band right after he got home in a few weeks. Now his leg was nearly blown off. Only gristle and bone remained where the man's knee had been.

"Did you say a prayer for me, Father?" the medic asked.

"Of course, I did. You'll be all right, you'll make it," Liteky told him. Then the priest pulled him and the other man to safety.

A witness to Father Liteky's bravery later said, "When Captain Liteky went out there the first time, we thought we'd never see him again. By the end of the day we just knew he could walk on water."

When the chaplain came upon one casualty, the savage enemy fire kept him from getting the man to safety. Determined to save the man's life, Father Liteky flipped over on his back, manhandled the bleeding man onto his chest, then, using his elbows and heels, pushed himself thirty yards toward an evacuation site. Once out of the line of fire, he carried the man the rest of the way.

All afternoon Father Liteky brought up stretchers, ammunition, and rations. Helmetless, he moved upright throughout the battlefield, anointed the dying, and gave aid to the wounded.

At one point, after Father Liteky had given the Last Rites to a man who had a huge hole in his back, he came upon an abandoned M-16. He picked it up. For a moment he was ready to use it to defend the wounded, but then he thought better of it. If a priest is going to buy it today, he told himself, they won't find a rifle on him.

Later, in the face of rockets and small-arms fire, the priest stood exposed in an open area to guide in the medevac helicopters. Under his direction the medics loaded up the wounded.

The fight lasted from early afternoon to late evening. Chaplain Liteky, despite painful wounds in the neck and foot, rescued twenty wounded soldiers. Many would have died without his help.

After he completed his Vietnam tour in October 1968, Father Liteky was sent to Fort Bragg, North Carolina. In early November 1968 he learned he was to receive the Medal of Honor. He had mixed feelings about the award.

"The company commanders who write up these medal nominations, they know how to pump it up," he said several years later. "I'm not saying some of these things didn't happen. I'm just saying it makes *them* look good, too."

Despite his misgivings, Father Liteky accepted the medal from President Johnson on November 19, 1968.

Liteky returned to South Vietnam in 1970. What he saw there greatly disturbed him. "When I got back over there, I really got turned off by the war," he later said. "I thought we should get out of there with all possible speed. I really got disgusted with things I saw. The insensitivity toward life; the emphasis on body counts—a mania."

It was about this time, too, that Liteky acknowledged another problem—his vocation. "One of my biggest problems in the priesthood all along was that my identity had pretty much gotten swallowed up," he said.

Born Charles J. Liteky on February 14, 1931, in Washington, DC, he grew up in Jacksonville, Florida. As a youth he had been a good football player. He was being groomed for the starting quarterback slot at the University of Florida when he decided to enter the priesthood. Ten years after his 1956 ordination he entered the army.

Upon returning from his second Vietnam tour, Liteky decided to face both problems. He resigned his army commission, left the priesthood, and eventually married. He worked at a variety of jobs, including pumping gas, then ran a halfway house in Cleveland for drug-addicted veterans. For a while he lived in a shack on a deserted Florida beach. He even spent time working as a benefits counselor for the Veterans Administration (after World War II, President Harry S. Truman had issued an order that guaranteed all Medal of Honor recipients a job with the VA whenever they wanted one).

In a well-publicized demonstration of his opposition to President Ronald Reagan's Nicaraguan policy, Liteky renounced his Medal of Honor in July 1986. Liteky placed the medal at the base of the Vietnam Veterans Memorial in Washington, DC. To the assembled reporters Liteky said, "I find it ironic that conscience calls me to renounce the Medal of Honor for the same basic reason I received it—trying to save lives."

Liteky has continued his leadership role in opposing the U.S. government's activities in Central and South America, and is an advocate for homeless veterans and other downtrodden members of the lower rungs of American society.

During a recon-in-force mission in Dinh Tuong Province on January 10, 1968, 9th Infantry Division medic *PFC Clarence E. Sasser* repeatedly ignored enemy fire to bring the wounded to a place of safety. Even when jagged shrapnel from an exploding mortar shell immobilized his legs, the twenty-year-old from Angleton, Texas, never stopped. He crawled more than one hundred yards through exposed terrain to reach one casualty. He pulled that man to safety, then called to a group of others to work their way to him. For the remainder of the action—five hours—Sasser dragged himself from casualty to casualty and treated their wounds. When medevac choppers finally made it in, Sasser refused evacuation until all the other wounded were pulled out.

Sasser spent ten months in the hospital recovering from his painful injuries, but on March 7, 1969 he stood proudly as President Nixon awarded him the Medal of Honor.

On May 18, 1968, near Khe Sanh in Quang Tri Province, *Corpsman Donald E. Ballard* from Kansas City, Missouri, had just finished evacuating two heatstroke victims when his unit, Company M, 3d Battalion, 4th Marines, 3d Marine Division, was surprised by an NVA ambush. Ballard immediately raced to the aid of a casualty lying in a bomb crater. He applied a field dressing and was directing four Marines in the removal of the wounded man when an enemy soldier tossed a grenade into the crater. Ballard yelled "Grenade!" then vaulted over the stretcher. In one swift motion he pulled the grenade under his body. He lay there for what seemed an eternity before he realized the missile was a dud.

Ballard calmly picked himself up, tossed the grenade away, and turned back to the wounded man. A sharp explosion erupted from behind him. "Whether it was the grenade I dropped on or not, I never knew for sure," he said.

Regardless, Ballard sent the stretcher-bearers on their way, then returned to treating the other wounded.

It was not until a few days later that the impact of his brush with death hit him. "I was shook up, that's for sure," he said.

Ballard is only the second man whose valor was not discounted because the deadly missile he chose to cover with his own body did not explode.

THOMAS W. BENNETT

During the Vietnam War conscientious objectors were allowed to choose between military service as a medic or community service, usually in a local hospital. Twenty-one-year-old *Thomas W. Bennett* chose military service when he flunked out of West Virginia University in his hometown of Morgantown after the fall 1967 semester.

Bennett was not an overly religious youngster, but he did hold dear the sanctity of human life. And he was not opposed to military service. He simply felt he could better serve his country by saving lives rather than taking them.

Bennett reported for induction on July 11, 1968. Though he hoped he would remain in the States or be sent to Europe, Bennett knew his chances of going to South Vietnam were good. From Fort Sam Houston, Texas, he wrote his parents on November 1, 1968: "If I am called to go to Nam, I will go. Out of obligation to a country I love I will go and possibly die for a cause I vehemently disagree with."

Bennett felt some need to explain his position, for he added, "It is my obligation to give service to my country. That's why I am here—to help provide freedom for dissenting voices . . . I believe in America. I believe that our process of government can respond to the people's needs—if we each assume our responsibility."

Bennett assumed more than his responsibility. On January 10, 1969 he arrived in South Vietnam. Two weeks later he joined Company B, 1st Battalion, 14th Infantry, 4th Infantry Division, in the Central Highlands. On February 5, Company B and two other rifle companies began a sweep of the rugged Chu Pa Mountains. For four days the grunts searched the dense jungle for the NVA, without any contact.

On February 9 the NVA ambushed another company. Bennett's Company B was sent to their aid. They walked into a trap.

Enemy fire hit Bennett's company as it closed on its sister unit. Three members of the point platoon fell, seriously wounded. The cry of "Medic!" "Medic!" traveled down the line of men.

From his position near the company command group, Bennett bounded forward, ignoring the enemy bullets flying through the air. His only concern was the wounded.

Bennett dressed the casualties' wounds. He then made

three trips across the battlefield to carry the men to an evacuation site.

With the help of friendly artillery, the riflemen drove the enemy off. After medevac choppers pulled out the five dead and six seriously wounded, the troops dug deep holes, fearing an enemy night attack. Bennett, however, spent most of the night above ground tending those wounded who had not been evacuated.

On February 10, after a night of relative calm, Company B set off in pursuit of the elusive foe. In a repeat of the previous action, the men were again ambushed. Five grunts dropped in the initial blast of enemy fire.

Through the exploding rockets and hand grenades and AK-47 rifle fire, Bennett kept up his work. Ever fearless, constantly ignoring the danger, unmindful of the deadly lead slugs filling the air, the pacifist slapped bandages on wounds, injected morphine to dull the horrible pain, and offered words of encouragement.

The enemy pulled back. Company B's survivors were exhausted. Bennett remained awake all night so he could tend the wounded.

Soon after dawn on February 11, enemy snipers began to fire at any Company B grunt who showed himself. Several men cried out in pain. Each time Bennett selflessly went to their aid.

A recently arrived man—so new that no one even knew his name—suddenly screamed in pain. He had been hit by a sniper's round. He was lying about thirty yards from Bennett. As the West Virginian looked toward the casualty, Sgt. James McBee grabbed him. "Don't go out there. He's gone," the sergeant warned.

Bennett shrugged him off. Without a word he jumped up, intent only on saving the wounded man. A flurry of AK-47 shots rang out. Bennett collapsed on the jungle floor, his young body riddled with bullets.

On April 7, 1970, which would have been Tom Bennett's twenty-third birthday, President Nixon presented his well-earned posthumous Medal of Honor to his proud parents. In

August 1988 a youth center at Schofield Barracks, Oahu, Hawaii, was named in his honor.

An NVA human-wave assault ripped into the fire support base manned by cannoneers of Battery D, 2d Battalion, 11th Marines, 1st Marine Division, at Phu Loc 6 near An Hoa in Quang Nam Province during the early morning hours of March 19, 1969. *Corpsman David R. Ray* ignored the NVA sappers racing through the wire and went from parapet to parapet treating the wounded. Even though he had been hit by shrapnel himself, Ray continued to care for the other casualties. While he huddled over one man, two NVA surprised him. Ray killed one and wounded the other enemy soldier with two well-placed pistol shots. Later, when an enemy grenade landed near a patient, Ray threw himself over the man and protected him from the explosion. The twenty-four-year-old former University of Tennessee student died from the wounds he received in that blast.

GARY B. BEIKIRCH

Deep in a remote section of Kontum Province, the Special Forces established an outpost to interdict NVA supply lines coming into South Vietnam from Laos. Manned by twelve Green Berets and 450 Montagnards, the camp had a definite effect on NVA troop movement into the province. The Green Berets could tell their tactics were working because NVA attacks on their outpost were increasing.

The medic attached to Camp Dak Seang was twenty-two-year-old sergeant *Gary B. Beikirch*. In 1967, Beikirch had quit college in his native Greece, New York, to join the Special Forces. "To broaden my experience" is what he said.

After Beikirch arrived in South Vietnam in July 1969, he became intensely involved in the war because he believed in it. In addition, there were numerous worthwhile medical projects that could be carried out among the primitive Montagnards. Beikirch developed a deep personal commitment to the people he worked and fought beside.

"I was chided for going 'native'," he said. "I'd do things like take the kids down to the swimming hole for an afternoon of fun."

Beikirch also remembered being on patrols near the Laotian border, all alone except for his 'Yards. A rare mutual trust existed between the two diverse peoples. At times Beikirch's life was completely in their hands. He never worried.

All through March 1970 evidence was mounting that the NVA were planning a major attack on the camp. Routine patrols were fired on with more frequency. Jungle trails indicated the presence of large bodies of enemy soldiers. The Green Berets knew that the NVA were coming—it was just a question of when.

They came on April 1, 1970.

Beikirch instinctively knew when the first mortar shell crashed down that this was no ordinary attack. Seconds later, the crack of AK-47s and the chatter of machine guns filled the air. Rocket-propelled grenades and hand grenades added their explosions to the din. From positions well concealed in the jungle around the camp, the NVA launched a full-scale attack designed to annihilate the defenders.

Beikirch grabbed his medical kit and went to work. Carefully threading his way through the barrage of exploding mortar rounds, he raced to the wounded. In full view of the enemy he patched up wounds, offered encouragement, and carried casualties to the safety of the medical bunker.

Midway through the eight-hour battle, Beikirch learned that an American officer was lying unconscious and dangerously exposed in the open. Concerned only with saving the man's life, Beikirch immediately ran to the officer's aid.

A mortar shell exploded directly behind Beikirch before he reached his destination. Flying metal ripped into his spine and right hip. A third red-hot chunk pierced his back and exploded out through his stomach.

Though stunned by the intense pain, Beikirch still thought

only of the wounded officer. Somehow he made his way to the man, applied a field dressing, and then carried him to safety.

After Beikirch applied bandages to his own wounds, he returned to the bullet-swept camp. He searched for and evacuated the other wounded. He was hit again as he dragged a Montagnard soldier to safety—while at the same time giving him mouth-to-mouth resuscitation. Beikirch's determination saved the man's life.

Finally, as the battle waned and the NVA pulled away from the battle site, Beikirch collapsed from the loss of blood.

When he awoke seven days later, Beikirch went through a crisis of spirit that changed his life.

"I was a Green Beret, the epitome of ego and self-sufficiency, lying in a hospital bed with my guts hanging out, cauterized, IVs stuck into both arms and both sides," he recalled. "I was battling for life and I looked for strength inside myself. I couldn't find it and I was scared."

Beikirch began to pray. Through prayer he found peace and calmness. "I felt someone was there who cared for me. I knew some kind of God was real."

After eight months in the hospital, Beikirch finished his military obligation and then began his "trek." He explored Eastern philosophies and tried meditation. For a time he worked with quadriplegics in a VA hospital. Finally he returned to college to study counseling.

By the time Beikirch received his Medal of Honor on October 15, 1973, he knew where he was going.

He became a minister in the United Baptist Fellowship. He went to work as a guidance counselor at a private Christian school and at a community veterans outreach center.

The last medic to earn a Medal of Honor in the Vietnam War was *PFC David F. Winder* for his actions in Quang Ngai Province on May 13, 1970.

Winder's unit, Company A, 3d Battalion, 1st Infantry, Americal Division, was searching for an NVA company when it was ambushed. Responding instantly to the frantic cries of "Medic!" Winder, the son of a Mansfield, Ohio, doctor, low-crawled through a rice paddy toward the casualty.

Winder was hit but kept going. Somehow he reached the man and gave him treatment. Undaunted and oblivious to the pain of his own wound, he set off toward another casualty.

A second bullet slammed into Winder. He went down. Unable to ignore the desperate call for help, Winder arose again. Struggling forward slowly but with tremendous determination, he made it to within ten yards of the casualty before a burst of machine gun fire killed him.

Inspired by Winder's selfless concern for others, his company broke from cover, attacked, and overran the NVA positions.

CHAPTER EIGHT

The War Winds Down

The year 1969 was one of transition for U.S. involvement in South Vietnam's civil war. The tactic of battalion-size sweeps against the VC and NVA in specific land areas, General Westmoreland's "search-and-destroy" tactics, would no longer be employed.

Instead, American forces would now primarily operate from fixed bases strategically located along well-traveled routes to thwart North Vietnam's infiltration of South Vietnam. Although there were offensive operations throughout each year, most combat actions came as the result of aggressive patrolling by company-size or smaller units. This was consistent with the new administration's policy of Vietnamization.

President Richard M. Nixon had been elected in November 1968 after promising the voters that he had a plan to end American involvement in South Vietnam. Although no such plan ever existed, popular support for the withdrawal of American troops forced Nixon to act. Under "Vietnamization," major responsibility for the military conduct of the war would be turned over to the Army of the Republic of Vietnam. It would take more than four years and cost tens of thousands of American lives, but at last there was light at the end of the long, dark tunnel that had become the war in Vietnam.

In early June 1969, President Nixon announced the first withdrawal of American military units from South Vietnam. One battalion of the 9th Infantry Division left the swamps and rice paddies of the Mekong Delta for the pine forests of

Fort Lewis, Washington. By the end of the year, the rest of the 9th Infantry Division and most of the 3d Marine Division had left South Vietnam. American troop strength had been reduced by 15 percent. (The ranks of the units that went home were actually filled with men from other units whose tours of duty had ended, i.e., "short-timers"; troops from the rotating units who had more than thirty days left in-country were transferred to other line units to complete their tours of duty.)

Those troops who remained in South Vietnam faced a perplexing situation. Fully aware that their country no longer supported their efforts, they still had to fight a determined and dangerous enemy. The beginning of the end of America's presence in Vietnam was not accompanied by a lessening of the brutality of the war.

Indeed, some of the most bitter fighting of the war lay ahead. Fifty-four American men earned Medals of Honor during 1969. Despite the daily hardships they experienced as players in an unpopular war, young Americans repeatedly covered themselves in glory.

One of 1969's first Medals of Honor was earned by *PFC Don J. Jenkins,* a twenty-year-old from Quality, Kentucky. On January 6, using an M-16, an M-60 machine gun, two antitank weapons, and a grenade launcher, the gallant Jenkins destroyed several enemy bunkers that had pinned down his unit, Company A, 2d Battalion, 39th Infantry, 9th Infantry Division, during a patrol in Kien Phong Province. Undeterred by a severe shrapnel wound, Jenkins then went to the aid of a squad isolated only a few yards away from the enemy's line. Jenkins pulled three casualties to safety before his wounds caused his collapse. He survived to wear his Medal of Honor.

On January 11, 1969, seven armored personnel carriers from Troop A, 1st Squadron, 11th Armored Cavalry Regiment were escorting a column of fuel and supply trucks along Route 13 to Quan Loi in Binh Long Province. Since this route was considered a hotbed of NVA activity, the tankers felt lucky to have made the run without any trouble. Now, if only the return trip would go as well.

HAROLD A. FRITZ

Leading the column of APCs was a twenty-four-year-old first lieutenant from Lake Geneva, Wisconsin. *Harold A. Fritz,* executive officer of Troop A, had volunteered the previous evening to take the place of a sick officer. Fritz was an experienced combat veteran, in his twelfth month with the 11th ACR. The previous August he had earned a Silver Star as commander of an M-48 tank platoon.

Now, as Fritz raced back down Highway 13, he felt that something was about to happen.

A sudden explosion threw Fritz violently against the side of his APC. His flak jacket was blown off his body. Red-hot shrapnel ripped into his back and legs. At first he thought his vehicle had hit a mine. A barrage of explosions that crippled the other vehicles under his command told him it was an ambush—and a well-executed ambush, as he soon discovered. NVA bunkers lined both sides of the road for five hundred yards in either direction. The twenty-nine soldiers manning the APCs were caught in a deadly cross fire.

As flames leaped over the front of his APC, Fritz pulled his driver from the wreckage. He thrust a rifle into the dazed man's hand, then set about to organize a defense.

One of the first things Fritz learned was that all of his radios had been knocked out. He could not report his situation or call for help. He was on his own.

Fritz dashed back and forth among the blazing APCs and put his men into position, passed out ammunition, and treated the wounded. He pulled all the weapons and ammunition he could off of the APCs; he knew his unit did not have a lot of ammunition—so he wanted to ensure that his men gathered every round possible.

The enemy continuously probed Fritz's defenses. They

would have overrun one position if he had not stood up, completely exposed to the enemy, firing a machine gun cradled in his arms. His accurate fire sent the NVA scurrying.

A few minutes later another NVA probe threatened to overrun the medic's position. Yelling "Come with me!" to a small group of men, Fritz, armed with only a .45-caliber pistol and a bayonet, waded into the NVA.

Slashing and blazing away at point-blank range, Fritz drove the NVA back into the jungle.

By 11:30 A.M., after the battle had raged for over an hour, Fritz knew the situation was desperate. Only he and five others remained standing. His radioman had tried to fix one of their radios but had no idea if any of the distress messages he sent out had been received. Ammunition was low. There were few choices left.

During a brief lull in the enemy firing, Fritz explained the options to his men. "We can try pulling back through the jungle," he told them, "or we can stand and fight it out."

To a man, they elected to fight it out.

Fritz was ready to lead another charge when he spotted a cloud of dust coming down the road. "It was a scene right out of a John Wayne western," Fritz recalled. "Our radio had worked. Headquarters had sent a relief column."

The column of APCs and tanks stopped about one hundred yards away from Fritz; they were unable to distinguish friend from foe in the melee. Fritz ran toward the vehicles, intent on deploying the tanks. Behind him, out of his view, an NVA sapper team was preparing to fire a rocket at the lead tank. The tank fired first.

"The muzzle blast blew me twenty-five feet off the road into the bushes," Fritz remembered. "I thought they were shooting at me. My ears were ringing like crazy when I ran up yelling at the tank commander."

Fritz used hand signals to set the tanks into offensive positions. They still were not enough. Two full companies of infantry from the 1st Cavalry Division (Airmobile) were needed before the NVA broke contact.

Fritz was medevacked to a hospital that afternoon, but later in the evening he went AWOL from the hospital, stole a jeep, and made his way back to his unit. It took a direct order from his commander to send Fritz back for treatment.

Three years earlier Fritz had run his own successful contracting business in Lake Geneva. With a pregnant wife, he was not too concerned when his draft notice arrived. Certainly he was entitled to a deferment. He took his case to the local draft board.

To his surprise, one of the board members was a man Fritz had recently taken to court over an outstanding debt. There's no way you're going to win this one, he told himself.

He was right. His appeal was denied.

To avoid the random process of conscription, Fritz enlisted in April 1966. One year later he was commissioned a second lieutenant.

After he received his Medal of Honor on March 2, 1971, Fritz decided to make the army his career. "With my experiences I felt I could help soldiers. And, I enjoyed the military life."

Fritz eventually retired as a lieutenant colonel, then became the director of Veterans Affairs for the state of Illinois.

In Quang Tri Province the 3d Marine Division launched a major operation into a previously untouched region south of Khe Sanh. Intelligence data had revealed that the NVA were infiltrating vast quantities of men and matériel into the far southwest portion of the province along the Da Krong River valley. Beginning on January 18, elements of the 9th Marines began to leapfrog into this area via a series of mutually protective fire support bases. Originally the operation was named Dawson River South. It was soon changed to Dewey Canyon. The Marines found the Dewey Canyon region, which sat north of the notorious A Shau Valley, to be as rugged as any they had experienced in South Vietnam. Thick, nearly impenetrable jungle growth cloaked jagged mountains that soared three thousand or more feet into the sky.

On January 31, Company G, 2d Battalion, 9th Marines, received orders to scale one of those peaks, the nearly vertical five-thousand-foot-high Co Ka Leuye Ridge. This promontory straddled the border and allowed anyone on its summit an incredible view into both countries.

Unfortunately, after the Marines made a laborious climb up the peak's side, rain set in and they found themselves unable to observe anything. Company G remained there for two days before receiving orders to abandon the peak.

Late on the morning of February 5 the Marines began the descent down the slippery slopes.

THOMAS P. NOONAN

Thomas P. Noonan was born in Brooklyn, New York, on November 18, 1943. He graduated from Grover Cleveland High School in 1961 (one of his classmates was Marine hero Robert O'Malley), then entered Hunter College in the Bronx.

When he graduated with a bachelor's degree in physical education in June 1966, Noonan could have sought a commission in any branch of the service. Instead, he enlisted in the Marine Corps. He went to South Vietnam as a rifleman in June 1968. He served initially with the 1st Marine Division, then was transferred to Company G, 2d Battalion, 9th Marines, 3d Marine Division.

Torrential rain poured down as the Marines of Company G worked their way downhill through the jungle growth. The lead elements of the company were suddenly fired on by NVA. Four Marines went down. Repeated attempts to rescue them were repelled by heavy enemy fire.

A corpsman rushed forward. As he treated the first man, an enemy rifleman shot him.

From behind a nearby boulder, Noonan watched in horror as blood spurted from the corpsman's neck wound. Concerned only with saving the man, Noonan broke from cover. He ignored calls from his squad leader and nimbly made his way down the slippery slope. He found cover behind an outcropping of rocks just a few yards away from the corpsman.

"Hang in there," Noonan yelled. "I'm coming to get you. Just hang on."

Noonan's fellow Marines sent out a heavy volume of fire that forced the NVA to take cover. He raced out from behind the rocks. In a few steps he reached the man.

"I've got you. You're going to be okay."

The ground proved too slippery for Noonan to carry the casualty, so he began to pull him to safety. An AK-47 cracked. Noonan spun to the ground, blood gushing from a deep wound.

Rather than seek cover, Noonan turned back to the man whose life he was determined to save. He offered more words of encouragement, then resumed pulling the man to cover. He had almost reached safety when a burst of machine gun fire stopped him. He died with his hands still clenching the wounded man's utilities.

Outraged at the slaughter, the other Marines charged down the slope, rifles blazing. They drove the enemy off. The original four casualties and the corpsman survived.

Noonan's parents accepted his posthumous Medal of Honor on February 16, 1971.

Contact with the NVA continued sporadically throughout the Dewey Canyon area of operation. On the morning of February 22, *1st Lt. Wesley L. Fox,* a former enlisted Marine, ignored painful wounds to continue to lead his battered company against NVA attackers. With all the other officers in the company wounded or killed, Fox personally led his men in a grenade charge that drove the enemy off. Under his spirited leadership the men of Company A, 1st Battalion, 9th Marines, pursued the NVA, destroyed a large bunker complex, and captured a large quantity of supplies.

At the western edge of the Dewey Canyon AO, the 2d Battalion, 9th Marines, pushed south against stiffening enemy resistance until they reached a position on a ridgetop that overlooked the Da Krong and Laos Highway 922 that paralleled it (the international border runs east and west here).

On February 21, Company H, 2d Battalion, 9th Marines, conducted the first official cross-border raid. The Marines shot up an NVA truck column on Highway 922, then high-tailed it back into the mountains and South Vietnam. Two days later, when there were no repercussions from the incursion, the company received orders to return to Laos and sweep eastward down Highway 922.

WILLIAM D. MORGAN

William D. Morgan enlisted in the Marine Corps to go to sea. That is what he had put on his enlistment papers when he signed up in November 1966. After completing his basic training in March 1967, he went to Sea School at Portsmouth, Virginia.

In July 1967 the nineteen-year-old Pittsburgh, Pennsylvania, native joined the Marine detachment aboard the USS *Newport News*. The next year passed too quickly for Morgan. He greatly enjoyed the spit-and-polish discipline aboard ship. Traveling across the seas as part of an elite unit was duty that many others envied.

But there was a war on. Like all Marines, Morgan was first and foremost a rifleman. In July 1968 he joined the 9th Marines as a machine gun section leader.

On February 25, Morgan was a member of a flanking patrol screening Company H's movement along the highway (actually, little more than a wide dirt path). As the Marines advanced through the thick undergrowth, heavy fire from a well-concealed NVA bunker broke the silence. Two Marines fell dangerously close to the enemy position.

Repeated attempts to pull the men to safety were stopped by heavy bursts of machine gun fire and RPGs. Unwilling to leave his fellow Marines at the mercy of the NVA, Morgan sprang into action.

He crashed through the jungle and made his way to the road in front of the enemy bunker. Morgan yelled "Pull 'em in" to some nearby Marines, then charged across the road directly at the bunker, his M-60 pouring out hot lead.

In full view of the enemy, Morgan sent a stream of rounds into the bunker. Other NVA positions took him under fire. Morgan fell, mortally wounded in a hail of bullets.

Although it lasted only a few moments, Morgan's charge allowed other Marines to pull the casualties to safety. His deliberate self-sacrifice inspired his fellow Marines to crush the NVA defenders.

When Morgan's parents accepted their son's posthumous Medal of Honor on August 6, 1970, they were not told that he had died in Laos. Instead, the citation pinpointed the action as occurring in "Quang Tri Province, Republic of Vietnam . . . southeast of Vandegrift Combat Base."

It would be years before they learned the truth.

The North Vietnamese response to the unilateral bombing halt announced by President Johnson on November 1, 1968 was to rush a torrent of supplies south to support a new offensive. The attacks began on February 22, 1969. Aimed primarily at U.S. logistical bases, the offensive was designed to disrupt the Allied supply lines.

Unlike the 1968 Tet Offensive, however, these attacks lacked the depth necessary to do any lasting harm. Damage was minimal and American casualties were relatively light. Regardless of each attack's duration, these offensive actions once again demonstrated the enemy's ability to dictate where and when the battle would be joined. And, they allowed America's fighting men to again demonstrate their incredible courage.

On February 22, *Sp4. George C. Lang,* a draftee from Hicksville, New York, led his squad of Company A, 4th Battalion, 47th Infantry, 9th Infantry Division, in an attack on enemy positions in Kien Hoa Province. Lang repeatedly exposed himself to hostile fire to wipe out three bunkers and capture a large cache of enemy weapons. As he examined the captured weapons, retaliatory Viet Cong rockets crashed down around him. In spite of severe wounds that left him permanently paralyzed, Lang directed his men in an assault on the enemy.

On that same day, on a long-range reconnaissance patrol deep in enemy territory in Binh Long Province north of Saigon, twenty-four-year-old *Sp4. Robert D. Law* threw himself on an enemy grenade to save his fellow patrol members from Company I, 75th Infantry, 1st Infantry Division. He died in the blast, but the others lived.

During the early morning hours of February 23, the NVA hit an observation post outside Da Nang manned by Marines from Company E, 2d Battalion, 7th Marines, 1st Marine Division. *PFC Oscar P. Austin,* a twenty-one-year-old from Phoenix, Arizona, went to the aid of a fallen Marine. As he neared the man, a grenade hit the ground nearby. Austin, who had been wounded a few months earlier performing a similar deed, threw himself between the injured Marine and the grenade. He caught the full effect of the explosion. Still concerned only with the other man, Austin was turning toward him when he saw an enemy soldier aiming a rifle at the Marine. Austin deliberately placed himself in front of the man. He died from the burst of rifle fire.

At almost the same time Austin was dying, the VC hit the 25th Infantry Division's base camp at Dau Tieng in Hau Nghia Province. A twenty-four-year-old dog handler with the 44th Scout Dog Platoon, *S.Sgt. Robert W. Hartsock,* spotted a sapper team advancing on the tactical operations center. Accompanied by his platoon commander, Hartsock set up an ambush for the enemy. When he opened fire, though, the VC tossed a satchel charge at the two men. Hartsock fell on the device as it exploded, protecting the officer. Gravely wounded, Hartsock continued to fire his rifle at the enemy until he succumbed to his wounds.

On the afternoon of February 23, the 2d Platoon, Company M, 3d Battalion, 7th Marines, 1st Marine Division, went to the rescue of another squad pinned down by the enemy in Bo Ban village in Quang Nam Province. While the Marines moved through a rice paddy, they too came under attack. *L. Cpl. Lester W. Weber* set off on a single-handed assault that broke the enemy's attack but cost him his life. Twice the twenty-year-old wrestled with Viet Cong soldiers, killing them in violent hand-to-hand combat. Weber also destroyed four enemy emplacements and was moving toward a fifth when a burst of machine gun fire killed him.

"Puff the Magic Dragon" was the name given by ground troops to the specially equipped C-47s used by the air force in the Vietnam War. First flown in 1935, the C-47 had been the backbone of the army air force in World War II. Now flying in its third war, the venerable aircraft was seeing service as a passenger plane and a supply plane, and was being flown on leaflet-dropping missions and on loudspeaker broadcast missions.

Late in 1965 the C-47 assumed a new role. Three 7.62mm machine guns were mounted in the cargo door. Their combined firepower was a devastating six thousand rounds per minute. This awesome display of might denied the enemy the cover of night. While the tracer rounds cut a neon light–like path of destruction on the target, the plane's loadmaster dropped high-intensity flares overboard. The flares were twenty-seven pounds of magnesium that burned at four thousand degrees Fahrenheit and illuminated the countryside with 2 million candlepower of light. "Puff" became a welcome friend during night combat.

JOHN L. LEVITOW

On the evening of February 24, 1969, a C-47, "Spooky 71," took off from Bien Hoa Air Base north of Saigon. Several army compounds in the Long Binh area had reported that they were receiving fire from aggressive VC forces. Spooky 71 was called in to help the perimeter guards repulse the hostiles.

For four and one-half hours, pilot and aircraft commander Maj. Kenneth Carpenter flew his craft over the Long

Binh–Bien Hoa area in response to calls for help from the ground. In tight circles at altitudes that averaged only a thousand feet, Spooky 71 sent thousands of rounds burning into the enemy positions below. The crew dropped dozens of flares to give their comrades below the light they needed to defend their positions.

The crew of Spooky 71 would have been pleased to hear the cheers of the grunts on the ground.

In the rear of the plane, *Airman 1st Class John L. Levitow,* the loadmaster, was performing his duties routinely. After 180 missions, Levitow could do his job in his sleep. He would remove the Mark 24 flare from its rack, set the ejection and ignition controls, then pass the volatile missile to the gunner.

Spooky 71's gunner, Airman Ellis C. Owen, would then attach the flare to a lanyard. On command, Owen next pulled a safety pin, then tossed the armed flare out the cargo door. Twenty seconds later it would erupt in a blinding flash of light. It was a routine the crew had performed dozens of times on each previous mission.

Major Carpenter was banking his C-47 into a left turn when it was suddenly jarred by a tremendous explosion. A brilliant burst of light surrounded the plane.

They did not know it, but a mortar round had hit the plane's right wing and exploded inside the wing frame. Thousands of pieces of shrapnel ripped through the plane's thin skin.

In the cockpit, Carpenter and his copilot wrestled to regain control of the wildly yawing plane. Carpenter was not sure he could right the aircraft.

The cargo compartment was in even worse shape. Shrapnel had wounded four of the crew; Levitow had forty holes in his right side. "It felt like a large piece of wood had struck against my side. I really didn't know what it was," he later said.

Airman Owen was down, too. But he was suffering from an agony far greater than his wounds.

Owen had been ready to toss a fully armed flare out the cargo door at the precise instant the mortar hit. As he fell backward, the flare slipped from his grasp. It was now rolling crazily along the floor. In less than twenty seconds it would erupt, incinerating the crew and destroying the plane.

Levitow had just finished pulling a casualty away from the open cargo door when he spotted the errant flare. With no idea of how long it had been free, he knew only that he had to get it out of the plane.

Three times Levitow reached for the flare. Three times it slipped from his hand. Desperately he threw himself on the metal cylinder and trapped it under his body. Inch by painful inch Levitow dragged the flare toward the open door. A thick smear of blood marked his path along the plane's aluminum floor.

At last the door was within his reach. With a superhuman effort, Levitow heaved the flare outside. A split second later the flare erupted. Levitow collapsed in a heap.

In the cockpit, Major Carpenter finally stopped the wild gyrations of the wounded plane, then brought it back to Bien Hoa and a safe landing. The ground crew later counted over thirty-five hundred holes in the plane, some exceeding three feet in length.

"After the mission," Carpenter said, "I was able to reconstruct what happened by the blood trail left by John. I had the aircraft in a thirty-degree bank, and how he ever managed to get to the flare and throw it out I'll never know.

"In my experience, I had never seen such a courageous act performed under such adverse conditions. The entire eight-man crew owed their lives to John."

Levitow recovered from his wounds after a brief hospital stay. He was discharged from the air force in August 1969 and returned to his home in Glastonbury, Connecticut.

When President Nixon presented Levitow with the Medal of Honor at the White House on May 14, 1970, the gallant young airman became the first enlisted man since World War II, and the youngest airman ever, to receive the top award.

Levitow died on November 8, 2000.

Members of the navy's elite SEAL teams played an integral role in America's efforts in Southeast Asia. The equivalent of the army's special forces, SEALs (Sea, Air, Land) are elite counterinsurgency forces skilled in underwater demolition and parachuting. Some SEAL members were assigned to SOG, but most operated independently of MACV. Though the SEAL teams were administratively attached to various commands in South Vietnam, they remained under the direct operational control of their headquarters back in the United States. Thus the majority of their missions were independent of the overall strategy employed in the war.

JOSEPH R. KERREY

To the men who served with him in South Vietnam, *Joseph R. "Bob" Kerrey* was an "operator's operator." He excelled at making quick decisions in the field and continually exhibited coolness and courage under fire. As one of his team later said, "Kerrey could handle anything put before him."

Kerrey would have a better chance than most men to put that statement to the test.

A native of Lincoln, Nebraska, Kerrey took a degree in pharmacology at the University of Nebraska in 1966. In the fall of that year he enlisted in the navy. He completed officer candidate school and received an ensign's commission on June 9, 1967. Two weeks later Kerrey reported to Coronado, California, for the first stage of the grueling SEAL course.

Kerrey entered the Basic Underwater Demolition School with 141 classmates; sixty-eight graduated. Of those, fourteen were selected for further SEAL training.

Physical strength was an important asset to SEAL candidates, but was not as important as determination and drive to reach a goal. Kerrey possessed all three. As one trainee said of him, "There was never a task or duty Kerrey couldn't perform."

When Kerrey graduated from the tough course in December 1967, he was assigned to SEAL Team One. He went to South Vietnam in January 1969.

Originally assigned to the naval command at Cam Ranh Bay, the large port through which most supplies entered South Vietnam, Kerrey and his team soon realized there was little opportunity to use their expertise in that area. Kerrey took his team to Vung Tau, downriver from Saigon, where they could run operations in the Mekong River Delta area.

Although Kerrey and his team set up several ambushes along the waterways of the delta, they had no contact with the enemy until February 25, 1969. On that night they entered the village of Thanh Phong expecting to find a number of high-ranking Viet Cong officials. Instead they found nothing but civilians. As the SEALs attempted to withdraw, they came under fire from unseen insurgents. The SEALs returned fire and withdrew.

One week later Kerrey took his team back to Cam Ranh Bay. Soon after their return, reliable intelligence sources reported the presence of several key local VC political figures on an island in Nha Trang Bay. Kerrey said his team would capture or kill the enemy. They set out on the night of March 14. It would be Kerrey's second and last combat experience.

In order to surprise the enemy, Kerrey led his team straight up a sheer thirty-five-foot-high cliff. After several hours of arduous climbing—in complete darkness—the team silently gathered on a rocky ledge above the enemy's location. Through prearranged hand signals and hushed whispers, Kerrey split his team into two elements. The treacherous descent to the enemy camp began.

As they neared the end of the downward maneuver, Kerrey's point man bumped into an enemy soldier's hammock in the dark. The VC's shouted warnings instantly brought a heavy barrage of small-arms fire onto Kerrey and his men.

Kerrey had maneuvered his team into defensive positions when an unseen grenade suddenly exploded at his feet. The force of the blast threw Kerrey savagely against the jagged rocks. It also shattered his right leg beyond repair.

Although Kerrey suffered excruciating pain, he directed

his team's efforts in repulsing the enemy. He gave his radioman clear, precise instructions that brought his second team through the darkness to a position from which they could deliver a telling cross fire on the VC.

Using only the flashes of tracers cutting through the night, Kerrey and his men defeated the VC and captured a number of prisoners. Kerrey was weak from a massive loss of blood, but overcame his shock to organize an extraction site and defend it against VC snipers. A medevac chopper came in and pulled Kerrey out. He was rushed to the hospital at Cam Ranh Bay.

Kerrey's ordeal had just begun.

In an interview several years later, Kerrey spoke of that time period when he was recovering and how the ending of his proud life as a SEAL affected him. The "operator's operator" had been permanently crippled in a brief, violent moment.

"Flash, there was no health," Kerrey said. "All the bravado, all that high self-esteem was gone. Tuck a bedpan under you a few times and it brings you right down to earth."

It took seven months in the hospital for Kerrey to recover and learn to walk with an artificial leg. On December 1, 1969 he took his discharge from the navy.

Recovery from the pain of his war experience and his personal suffering gave Kerrey time to reflect. He began to have misgivings about the war and his role in it. His hurt caused him to think of the hurt he had caused others.

When word came of the Medal of Honor award, Kerrey thought he should reject it as unwarranted and unwanted. Instead, he accepted it as a symbol of the valor of his comrades. President Nixon made the presentation at the White House on May 14, 1970.

When Kerrey returned to Nebraska, he drove himself harder than ever to overcome his handicap. He took up running to build up the strength in his leg. Through mile after painful mile of work, he again proved himself to be the "operator's operator." Eventually he was able to participate in marathon races.

Determined to achieve similar success in the business world, Kerrey developed a chain of popular restaurants and health clubs in the Omaha area.

In the early 1980s, Kerrey turned his attention to politics. Summing up his philosophy, Kerrey said, "It is important to make a judgment about what is right and wrong, and then fight for those things you believe are right. You may be proven wrong, but you will have made an effort."

In November 1982, Democrat Bob Kerrey was elected governor of Nebraska. He served one term, then in 1988 successfully ran for the U.S. Senate. In 1992 he was a serious contender for the Democratic Party's nomination as its presidential candidate, the first and only Medal of Honor recipient to be so considered. He served two terms in the Senate, resigned in January 2001, and then became president of the New School University in New York. In 2002 he was appointed to the commission investigating the September 11, 2001 terrorist attacks.

On March 20, 1969 the nineteen-year-old son of a career army sergeant deliberately sacrificed himself to save his fellow soldiers. On that night a group of VC sappers attacked the 173d Airborne Brigade's base camp at Camp Radcliff at An Khe in Binh Dinh Province. When the enemy took his barracks under fire, *Cpl. Terry T. Kawamura* grabbed his rifle and returned the fire. An enemy mortar shell crashed through the barracks roof and exploded, stunning and wounding several paratroopers. A split second later a demolition charge came flying through the hole in the roof. Kawamura realized his injured buddies were not going to be able to escape the impending explosion. Unhesitatingly, he threw himself on the device, dying in the blast so that others might live.

Army *S.Sgt. James L. Bondsteel,* a native of Allen, Michigan, served in South Vietnam for four straight years. He spent his first two years as a communications specialist with the Signal Corps. In December 1967 he transferred to Company A, 2d Battalion, 2d Infantry, 1st Infantry Division, and remained with that unit until February 1970. On May 24,

1969, near An Loc in Binh Long Province, Bondsteel displayed tremendous courage in a vicious one-man assault on a series of enemy bunkers. In a violent four-hour battle he personally destroyed ten enemy bunkers and killed over a dozen of the enemy. Wounded twice, Bondsteel successfully rescued a number of casualties, carrying them to safety.

On April 9, 1987, Bondsteel died in an automobile accident in Alaska.

Near An Hoa in Quang Nam Province on May 27, 1969, Marine *PFC Jimmy W. Phipps* of Santa Monica, California, a member of the 1st Engineer Battalion of the 1st Marine Division, was defusing a 175mm artillery round planted by the VC as a booby trap. After he realized that the shell was attached to a secondary explosive device, Phipps elected to destroy it with a hand grenade. He had just prepared the grenade when the fuse of the secondary device ignited. Instantly sensing the lethal danger to those around him, Phipps dived forward and covered the secondary device and the artillery shell. He absorbed the full and tremendous explosion of both devices with his own body, thus saving the lives of his fellow Marines.

GORDON R. ROBERTS

On June 14, 1968, two weeks before his eighteenth birthday, *Gordon R. Roberts* left his home in Lebanon, Ohio, to enlist in the army. Trained as a rifleman, Roberts spent six months in Europe with the 8th Infantry Division before receiving orders to South Vietnam in April 1969.

Roberts joined the 101st Airborne Division's 1st Battalion, 506th Infantry, in time to fight at the bloody battle for Ap Bia Mountain, otherwise known as "Hamburger Hill," in the A Shau Valley just one mile east of the Laotian border, on May 10–20, 1969. He earned a Silver Star for his coolness and courage in that intense fight.

On July 11, 1969, Roberts's unit, Company B, moved along a ridgeline in Thua Thien Province near the A Shau on its way to help another company under heavy enemy fire. Suddenly from a nearby hill, the NVA unleashed a fury of small-arms fire and RPGs. Company B's members hit the dirt, unable to move.

Displaying incredible courage, Roberts crawled through the grass toward the nearest gun emplacement. He then jumped to his feet, rifle blazing, and headed straight into the enemy's fire. His accurate shots killed the two enemy gunners. He paused to load a fresh clip in his M-16, then moved toward a second bunker. A burst of enemy fire knocked his rifle from his hands.

Roberts raced back down the hill. Yelling "Gimme that," he grabbed a rifle from a buddy, then took off back up the hill.

The second bunker fell to Roberts's onslaught, then he knocked out a third with an accurate grenade toss. He was now cut off from his platoon, though, but continued on, adrenaline pumping through his veins. A fourth bunker fell.

Because Roberts's single-handed assault had carried him so far ahead of his own unit, he worked his way through the jungle to join the other company. He fought with them until the enemy pulled back.

The young soldier finished his one-year tour in South Vietnam in April 1970. On March 2, 1971 the slight-framed Roberts stood alongside his beaming parents as President Nixon draped the Medal of Honor around his neck.

Roberts later graduated from the University of Dayton and earned a master's degree from the University of Cincinnati. During the Gulf War in 1991, Roberts volunteered for active duty. The army accepted him in the Medical Service Corps. In June 2002 he was the oldest lieutenant colonel in the army and the last Medal of Honor recipient from any war or any service branch on active duty.

A week after Roberts's display of bravery, a 101st Airborne trooper earned a posthumous Medal of Honor for his gallantry over a three-day period. *S.Sgt. John G. Gertsch* took command of his platoon of Company E, 1st Battalion, 327th Infantry, after his lieutenant was killed during heavy fighting in the A Shau Valley. Over the next two days Gertsch repeatedly risked his life to maneuver his men against the enemy. He was wounded on July 18 but refused to be evacuated. His concern for his men overcame any feelings he had for his own welfare.

Gertsch proved that beyond any doubt on July 19. In the middle of a vicious firefight he saw an enemy rifleman firing at a medic who was treating a casualty. Gertsch raced through a barrage of small-arms fire to position himself between the two men and the NVA soldier. Under Gertsch's covering fire the medic pulled the wounded man to safety. The NVA then directed their fire at Gertsch and killed him.

A twenty-four-year-old Mexican-born Marine staged a one-man assault on August 28, 1969 that destroyed two enemy bunkers, an antiaircraft gun crew, and killed a number of NVA. *José Francisco Jimenez* moved to Eloy, Arizona, with his family in 1956 when he was ten years old. Although he never became a citizen, Jimenez enlisted in the Marines because he wanted to "show America how grateful" he was for all it had given him and his family.

When his unit, Company K, 3d Battalion, 7th Marines, 1st Marine Division, stumbled across the NVA in the Hiep Duc Valley west of Tam Ky in Quang Nam Province that August afternoon, Jimenez went to work. Over and over he moved alone against the enemy's strong points until he was hit too many times to continue. When his fellow Marines caught up to him, they found Jimenez mortally wounded, only ten feet away from a trench full of dead NVA.

Throughout most of 1969 the 1st Cavalry Division (Airmobile) operated northwest of Saigon. Repeatedly clashing with NVA units trying to slip across the Cambodian border, the cavalrymen fought in dozens of brief but violent firefights.

DONALD S. SKIDGEL

He tried to enlist several times in 1967, but neither the army nor the Marine Corps would take *Donald S. Skidgel*. He was married with a pregnant wife and one daughter. The military establishment was not interested in young married men—at least not then.

Born on October 13, 1948 in Caribou, Maine, Skidgel grew up in Plymouth, Maine. The rural area around Plymouth was an excellent place for a boy to mature. In the open fields and dense green forests of central Maine, Skidgel hunted small game from the time he was old enough to hold a rifle. Under his father's tutelage he developed a keen instinct for the outdoors.

Skidgel always looked for excitement and adventure. School did not offer him enough, so he quit at age sixteen. Within a matter of weeks he was off on his own, working in Connecticut.

Skidgel took up riding motorcycles for the thrill they provided. Barreling down the back roads of rural Maine, he would crank a two-wheeler up as fast as he could. He was always looking for more excitement.

In 1966, Skidgel married—another adventure. A year later his daughter was born. He was so excited he could hardly stop talking about her.

As proud as Skidgel was of being a father, he still sought excitement. He thought he could find it in the military—but the services were not interested.

At least not until January 1968. After the Tet attacks, the army reached out for anyone it could find. Skidgel soon received his draft notice. With his wife expecting the following month, Skidgel reported for induction in February 1968.

Skidgel completed his basic training and was learning to be a tank crew member at Fort Knox, Kentucky, when a recruiter from the Airborne School at Fort Benning, Georgia, made a pitch to Skidgel's class.

To Skidgel, airborne training was just another adventure.

Besides, it paid fifty dollars a month more. With a wife and two children, he could use the extra money.

Skidgel earned his jump wings in August 1968. By that time, though, one of his adventures had ended—his absence from home had caused his marriage to end.

Skidgel arrived in South Vietnam in May 1969. Although Airborne-qualified, he went to the 1st Cavalry's Troop D, 1st Squadron, 9th Cavalry. That division reconnaissance unit needed men more than the in-country Airborne units did.

On September 14, 1969, Troop D, in APCs, was providing road security to a truck convoy near Song Be in Binh Long Province. In a remote area, an NVA battalion lay concealed in the grass alongside the road. When the two-and-a-half-ton trucks of the convoy came into range, the enemy opened up. Small-arms fire and RPGs raked the column. Trucks and APCs swerved from side to side, seeking an escape.

All but Skidgel's.

Skidgel ordered the driver of his APC to steer the vehicle off the road directly into the middle of the enemy force. From his position atop the vehicle, Skidgel sent repeated bursts of machine gun fire into the NVA ranks.

After Skidgel had knocked out one key position, he dismounted the APC. He grabbed an M-60 machine gun, then ran through the bullet-swept field to a better firing position.

For more than fifteen minutes Skidgel stayed in the open, dueling with the enemy. His one-man attack diverted the enemy's attention long enough for the rest of the convoy to organize a defense.

When he ran out of ammunition, Skidgel headed back to his APC for a resupply. He had just finished loading up when a cry for help came over the radio. The command element's APC was under strong attack.

Ordering "Let's go" to his driver, Skidgel boarded his vehicle. Using his machine gun with brutal effectiveness, he knocked out several more enemy positions. He was still urging the driver forward when an RPG hit the APC. The blast blew Skidgel out of the gunner's seat and onto the rear fender.

With blood streaming down his body from multiple wounds, Skidgel crawled back to his gun. His driver called for him to quit, but Skidgel would not. This was an adventure he wanted to finish. He ordered the driver forward.

Onward they pressed. Skidgel's selfless actions had the desired effect. The NVA turned their attack away from the command vehicle and focused on the lone vehicle moving toward them. They concentrated their fire on Skidgel, at last shooting him from his perch.

In the meantime, the command vehicle withdrew to a better position. There it reorganized the elements of the convoy into a counterattacking force that drove the enemy off the field.

Skidgel's bravery had saved the convoy.

On December 16, 1971, Vice President Spiro Agnew, in the presence of Skidgel's parents, presented Skidgel's posthumous Medal of Honor to the three-year-old son he had never seen.

MICHAEL J. NOVOSEL

Michael J. Novosel flew off to war for his country for the first time in 1945 when he was the twenty-two-year-old pilot of a B-29 bomber bound for Japan. He spent the last four months of World War II flying similar missions, then served another two years in the South Pacific as commander of a bomber squadron.

It was pretty heady stuff for a youngster who had grown up in the Pittsburgh suburb of Etna, Pennsylvania. Novosel vividly recalled his homecoming six years after he had enlisted: "The treatment was unbelievable. Everyone was so grateful for what we had done over there."

Novosel was transferred to Florida to serve as a test pilot at Eglin Air Force Base before he departed active duty in 1949. By the time the Korean War broke out a year later, he owned a very successful restaurant in Fort Walton Beach, Florida, was a partner in an appliance store, and a major in the air force reserve. Those ventures did not keep Novosel from volunteering for active duty, however.

"I didn't get into combat—not that I didn't want to," Novosel said. "It's just that the air force didn't pick me up until 1953. And then it was to attend the Air Command and Staff School."

When the air force released Novosel in 1955 as a lieutenant colonel, he became a pilot for a major commercial airline. It was a way for him to spend some more time with his growing family.

Less than ten years passed before Novosel again went on active duty—and found himself in his second war. "I was a great fan of John Kennedy. I took him at his word when he said to do something for your country. When I found out there was a war going on in Vietnam, I volunteered," he said.

The air force did not have much use for forty-two-year-old lieutenant colonels, so Novosel went to the army. "They were desperate for pilots, so they took me," he said.

Newly commissioned army warrant officer Mike Novosel spent a year in the United States flying helicopters with the Special Forces before being sent to South Vietnam as a medevac pilot.

Novosel finished his twelve-month tour in January 1967. This time when he came home, there were no bands. "There wasn't even anyone to say 'Hello' or 'Congratulations, you made it back from 'Nam after a year.' "

Novosel spent two years training new helicopter pilots before deciding to resume his civilian flying career. Fate changed his plans. His separation physical revealed that he had glaucoma.

"For civilian airlines it's a grounding condition. But the army gave me a waiver and let me continue flying," Novosel said.

In March 1969, Novosel began his second tour of duty in South Vietnam. He went to the 82d Medical Detachment, 45th Medical Company, 68th Medical Group at Binh Thuy, upriver from Can Tho, about seventy-five miles southwest of Saigon.

On October 2, 1969, Novosel had already been at the controls of his Huey for seven hours when word came that three ARVN infantry companies had stumbled across an NVA training area in the Plain of Reeds, Kien Tuong Province, near Cambodia's Parrot's Beak. There were heavy casualties, and they needed to be pulled out.

Novosel turned to his copilot, WO2 Tyron Chamberlain, and said, "Let's go get them."

On the flight to the battle site, Novosel learned that heavy enemy fire had already brought down two Cobra gunships and hit two air force F-100 jets. But that did not lessen his determination to save the wounded.

Once at the battleground, an open area alongside the Cambodian border covered with six-foot-tall elephant grass, Novosel flew slowly at grass-top height looking for the wounded. The thick vegetation made it difficult. "We spotted the first one finally," he recalled, "and then all of a sudden we started seeing others all over."

Back and forth across the battlefield Novosel flew, picking up wounded. His crew chief, Sp4. Joseph Horvath, remembered, "I never heard so much enemy fire before. I saw gun flashes from bunkers all around us."

Completely disregarding the enemy fire, Novosel hovered while Horvath and the medic, Sp4. Herbert Heinold, pulled the wounded Vietnamese aboard.

"As soon as we touched down we started receiving fire," recalled Heinold, "but Mr. Novosel stayed until we got the wounded aboard. Several times the intensity of the fire forced us out. At one point I saw gun flashes from at least a half dozen places."

Six times enemy fire forced Novosel to pull back. Six times he came in from another direction. Each time his ruse worked.

As soon as Novosel had a full load of wounded, nine or ten men, he flew them to the medics waiting at the Special Forces camp at nearby Moc Hoa. Then he flew back into the carnage. Three times during the two and one-half hour ordeal Novosel made the round trip.

Novosel had just decided that it was too dark to search for casualties when a wounded ARVN suddenly stood up in the grass, waving his shirt. From twenty yards behind the man, an NVA machine gun fired at the chopper. Novosel never hesitated.

In order to save the ARVN and protect the wounded who already filled his ship, Novosel brought his Huey in low, then began to back up. He wanted as much metal between him and the machine gun as possible.

Horvath had started to pull the casualty into the chopper when an enemy rifle round slammed into the cockpit. Plexiglas and bullet fragments flew through the compartment, some embedding themselves in Novosel's right calf and thigh. Shock and the impact of the shrapnel caused him to lose control of the Huey.

"Aw hell! I'm hit," Novosel remembered saying. He was afraid he would pass out, but somehow he managed to regain control of the chopper, then climbed rapidly out of the area. Horvath finished pulling the ARVN soldier aboard sixty feet above the ground.

Altogether Novosel made fifteen extractions that afternoon, bringing twenty-nine casualties to safety. With his wounds patched up, he returned to flying the very next day. "I didn't think much of it at the time. I've had other missions just as tough," he said of the rescues.

During his two tours in South Vietnam, Novosel received credit for extracting more than fifty-five hundred casualties. Few men have amassed such an enviable record.

Before Novosel left South Vietnam in March 1970, his eldest son, Michael, Jr., joined the unit as a medevac pilot. They have the unique distinction of having rescued one another. "My son was shot down one day and I picked him up," Novosel said. "When I was shot down the same week, he picked me up."

Once Stateside again, Novosel served for three years as the aviation officer and pilot for the army's prestigious Golden Knights parachute team. He was still serving with them when he was summoned to the White House on June 15,

1971 to receive his Medal of Honor. He was the oldest recipient for Vietnam service.

When Novosel retired in March 1985 after forty-four years of service to his country, he was the last military aviator on active duty who had flown combat missions in World War II.

CHAPTER NINE

POWs Fight Back

Americans captured and held as prisoners of war by the North Vietnamese or Viet Cong were a very special group of warriors who engaged the enemy on a different level. Over seven hundred men became POWs, with some spending up to nine and one-half years in the hands of their captors. They were held in camps ranging from isolated VC outposts in South Vietnam to the infamous "Hanoi Hilton"—the block-long French-built prison complex in downtown Hanoi, which the North Vietnamese called Hao Lo, or "Fiery Furnace." While in captivity the POWs were subjected to incredible brutality and deprivation.

Throughout their period of confinement, most POWs lived in a small cell. Only a handful of men were fortunate enough to have a cell mate. A concrete slab served as a bed, an old bucket as the toilet. Meals were served no more than twice a day. Usually these consisted of a thin, watery soup along with a meager portion of rice. Meat, or any protein, was available only rarely.

Although isolated from one another, the POWs developed elaborate methods of communication. By tapping on walls or using hand signals, they laboriously sent messages to one another. Thus they could keep each other informed and organize against their captors. To be caught sending messages, though, invited swift and inhuman torture.

Resistance to the enemy's attempts to extract military information proved to be a difficult task. Some men completely resisted the North Vietnamese interrogators, revealing only their name, rank, and service number. Most, though, held out only as long as they could endure the pain of torture. Even then they were often able to give their captors false information.

The five POWs who earned Medals of Honor displayed unique valor. They were cited for *sustained* bravery rather than for specific acts of gallantry. These heroic men repeatedly resisted the enemy by overcoming unimaginable hardships. They demonstrated great courage in organizing their fellow captives against their captors, and although horribly injured, they attempted to escape. Their indomitable courage provided dramatic inspiration to the other POWs.

DONALD G. COOK

Born in Brooklyn, New York, on August 9, 1934, *Donald G. Cook* grew up in Burlington, Vermont. An avid football player, he played on teams both at his high school and at Saint Michael's College in Winooski, Vermont.

After Cook graduated from Saint Michael's in June 1956, he entered Marine Corps Officer Candidate School. He went on active duty in January 1957 and received his commission as a second lieutenant five months later.

Cook selected communications as his specialty and drew an assignment with the 1st Marine Division. When he showed a talent for languages, the Marine Corps sent him to the U.S. Army Language School in Monterey, California. The difficult Mandarin Chinese course required one year of intense study, but Cook persevered and graduated in May 1961. He next attended the army's Intelligence School at Fort Holabird, Maryland. In September 1961 he returned to the 1st Marine Division as head of its Interrogation Team.

On December 11, 1964, Cook left his Hawaii duty station with eight other Marines for a temporary thirty-day assignment in South Vietnam. The Viet Cong captured him on December 31, 1964.

Years passed without any further word of Cook. Only

when the other POWs came home in 1973 did the story of Cook's heroism while a prisoner become known.

Cook had served as the senior Marine adviser to a South Vietnamese Marine battalion. On that last day of December, while his unit conducted an offensive sweep in coastal Phuoc Tuy Province, the VC shot down a U.S. helicopter. Cook led a rescue platoon toward the crash site. The VC sprang an ambush.

Most of the South Vietnamese Marines turned and ran. Cook tried to organize the few remaining South Vietnamese into a workable defense but took a round in the left leg before he could get them into position. With that, the rest of the Marines took off. Alone and immobile, Cook was carried off by the VC.

As soon as Cook arrived at the first POW camp, he established himself as the commanding officer of all the other POWs held there. His assertiveness thwarted the VC's efforts to break down military discipline among the prisoners. Even though he was beaten and tortured by sadistic guards, Cook still refused to step aside. He insisted on acting as the POWs' commanding officer and demanded the appropriate respect.

According to one former POW, Cook "wouldn't even give the VC the time of day."

In their propaganda meetings, the VC characterized American officers as members of the elite class, unwilling and unable to perform manual labor. Cook undermined that effort when he organized calisthenic classes for the POWs and led them himself. On other occasions Cook purposefully stepped up the pace of work details in order to embarrass the VC interpreter working alongside him.

The results not only proved Cook's point, but earned him more physical abuse.

Cook's courage also impressed his captors. The VC forced Cook to hike several hundred miles through jungle and mountain terrain to a new camp in Phuoc Long Province even though he was weak with malaria. Witnesses expressed amazement at Cook's stamina. His deteriorating health caused him to stagger, yet he refused to accept help or to allow anyone to carry his pack. He would not show any weakness to the enemy. Once at the new camp, the VC commander praised Cook for his perseverance.

During his stay at the new site, Cook used his limited medical knowledge to give first aid to his fellow prisoners. At times he even gave heart massages to revive malaria victims. More than once Cook shared his meager rations with those sicker than himself. At other times he sacrificed his small allowance of penicillin so that another man might benefit from a larger dose.

Cook recognized the need to maintain communication among the prisoners. He set up message drops and developed a simple code. Always his message contained the same theme: Resist.

One time the guards caught Cook as he passed a message. Furious at his constant insubordination, they knelt him in front of the other prisoners. A VC officer held a pistol to Cook's head. To the amazement of the other prisoners and the VC, Cook defiantly recited the pistol's nomenclature in a calm, strong voice. The guards gave up.

In spite of Cook's mental strength, disease extracted its inevitable toll. Unable to counter the crippling effects of malaria, Cook died on December 8, 1967. The other POWs buried him in a jungle grave.

Although repatriated POWs reported Cook's death, and the Provisional Revolutionary Government of South Vietnam confirmed it in January 1973, his widow refused to accept the news. Without his body, she held out hope that he might still be alive. At her insistence, the Department of Defense kept Cook listed as missing-in-action.

A Medal of Honor recommendation had been prepared for Colonel Cook, who was promoted regularly while carried as MIA, soon after reports of his courage were verified. It was approved, but the award was held in abeyance at the family's request.

On February 26, 1980, with his widow's approval, the Defense Department officially declared Cook deceased. Mrs.

Cook accepted her husband's posthumous Medal of Honor from Navy secretary Edward Hidalgo on May 16, 1980.

JAMES B. STOCKDALE

When antiaircraft fire blew his Skyhawk jet apart on September 5, 1965, ice-cold fear gripped navy *Cmdr. James B. Stockdale*'s stomach. It was not fear of capture that hit him—after all, as a navy fighter pilot on his 201st mission over North Vietnam, Stockdale had learned to accept the risks of being shot down and captured.

It was far worse than that. "I had the most damaging information a North Vietnamese torturer could possibly extract from an American prisoner," he remembered.

Stockdale knew the truth about the Gulf of Tonkin incidents.

Thirteen months earlier, Stockdale had been commander of Fighter Squadron 51 aboard the aircraft carrier USS *Ticonderoga*. On August 4, 1964 he had scrambled into the air in response to a call for help from the destroyers USS *Maddox* and *Turner Joy*. They reported that they were under attack by North Vietnamese PT boats.

For two hours Stockdale and the other jets flew back and forth above the black waves. He fired his rockets where the destroyers' radar said the enemy boats should be. Always his eyes, and his radar, told Stockdale the same thing: There was nothing out there.

When Stockdale returned to the *Ticonderoga,* he threw his helmet against the bulkhead in disgust. "Nothing but a damn Chinese fire drill!" he swore. "Spooked operators and spooked equipment."

In spite of what Stockdale reported to his superiors, President Johnson ordered reprisal attacks against North Vietnam. A few days later the president's Gulf of Tonkin Resolution sailed through Congress. The United States was at war—an undeclared war, to be sure—but still a war.

If the North Vietnamese could pry that information from Stockdale, they would possess tremendous ammunition for their propaganda campaign.

Born in the small central Illinois town of Abingdon on December 23, 1923, Stockdale entered Annapolis with the class of 1947. His frustration at missing out on action during World War II peaked when his cousin, Robert H. Dunlap, received a Medal of Honor for his heroism as a Marine officer during the vicious battle for the island of Iwo Jima in 1945.

A Stateside instructor's berth kept Stockdale out of the Korean War. Sometimes he thought he would never get a fighter command. Finally in February 1963 his assignment to a fighter squadron came through.

Now, as Stockdale drifted below his parachute, he vowed not to reveal what he knew.

Stockdale hit the ground hard, discovering for the first time that the force of the ejection had shattered his left knee and broken his left shoulder. Before he could pull himself free from his chute, a crowd of peasants descended on him. They beat him with clubs and their fists until North Vietnamese soldiers pulled him away—eventually transferring him to the notorious Hanoi Hilton.

Eight years would pass before Stockdale again knew freedom. Three of those years would be spent in complete isolation. For two years he stayed locked in leg irons. His injured leg never received treatment. As a result, he has a permanent limp.

"If you really want to turn a person to putty," Stockdale said, "isolation is best. I spent a month blindfolded. The Vietnamese never knew how close I came to giving up and spilling my guts."

But Stockdale did not. As the senior POW in the camp, he organized the others into military units. Unit commanders were appointed. Orders were issued. The chief order demanded defiance of the enemy. Captives were expected to resist torture as long as they could.

Stockdale instituted a simple but effective code for communication. "It was a tap code keyed to a five-by-five matrix. Through tapping we could pass messages, keep each other's morale up," he recalled.

Stockdale knew that without discipline, the group would fall apart. He had to provide an example of resistance so that the others would know what was expected of them.

Early in 1969 the North Vietnamese made it clear they were going to use Stockdale in propaganda pictures. To foil their efforts, Stockdale beat his own face to a bloody pulp with a wooden stool; he then used a razor blade to tear up his scalp. The result: No pictures.

According to Stockdale, the North Vietnamese applied fear, guilt, pain, solitude, and degradation to turn prisoners against each other and to pry loose military information. Whenever they caught a prisoner in any act considered a violation of the Hanoi Hilton's many petty rules, the guards cruelly tortured the offender. The worst crime was to cause other prisoners to oppose the camp authority.

Almost as soon as Stockdale's imprisonment began, he was recognized as a leader of the resistance. Twice the guards identified him as the organizer of elaborate secret resistance groups. Each time a dreadful purge followed. Stockdale and the other leaders were horribly tortured, then cast into solitary. The other prisoners suffered as well. At least one died during the purges.

"In September 1969, I had been caught in a third prison bust. I was at the end of my string. I had been through thirteen different torture sessions. I didn't want any more men to suffer as a result of my actions," Stockdale recalled.

Stockdale feared he would reveal the names of his fellow conspirators. He took a drastic step to prevent that. When he was temporarily left alone in the small room used for torture sessions, Stockdale crawled to its tiny window. Even though he was hampered by leg irons that cut deep into his flesh, Stockdale somehow managed to break the glass. He slashed his wrists with the shards.

"It was clear to me that I had to stop the interrogation. If it cost me my life, it cost it," Stockdale said matter-of-factly.

The North Vietnamese found Stockdale before he bled to death. His willingness to sacrifice his own life deeply impressed his captors. And the publicity-conscious North Vietnamese could not afford to have the world learn of the senior POW's suicide. They turned off the torture machine. While Stockdale's ordeal would not completely end until his release on February 12, 1973, the North Vietnamese did treat him with considerably more respect after this incident.

For his "valiant leadership and extraordinary courage in a hostile environment," Stockdale received the Medal of Honor from President Ford on March 4, 1976.

Stockdale had looked forward to resuming his naval career after his release, but it was not to be. His one dream—to command an aircraft carrier—never materialized. "They patted on three stars and patronized me. I'd been away too long. I was destined to be on the second team."

After thirty-three years of active naval service, Admiral Stockdale retired in 1977. He then spent three years as president of The Citadel Military Academy in Charleston, South Carolina, before accepting a position as a senior research fellow at the Hoover Institute on War, Revolution, and Peace at Stanford University in Palo Alto, California.

In 1984, Stockdale's account of his years as a prisoner of war were published. Written in conjunction with his wife Sybil, *Love and War* examined the POW experience not only from his perspective but from Sybil's as the wife left behind to deal with a government that offered no help to the POW families. A few years later it was made into a television movie.

In 1992 billionaire activist and presidential hopeful Ross Perot tapped Admiral Stockdale as his running mate on the Reform Party ticket. Stockdale, who understood he was only a temporary part of the ticket until a more politically experienced candidate could be persuaded to run, is best remembered for his opening remarks during a vice presidential debate when he asked, "Who am I? Why am I here?"

The Reform Party lost by a wide margin.

GEORGE E. DAY

On August 26, 1967, *Maj. George E. "Bud" Day* was flying an F-100 jet on a forward air control mission about fifty miles north of the DMZ. A pilot since 1952, Day had over 5,000 hours of flying time, with 4,500 of those in single-engine jets. His experience included time in almost every jet fighter in America's aerial arsenal.

Day was no stranger to the military, either. Born in Sioux City, Iowa, on February 24, 1925, he left there to enlist in the Marine Corps in 1942. He spent thirty months as a noncommissioned officer in the South Pacific during World War II.

Day returned to Iowa after the war to earn his bachelor's degree, then took a law degree from the University of South Dakota in 1950. He also accepted an air national guard commission as a second lieutenant.

After hostilities erupted in Korea in 1950, Day was called to active duty and selected for flight training. By the time the Korean War ended three years later, Day had spent two tours there as a fighter-bomber pilot.

In April 1964, Day went to South Vietnam for the first time to serve as an F-100 squadron's assistant operations officer at Tuy Hoa Air Base. Later he went to Phu Cat Air Base to organize and command the first squadron of F-100s used as forward air controllers (FACs).

The F-100, a vintage Korean War–era jet, was used as a high-speed FAC on missions where slower FAC planes proved too vulnerable to ground fire. Day's men called themselves "the Huns."

On that hot August day, ground fire hit the head Hun. Day knew immediately that he would have to bail out. On ejecting, he slammed into the plane's fuselage. The impact broke his right arm in three places and sprained his left knee. He was captured as soon as he touched down.

For two days the North Vietnamese tortured and interrogated Day. He suffered intense pain from his untended injuries but still thought about escape. All he needed was the right opportunity.

On Day's third day in captivity, an enemy medic crudely set his broken arm. Day thought the cure was worse than the injury.

Day's captors were members of a local militia unit. Mostly teenagers, they were undisciplined and easily deluded. Day convinced his guards that his injuries left him incapable of moving. As a result they left his hands untied, securing only his feet.

On the sixth day after Day was shot down, he undid the knots and headed south.

Day walked for two days, going without sleep the first night out of fear that the enemy would find him. On the second night he crawled under a bush to sleep. In the middle of the night, a bomb, rocket, or artillery shell (he never did know which) exploded nearby. Red-hot shrapnel ripped into his right leg. The concussion ruptured his sinuses and eardrums. He vomited blood.

Day holed up for two days until he regained his senses. Then he restarted his southbound trek.

As Day drew closer to the Ben Hai River that marked the DMZ, the terrain grew rougher. Where before he had traversed rice paddies, he was now walking through heavy jungle. The only food he had during this odyssey was the occassional raw frog he caught and berries he found growing on bushes along his route.

Day knew that he was close to starving when he began to hallucinate and talk out loud. Still, he pressed onward.

At last Day reached the river. By using a bamboo log as a float, he waded across.

Because Day was growing more delirious with each passing hour, he found it increasingly difficult to maintain his bearings. The no-man's-land of the DMZ was harsh country, pockmarked by numerous bomb craters. Day, weakened by hunger, stumbled and fell frequently.

One day, two slow-moving FAC planes flew directly overhead at a low altitude. Day screamed, shouted, and jumped around. The pilots did not see him.

Near the end of his ordeal Day heard choppers nearby. He

headed toward the sound. He did not know it, but the helicopters were picking up a Marine patrol a short distance away.

Day limped through the underbrush, every fiber of his body intent on reaching the pickup zone. As he drew closer he yelled, but his voice could not be heard above the noise. He burst into the clearing just as the last chopper disappeared over the trees.

Filled with despair, Day staggered back into the jungle—still determined to find help.

Perhaps if Day had not been so weak, so unable to orient himself, he might not have stumbled into an NVA ambush a few days later. He had been able to avoid other enemy positions by going around them. This time he used a trail well worn by American patrols. Before he knew it, he walked right into the middle of an ambush position.

Day always thought he must have scared the enemy as much as they scared him. Here he was, an unexpected apparition stumbling out of the jungle, with matted hair, filthy skin, clad in shorts, and staggering around as if he were drunk.

The NVA hesitated before they reacted. When they called to him, Day ran back into the jungle. The NVA opened fire. Day made it about thirty feet before bullets hit his left hand and thigh. His escape attempt was over.

Day never did know exactly how long he had stayed on the run. The closest he could ever determine was somewhere between eleven and fifteen days. What Day does remember is that it took the enemy only a day and a half to return him to the original prison camp.

Cruel torture awaited Day. A starvation diet dropped his weight from 170 to 110 pounds. The North Vietnamese refused Day all medical treatment for his gunshot wounds. The injuries festered and became infected.

Day met with stoic resistance all attempts by the North Vietnamese to extract information. He simply refused to talk.

The North Vietnamese resorted to two full days of barbaric torture to try to break Day, but he still resisted. At one point the torturers bound Day's hands behind him, tied a rope to his wrists, then used that rope to hoist him off the ground, leaving him suspended from an overhead ceiling beam. Day's shoulders dislocated. When he still would not cooperate, the interrogation officer ordered a guard to twist Day's mangled right arm. The pop of the wrist bone could be heard across the room.

Stretched to the limit of human endurance, Day agreed to talk. The North Vietnamese were sure they had broken the stubborn lawyer.

But they had not. Even though Day knew he faced death if discovered, he answered his captors' questions with false information and revealed nothing of military significance.

When Day arrived at Hoa Lo Prison in Hanoi two months later, he was a complete physical wreck. Even though he could not perform the simplest tasks for himself, the North Vietnamese continued to torture him.

Day's ordeal continued until his release from captivity on March 14, 1973.

Day's incredible resistance to the unspeakable cruelties of the North Vietnamese was rewarded with the Medal of Honor on March 4, 1976.

Colonel Day is one of the most decorated men in air force history. Among his sixty decorations and awards—which include forty for combat—are: the Air Force Cross, the Distinguished Service Medal, two Silver Stars, the Legion of Merit, the Distinguished Flying Cross, ten Air Medals, three Bronze Stars, and four Purple Hearts.

Today, retired air force colonel Bud Day resides in Florida, where he practices law and is a strong advocate for veterans' benefits.

LANCE P. SIJAN

"Sijan! My name is Lance Peter Sijan!"

The voice, raspy and filled with pain, spoke defiantly to a North Vietnamese interrogator. For over two hours the enemy officer had tortured the downed pilot. He would say to the POW, "Your arm, your arm is very bad. I am going to twist it unless you tell me."

American prisoners in nearby bamboo cells would hear the unseen air force officer respond, "I'm not going to tell you, it's against the code of conduct." Then they would hear him scream. They knew the guard was twisting the man's bad arm.

The other prisoners had no idea of their fellow captive's identity. All they had seen was a badly beaten and emaciated body thrown into a cell. Then the questioning started.

Amazingly, at one point the prisoner threatened his captor. "Wait until I get better, you SOB," he told the North Vietnamese. "You're really going to get it."

The other POWs could not believe a man could be so bold.

At last, when it seemed their fellow prisoner was about to break, he shouted out his name, rank, and serial number.

That was how the other Americans met air force *Capt. Lance P. Sijan.*

During his senior year in high school Sijan received an appointment to the U.S. Air Force Academy. The eighteen-year-old left his hometown of Milwaukee, Wisconsin, to join the class of 1965 in Colorado Springs, Colorado.

Sijan quickly proved himself a leader. He excelled not only academically but also on the gridiron. He spent two years on the varsity football team as a substitute end.

After graduation, Sijan entered flight training. He earned his pilot's wings in November 1966. Seven months later he was sent to South Vietnam.

On November 9, 1967, Sijan was in the backseat of an F-4 Phantom piloted by Col. John W. Armstrong, commander of the 366th Tactical Squadron. It was a routine bombing mission near Vinh, North Vietnam, until ground fire hit the jet. Armstrong ordered an ejection.

Armstrong was never seen or heard from again. Sijan suffered a skull fracture, a mangled right hand with three fingers bent back to the wrist, and a compound fracture of the left leg. To add to his ordeal, he had no survival equipment except his emergency radio.

Sikorsky HH-3 search-and-rescue helicopters, the famed Jolly Green Giants, raced to the area as soon as they received word of the shoot-down. The rescuers made contact with Sijan almost immediately. The SAR crews learned of Sijan's injuries. He was down but not out. By using the sound of the aircraft's rotors, Sijan directed the rescuers over the thick jungle canopy.

Suddenly one Jolly Green Giant crewman heard Sijan transmit, "I see you. I see you. Stay where you are. I'm coming to you."

Even though the helicopter pilot was now taking increasingly heavy ground fire, he hovered in place, his craft's rescue line disappearing into the jungle below. Bullets crashed into the chopper, a few at first, then more. After half an hour, with no further voice contact, the pilot turned his craft away.

But the SAR operation did not end. Over one hundred aircraft were used in the search on the first two days, fourteen more on the third. Enemy fire brought down one plane and several helicopter crewmen were hit by enemy ground fire. But the search was in vain. No further word was heard from Sijan.

Where was he?

The trauma from Sijan's injuries had overwhelmed him within a few feet of the rescue line. For the next three days he passed in and out of consciousness from the excruciating pain.

When Sijan at last regained consciousness, he realized that his freedom depended on his strength. Unable to stand or use his legs to crawl, he pulled himself backward through the jungle. Foot by painful foot, Sijan dragged himself along.

One of Sijan's future cell mates, Capt. Guy Gruter, recalled that "Lance said he'd go for two or three days—as long as he possibly could—then he'd be exhausted and go to sleep. As soon as he'd wake up, he'd be off again."

Sijan evaded the searching enemy for six full weeks. For almost forty-five days, without food and with very little water, Sijan moved over the rugged terrain. He was so emaciated that every bone in his body protruded through his gaunt skin.

Sijan finally collapsed along a dirt road. He lay there for more than a day before an enemy truck passed by and found him.

As Sijan later told Gruter, the North Vietnamese gave him food and shelter. After a few days, with his strength returning, Sijan's thoughts again turned to escape.

One day a single guard served him food. Sijan beckoned him over. When the guard bent down, Sijan told Gruter, "I just let him have it. Wham!"

After he knocked the guard unconscious, Sijan pulled himself back into the jungle. This time only a few hours passed before he was found. The guards severely beat him.

On New Year's Day 1968 the North Vietnamese threw Sijan into a cell near Captain Gruter. That very night Gruter and several other American POWs heard Sijan scream his name in defiance at his interrogators.

Over the next several days, according to Gruter, "the guy was always trying to push his way out of the bamboo cell. They'd beat him back with a stick. We could hear the cracks."

Finally the North Vietnamese were ready to transport their prisoners to Hanoi. Gruter and Col. Robert Craner were detailed to care for Sijan.

"When I got a look at the poor devil, I retched," said Craner. "Maybe twenty percent of his body was not open sores or raw flesh. He was so thin; every bone in his body was visible."

Gruter picked Sijan up to carry him to the truck. "He looked like a little guy, but when I picked him up I told Craner, 'This was one big sonofagun.'"

On the trip to Hanoi, Gruter realized that he had met Sijan at the academy. "I have never had my heart broken like that," said Gruter, who remembered Sijan as a 220-pound football player. Now Sijan "had no muscle left and looked so helpless."

Not once during the grueling, bouncy four-day truck ride to Hanoi did Sijan complain. Lucid for varying periods of time, Sijan responded weakly to Gruter's and Craner's questions about his forty-five-day ordeal.

Craner later said that through it all, Sijan never gave up his desire to seek freedom. "One of the first things he mentioned in Vinh was how we were going to get out. 'Have you guys figured out how we're going to take care of these people? Do you think we can steal a gun?'

"He had to struggle to get each word out. It was very, very intense on his part that the only direction he was planning was escape. Even later, he kept dwelling on the fact that he had made it once and he was going to make it again."

When the prisoners finally reached the Hanoi Hilton, they were thrown into a dank, unlit cell. A pool of water covered most of the concrete floor. Craner remembered, "It was the first time I suffered from the cold. Guy Gruter and I started getting respiratory problems right away. I couldn't imagine what it was doing to Lance.

"Through it all Sijan never talked about pain. In fact, I never heard him complain. He was so full of drive whenever he was lucid. It was always positive for him, pointed mainly toward escape."

Craner remembered one night in particular. "A guard opened the little plate in the door and looked in. Lance beckoned to him. I recognized it as the same signal he had given the guard in the jungle. It was clear what was on his mind."

Near the end, Sijan asked for help to exercise so he could build up his strength for another escape attempt. "We got him propped up and waved his arms around a little," Craner said. "That satisfied him. Then he was exhausted."

About eight days after they arrived at the Hanoi Hilton, Craner knew the end had come. Pneumonia gripped Sijan's lungs. He started to make strangling sounds. His two roommates rushed to sit him up.

"Then, for the first time since we'd been together his voice came through loud and clear," Craner recalled. "He said, 'Oh my God, it's over,' and then he started calling for his father. He'd shout, 'Dad, Dad, where are you? Come here, I need you!'" (That night, in Milwaukee, Sylvester Sijan told his wife that as he was driving home from the family jewelry store, he was gripped with a nearly overwhelming sensation that Lance needed him.)

"I knew he was sinking fast," Craner continued. "I beat on the walls, calling for the guards, hoping they'd take him to a hospital. They finally came and took him away. As best as I could figure it was January 21. It was the last time we saw him."

While Gruter was on a detail a few days later, a guard told him, "Sijan die."

When Craner and Gruter were released in early 1973, they immediately initiated a recommendation for Sijan to receive a Medal of Honor. Craner said it was because "Sijan survived a terrible ordeal, and he survived with the intent, sometime in the future, of picking up the fight. There is no way you can instill that type of performance in an individual."

On March 4, 1976, after he presented Medals of Honor to former POWs Admiral Stockdale and Colonel Day, President Ford turned to Mr. and Mrs. Sylvester Sijan of Milwaukee. "I deeply regret," the president said, "that one of the awards today is posthumous."

Then he handed the father his son's medal.

CHAPTER TEN

America Withdraws

The main U.S. effort in the final three years of the Vietnam War, 1970 to 1973, concentrated on pushing the South Vietnamese army into battle as fast as possible—and withdrawing American units even faster. Though several U.S. divisions occupied potentially volatile territory along the Laotian and Cambodian borders, they were there primarily to train the ARVN.

Over 380,000 U.S. troops were in South Vietnam at the beginning of 1970. Twelve months later only 265,000 remained. In 1970 the 1st Infantry Division, most of the 4th Infantry Division, the 25th Infantry Division, and several separate infantry brigades all departed South Vietnam.

The withdrawal of troops and the deemphasis on American involvement resulted in a reduction of combat deaths in 1970 to 4,221 from the 9,414 suffered in 1969. This was the lowest level since 1966, when 5,008 Americans were killed in action.

The major combat in 1970 came during the invasion of Cambodia in May and June. Elements of the 25th Infantry, 1st Cavalry, and 4th Infantry Divisions penetrated up to thirty-five miles into the previously off-limits area. While the invaders recorded no major military victories, they did destroy huge quantities of supplies—seriously hampering the NVA's ability to wage war. The incursion had the secondary objective of enhancing the South Vietnamese military's self-confidence. That goal was only partly met.

The Cambodian invasion produced no Medals of Honor. Almost all of the medals earned during the final three years of U.S. participation in South Vietnam came during static defense missions performed by American troops.

There were combat battalions engaged in reconnaissance-in-force missions in areas hotly contested by the NVA, but most units were assigned security roles near towns, roads, bridges, and military installations. The days of aggressive offensive operations were in the past.

The Studies and Observation Group did maintain an offensive schedule. Its elite counterintelligence troops continued their efforts behind enemy lines and across international borders.

A twenty-four-year-old staff sergeant from SOG's Command and Control–Central, *Franklin D. Miller,* led one such mission into Laos on January 5, 1970. From their base at Kontum, Miller headed his American and Vietnamese long-range recon patrol across the border. No stranger to combat in South Vietnam, Miller wore a Purple Heart earned on one of his two previous tours.

Soon after the team landed in Laos, one of the Vietnamese tripped a booby trap; the explosion wounded four team members. Within minutes an NVA platoon arrived to investigate the blast. Miller sent his team up a hill into a defensive position, then turned to meet the enemy. Twice the Santa Fe, New Mexico, resident single-handedly fought them off.

Miller led his team to an evacuation site, but the NVA hit them a third time. The enemy fire drove off the rescue chopper and wounded the rest of the team, including Miller. Alone and unaided, he repulsed three more attacks before a relief force reached them. Through Miller's gallant efforts seven lives were saved.

During the final days of the war, patrols and ambushes occupied most of the average grunt's combat time. Unable to offensively engage the NVA, American troops were not ready to concede the countryside to him, either. As long as they were there, U.S. troops would battle the enemy.

1st Lt. Russell A. Steindam of Plano, Texas, led one of his squads from Troop B, 3d Squadron, 4th Cavalry, 25th Infantry Division, to an ambush site in Tay Ninh Province on the night of February 1, 1970. Before the soldiers reached the site, enemy fire ripped into their ranks, wounding several. Steindam ordered his men to return fire, then helped move the casualties to the safety of a bomb crater. He was on the radio to his CO when an enemy grenade landed among the wounded. Steindam shouted a warning, then jumped on the grenade. He died saving his men.

Ten days later *Sp4. John P. Baca* also jumped on a grenade to save eight men but—amazingly—he survived his grievous wounds. The 1st Cavalry Division (Airmobile) trooper was on a night ambush in Phuoc Long Province along the Cambodian border with his platoon from Company D, 1st Battalion, 12th Cavalry, when a fragmentation grenade landed near him. Baca whipped off his helmet, covered the grenade with it, and fell on the helmet as the grenade exploded. Baca spent a year in the hospital recovering from his wounds.

Throughout the Vietnam War, incredible acts of heroism often occurred during tough fights that had no lasting consequence. This was the case when a company of Chinese Nungs—with Special Forces leadership—attacked a strategic mountain pass in Chau Doc Province on the Cambodian border.

BRIAN L. BUKER

Only twenty years old when he died, Special Forces sergeant *Brian L. Buker* was one of thousands of soldiers serving a second tour in South Vietnam. He had been there before as a paratrooper with the 173d Airborne Brigade in 1968 and 1969.

What Buker witnessed on that first tour convinced him of the need to stop the spread of communism before it engulfed all of Southeast Asia. He had also learned that conventional warfare had little impact on the insurgents. The only way to aid the South Vietnamese seemed to be at the village level. The native tribesmen needed training to resist the VC and the NVA. The Special Forces offered the type of training

Buker felt would let him help the South Vietnamese help themselves.

During his first tour in South Vietnam, Buker volunteered for the Special Forces. He entered training in July 1969. By November he was back in the war zone, this time wearing the coveted green beret.

Buker joined Detachment B-55, which controlled the Mobile Strike Force companies. Organized around South Vietnamese and ethnic minorities, these companies operated in battalion-size combat operations in difficult terrain.

For years the NVA had reigned supreme in a mountain fortress just inside the Vietnamese border. As long as they were there, Chau Doc Province would never be free. Buker's company was going to try to change that.

Although technically an adviser, on this mission Buker took charge of a platoon. Up through the rugged mountains, through a series of enemy strong points, he pushed his troops forward. Buker repeatedly exposed himself to enemy fire while setting an example of personal heroism for his men.

Buker and his troops fought the enemy all day long. Bunker after bunker fell to the platoon's onslaught. By late afternoon the battle-weary troops had cleared the pass and established a hold on the crest of the mountain.

But Buker felt that the enemy would not give up the site easily—and he was right. Before he could complete preparation of his defensive positions, the NVA counterattacked and quickly reoccupied two bunkers.

Buker could have sent one of his squads out after the bunkers, but that was not his style. He went himself.

Bounding forward, ignoring the enemy fire, Buker closed on the first bunker and knocked it out with a grenade.

Buker moved toward the second bunker but was shot by an enemy machine gun. That did not stop him. He crawled on. He got to within grenade range and destroyed that bunker, too.

Rather than stop for badly needed medical attention, Buker began to organize his men for a drive on the remaining pockets of resistance. An enemy RPG killed him before he could complete his task.

Without Buker's dynamic leadership, the attack faltered. Under heavy fire, the Nungs pulled back. By that evening the NVA again controlled the mountaintop.

Buker's widowed mother, from Albion, Maine, accepted her son's posthumous Medal of Honor on December 16, 1971.

A special program that the Marine Corps used to promote Vietnamization was the Combined Action Platoon, where groups of three or four volunteer Marines lived in villages among the inhabitants. In addition to providing security, the Marines were expected to train the local males to defend their homes. Vigorous patrolling kept the nearby areas free of VC and the NVA. Obviously the enemy did not like this Marine effort to undermine their propaganda. They frequently targeted CAP villages for attacks.

When Marine *LCpl. Miguel Keith,* from Omaha, Nebraska, arrived in South Vietnam in November 1969, he volunteered for the CAP program. To him it seemed like a good way to help the South Vietnamese.

During the early morning hours of May 8, 1970, the NVA hit Keith's village in Quang Ngai Province. Wounded twice in the opening barrage, he still managed to support several defensive positions manned by the locals. Later he single-handedly attacked five enemy soldiers who were approaching the command post, killing three and wounding the others.

Determined to protect the South Vietnamese he had come to know and respect in the previous six months, Keith ignored a third wound to charge twenty-five NVA who were massing in the dark for another attack. His accurate rifle fire killed four and sent the rest scurrying for cover. Seconds later, though, an enemy soldier shot and killed Keith.

The remarkable bravery of eighteen-year-old Keith, the last Marine to earn a Medal of Honor in South Vietnam, completely disrupted the NVA plans for overrunning the village.

* * *

Although no member of the U.S. forces that invaded Cambodia received a Medal of Honor for that action, an army medic working with the ARVNs did. *SFC Louis R. Rocco,* of Albuquerque, New Mexico, volunteered on May 24, 1970 to accompany a medevac helicopter going to pick up eight wounded ARVN soldiers who were in Cambodia north of Katum, South Vietnam. Rocco manned one of the Huey's machine guns as the craft descended to the LZ, but his accurate fire did not keep the NVA from shooting the helicopter out of the sky.

Rocco broke a wrist and a hip in the crash. Unmindful of the pain, he pulled the crew and other passengers from the burning wreckage. Then, alone and completely unaided, Rocco ignored the enemy fire and carried three casualties into the ARVN perimeter. There, he administered first aid to the injured until he collapsed from loss of blood.

Rocco survived his severe wounds to wear his well-deserved Medal of Honor. He later served as head of New Mexico's Veterans Service Commission. He died on October 31, 2002.

ROBERT C. MURRAY

Unlike the typical soldier who served in South Vietnam— a high school graduate from a working-class family—*Robert C. Murray* left Harvard's Graduate School of Business to join the U.S. Army. Raised in upper-class Tuckahoe, New York, Murray had graduated from Fordham University in New York City with a bachelor's degree in June 1968 before entering Harvard that fall.

As an undergraduate Murray had been entitled to a draft deferment; he lost that when he entered graduate school.

Murray had already received his notice from the draft board when his brother enlisted in the army reserves. That inspired Murray to accept the inevitable and get his military obligation out of the way. On October 29, 1968 he enlisted in the army.

Murray could have used his education to go to OCS and get a commission in a noncombat field. Instead, in his own quiet, determined way, he elected to serve as an enlisted man. A well-trained one, too. He volunteered for Ranger training after basic.

"Even though he didn't participate in organized sports in college, Bob was always very athletic," his mother, Mrs. James P. Murray, said. "Ranger training was just a way for him to show he was as good at soldiering as he was at studying."

Murray excelled throughout the difficult and rugged Ranger and Airborne training. His selection as the outstanding graduate of his class earned him a meritorious promotion to staff sergeant.

In November 1969, Murray went to South Vietnam. He joined Company B, 4th Battalion, 31st Infantry, Americal Division, then operating in Quang Nam Province, as a squad leader. The division performed mostly security missions and operated out of fire support bases strategically placed throughout the province.

The daily patrols and nightly ambushes kept Murray's squad members busy. He worked particularly hard at preventing casualties. Like everyone else, he knew the war was winding down. He did not want anyone from his squad to be the last man killed in the Vietnam War.

On June 7, 1970, Murray's squad was on patrol near Hiep Duc village west of Tom Ky. The grunts were hunting an elusive enemy mortar team that had been dropping harassing fire on their company's position for several days. While moving through some thick brush, one man tripped a grenade rigged as a booby trap. "Take cover!" he yelled.

Murray instantly realized that several members of his squad could not get out of the way in time. Concerned only with their safety, he flung himself on the grenade. He died in the blast, but saved his squad members from death or serious injury.

"It was just like Bob to die for his men," his mother said

when she accepted his posthumous Medal of Honor on August 8, 1974. "He was always so worried about them."

Unfortunately, Murray's father never learned of his son's high honor: He died in 1971.

On September 7, 1970, four APCs carrying members of Company E, 3d Battalion, 503d Infantry, of the venerable 173d Airborne Brigade moved down a jungle road in the Phu My District in Binh Dinh Province. A mine suddenly blew up the lead vehicle. Seconds later, automatic weapons fire ripped into the APC, setting it on fire.

Thirty-year-old staff sergeant *Glenn H. English, Jr.,* who had already served more than two years in-country, leaped from the vehicle, his fatigues afire. Without stopping, he rallied several nearby soldiers and led them in a vicious counterattack that routed the enemy.

English returned to the road, where the cries of three men trapped in the burning APC caught his attention. He ignored the threat of explosion from stored ammunition and climbed inside the vehicle. As he lifted the first wounded man to safety, the ammunition blew up. The blast killed English and the men he was trying to save.

After nearly two years of Vietnamization, MACV concluded that the forces of the Republic of Vietnam were ready to launch a major offensive operation of their own. In order to reduce the supplies flowing down the Ho Chi Minh Trail to the NVA and insurgent forces in South Vietnam, MACV decided on a thrust into Laos. No Americans would accompany the ground forces; they would only provide artillery and aviation support.

Beginning on January 30, 1971, U.S. combat engineers opened Route 9 through Quang Tri Province. On February 8, ARVN tanks rolled across the border in Operation Lam Son 719.

In support of the ARVN, Troop D, 2d Squadron, 17th Cavalry, 101st Airborne Division, regarrisoned the Khe Sanh Combat Base. On the night of March 23, 1971, NVA sappers infiltrated the base. They tossed three satchel charges into a bunker occupied by *Sp4. Michael J. Fitzmaurice* and three other soldiers.

In the dim light, Fitzmaurice, from Cavour, South Dakota, grabbed two of the charges and threw them out of the bunker. When he came upon the third, he covered it with his flak jacket and his own body.

The subsequent explosion seriously wounded and partially blinded Fitzmaurice, but he continued to fight. He charged out of the bunker and fired at the enemy until an exploding grenade wrecked his rifle. While searching for another weapon, he killed a sapper in hand-to-hand combat. Fitzmaurice then returned to his bunker, where he manned a machine gun until the enemy fled.

Fitzmaurice spent thirteen months in the hospital recovering from his wounds. A well-deserved Medal of Honor was presented to the twenty-one-year-old on October 15, 1973.

For the first few weeks of Operation Lam Son 719, the South Vietnamese soldiers performed well. However, by the time they neared Tchepone, the NVA had begun a series of aggressive counterattacks. The ARVN faltered. MACV decided to retreat.

Instead of an orderly withdrawal, though, the movement turned into a rout. Whole ARVN units broke and ran. Medevac helicopters were mobbed by able-bodied troops. Equipment was abandoned.

The first major offensive under Vietnamization turned into a disaster.

Yet withdrawal of American units continued. In early 1971 the 11th Armored Cavalry Regiment, the Americal Division, and most of the elite 1st Cavalry Division (Airmobile) returned home. In August 1971 the 173d Airborne Brigade left. The 173d had been the first army combat unit to enter South Vietnam—and its departure symbolized the end of American involvement. In January 1972 the 173d was deactivated (it was reactivated in 2001 with headquarters in Italy; it participated in the Second Gulf War in 2003).

The colors of the 5th Special Forces Group were returned to Fort Bragg, North Carolina, in March 1971. Most of its personnel, though, remained in-country, performing the same functions but for different, newly created, agencies.

One of the new units established after the 5th Special Forces Group officially withdrew was the Vietnam Training Advisory. Like their brothers from the early days of the war, these Green Berets still provided guidance and leadership to ARVN units.

JON R. CAVAIANI

When he took his Selective Service physical in 1962, *Jon R. Cavaiani* learned he was 4-F. His allergy to bee stings meant that the army did not want him. That was fine with Cavaiani—he had a family and a good job selling agricultural chemicals. He did not want the army either.

An orphan of World War II born in 1943, Cavaiani immigrated to America from England with his adoptive parents in 1947. The family settled in Ballico, California, where they operated a very successful farm. After college, Cavaiani took a job as a district sales manager in central California for a major chemical company.

Cavaiani was well on his way to middle-class success when he took and passed his citizenship test in 1968. "After that, I felt a profound sense of responsibility to the country that had been so good to me," he later said.

Although Cavaiani had two daughters, he enlisted in the army in May 1969. He volunteered for Special Forces training to prove a point after his toughness was questioned in basic training. Cavaiani proved his detractors wrong—he graduated with the green beret while they did not.

With his farm background and his military specialty of medicine, the 5th Special Forces assigned Cavaiani to duty as agricultural adviser to I Corps when he first arrived in South Vietnam in August 1970. He traveled to the different Special Forces camps and helped the CIDG troops properly grow crops and raise their stock.

Cavaiani enjoyed that role until the NVA destroyed an orphanage where he had spent his off-duty time. The savagery of the slaughter sickened Cavaiani. His life would never be the same. He volunteered for SOG's Command and Control–North (later Vietnam Training Advisory Group). Soon he was leading clandestine cross-border operations and taking his revenge on the NVA.

Soon after the Laotian invasion, Cavaiani took command of the security platoon at radio relay station Hickory, north of Khe Sanh on Hill 950. Composed of Special Forces, Montagnards, ARVNs, and communications specialists, the camp operated deep within enemy-dominated territory.

For several days at the end of May 1971, Cavaiani's patrols reported the presence of large numbers of the enemy in the vicinity. Cavaiani himself had seen hundreds of enemy soldiers walking boldly through the jungle in broad daylight. "We knew we were going to get hit; it was just a matter of when," Cavaiani said.

The night of June 3–4 witnessed a torrential downpour that kept the outpost's defenders in their bunkers. The troops could see only a few feet in the driving rain. At dawn Cavaiani and another American set out to check the perimeter. Unknown to them, NVA sappers had converged on the camp in the rain. A deadly ring of claymore mines surrounded the Allied compound.

Halfway through his rounds, Cavaiani detected movement to his front. "Get down," he yelled to his companion.

A claymore detonated with a mighty roar. The mine's lethal steel balls flew harmlessly by. The battle for Outpost Hickory was on.

For the rest of that fateful day, Cavaiani led the seventy defenders in a spirited fight. While mortar shells crashed down, RPGs flew through the air, and small-arms fire cracked overhead, Cavaiani raced back and forth through the camp. He put people in position, cared for the wounded, distributed ammunition, and manned a variety of weapons.

At one point Cavaiani fired a twin .50-caliber machine gun into the enemy's ranks until an RPG blasted him off the position.

"You could see the RPGs coming in, they were so slow," Cavaiani remembered. "When I'd see one, I'd just slip off the weapon into cover. One time, I miscalculated." The exploding grenade wounded Cavaiani, but he never slowed down. He continued his valiant leadership, inspiring those around him.

By noon Cavaiani knew he could not hold out. He called for evacuation.

Under continual heavy fire, Cavaiani guided the choppers into the camp. Inclement weather hampered the process. By four that afternoon, Cavaiani and fifteen others remained on the ground at Hickory. If they could make it through the night, the helicopters would return in the morning. Cavaiani took advantage of a lull in the fighting to rig booby traps throughout the camp. Then he pulled back to a series of bunkers, conceding half the camp to the enemy.

The NVA came again at 7:00 P.M. They attacked every fifteen minutes for the rest of the night. Cavaiani had placed his men strategically about the area, where they prevented the enemy from gaining any more ground. Cavaiani put himself atop the ammunition bunker. "I figured if it went, I'd go quick."

By 2:00 A.M., Cavaiani knew the situation was hopeless. He gathered the handful of survivors together. "Take off," he told them. "Get away as best you can. I'll cover you."

The others fled into the night. When last seen, Cavaiani was kneeling on the bunker, an M-60 machine gun cradled in his arms. Back and forth he swept it, knocking down dozens of swarming NVA.

When the survivors reached American lines they told the story of Cavaiani's heroism. They also reported his death.

But the rugged farm boy was not dead.

Cavaiani stayed atop the bunker, his fire forcing the enemy to cover. When he stood up to make his own escape, he was shot in the back. Suffering intense pain, he crawled into the dark bunker.

From his hiding place, Cavaiani shot several NVA who came looking for him. Then a grenade bounced in through the sandbagged doorway. The explosion drove dozens of pieces of shrapnel into Cavaiani's body.

Two NVA then entered the bunker. Cavaiani played dead. The enemy soldiers inspected the "corpse," then set the bunker on fire.

Cavaiani remained in the bunker as long as he could. "Soon my hands were blistering and my pant legs were on fire," he said. "I crawled out."

Somehow Cavaiani made it to a nearby bunker and hid himself. He killed one NVA who came snooping around, then played dead again when two more arrived. They ignored his bloody body to loot some abandoned field packs.

When they left, Cavaiani crept out of that bunker and into the jungle. For the next week he struggled eastward through the dense forest. He covered thirty-five miles before he reached Camp Fuller, the nearest fire support base. Since it was before dawn, Cavaiani chose to wait outside the friendly wire. He did not want some nervous sentry to shoot before he could identify himself.

As the sun rose, Cavaiani prepared to get the attention of the guard. "I happened to look on the ground. I was quite startled to see two shadows."

Within hailing distance of safety, Cavaiani was captured. "It was an old man armed with a rifle even older than he was. But it worked," he recalled.

Taken back to Outpost Hickory, Cavaiani learned that half a dozen of his comrades, including his ARVN interpreter, had also been captured. All, including Cavaiani, were sadistically tortured. Six of Cavaiani's vertebrae and as many ribs were broken during the beatings. Two of his Montagnard soldiers were executed in front of him as an example of his pending fate, but Cavaiani never broke.

After several weeks, Cavaiani and the remaining friendly soldiers were sent north. Barely able to walk due to his severe injuries, Cavaiani received no mercy from his guards. When the pain caused him to falter, the NVA just beat him some more.

The ragged group finally reached Vinh, where a train waited to carry them to Hanoi. After the group boarded, Cavaiani's ARVN interpreter was suddenly removed from the railroad car. Just as suddenly he returned. This time, though, he was wearing the uniform of an NVA sublieutenant.

"I was never more shocked in my life," Cavaiani said. "So many things became clear after he revealed his treason. If I could have gotten my hands on him, I'd have killed him. The NVA were smart enough to keep him away."

Twenty months of imprisonment passed before Cavaiani was released in March 1973. The well-deserved Medal of Honor for his gallant stand at Outpost Hickory was presented by President Gerald R. Ford in White House ceremonies on December 12, 1974.

A few months later Cavaiani decided to make the army his career. "If my experiences could help keep one kid alive, it would be worth it," he explained.

Cavaiani continued his successful career and reached the rank of sergeant major before retiring in 1990. He then returned to central California and a farm.

LOREN D. HAGEN

Loren D. Hagen enlisted in the army in June 1968, two months after he had graduated from North Dakota State University in his hometown of Fargo. He believed so sincerely in the U.S. war effort that he volunteered for Special Forces. Two and one-half years of training preceded his transfer to South Vietnam in December 1970.

Like all new members of the Vietnam Training Advisory Group, First Lieutenant Hagen was assigned to a seasoned team before getting his own command. Hagen's training team was led by S.Sgt. Jon Cavaiani.

"I remember Lieutenant Hagen very well," Cavaiani said. "On our very first patrol I knew he had what it takes to be a good team leader. In fact, I recommended he be given his own team sooner than normal. He was that good."

At last light on August 6, 1971, Hagen's fourteen-man team was inserted by helicopter at a long-abandoned fire support base east of Khe Sanh. Their mission was to capture a prisoner so U.S. intelligence experts might learn more about the increased enemy activity in the area. What Hagen did not know was that he had landed in sight of the enemy's newest effort—the laying of a six-inch fuel pipeline across the DMZ and into Quang Tri Province. The local NVA commander could not let this project be discovered.

Throughout that night Hagen and his team members heard sounds that indicated the enemy was planning a major attack on their position. Indeed, over two thousand enemy soldiers had ringed the hill. Just after dawn on August 7, the enemy started up after the team.

In the blink of an eye, thousands of enemy rounds crisscrossed the hilltop. Hand grenades and RPGs fell from the sky in a near-constant barrage. An RPG round slammed into a bunker that housed an American sergeant and several Montagnards. They could not be reached by radio. Hagen had no way of knowing if the men were alive or dead. He had to find out, though. If they were alive, he could not leave them unattended. He told those with him that he was going to check on the damaged bunker. One Montagnard agreed to accompany him.

Hagen must have known the odds of reaching the bunker were against him. With the tremendous amount of enemy fire impacting the area, it would take a miracle to make it across the open ground. But Hagen never hesitated. His men were hurt and he had to help them.

A few minutes later the Montagnard returned alone. "The lieutenant is dead," he announced.

The fight for the hilltop raged into the morning. When it became apparent the team could not hold out, they called for a helicopter extraction. Only under the cover of heavy bombing and strafing by jet fighters were the eight survivors pulled out.

When he accepted his son's Medal of Honor from President Ford on August 8, 1974, Loren H. Hagen said, "While I regret losing my son, I have the satisfaction of knowing he died doing exactly what he wanted to."

Lieutenant Hagen was the last member of the U.S. Army to earn a Medal of Honor in the Vietnam War.

* * *

By the end of 1971 only a handful of American combat troops remained in South Vietnam. Elements of the 101st Airborne and 1st Cavalry Divisions formed the bulk of American maneuver units. These were assigned primarily to the defense of critical areas near major cities. The units witnessed little combat; most experienced only brief skirmishes with enemy forces.

North Vietnam took full advantage of the U.S. withdrawal to press its war in the South. In what became known as the Easter Offensive, six NVA divisions poured into South Vietnam in late March 1972. Without American support and strength, one ARVN unit after another collapsed in front of the enemy. Within six short weeks, Quang Tri Province, most of the Central Highlands region, and the area northwest of Saigon were in NVA hands.

On April 2, 1972 a U.S. Air Force EB-66 electronic jamming plane was shot down south of the DMZ. Only one of the aircraft's six crew members, fifty-three-year-old lieutenant colonel Iceal Hambleton, survived. His parachute brought him down in an area north of Route 9 between Dong Ha and Cam Lo that was swarming with NVA. Hambleton escaped detection and hid in thick foliage near the Mien Gang River.

The ensuing effort to rescue Hambleton, call sign Bat-21, developed into the largest air rescue operation of the entire war. Over the next week, three helicopters and two airplanes were shot down and destroyed while supporting the rescue mission. At least eleven men died and two were captured in the attempt to pick Hambleton from the midst of the NVA forces. One man, air force 1st Lt. Mark Clark, had also survived his own shoot-down and was in hiding less than a mile east of Hambleton.

By April 8 senior authorities had decided it was too costly and too risky to continue the rescue efforts. If Hambleton and Clark were to be saved, it would be up to a little-known department of SOG.

The Joint Personnel Recovery Center was a part of

MACV's J-2 (Intelligence) section. On the surface it analyzed post–search-and-rescue personnel recovery missions. In reality, it was the cover organization for SOG's Recovery Studies Division, which ran covert missions to recover lost personnel. Because of America's withdrawal from South Vietnam, SOG had been ordered to cease all operations as of March 31. The group was to deactivate on April 30, 1972. In the interim, the remaining SOG personnel were transferred to Strategic Technical Advisory Team 158. This was the team that would go after the two Americans.

THOMAS R. NORRIS

Thomas R. Norris enlisted in the navy in September 1967 to be a pilot. The twenty-three-year-old from Silver Spring, Maryland, had a degree in criminology but wanted to fly. He spent a year training at Pensacola, Florida, before his faulty depth perception washed him out of the program.

While Norris waited for reassignment, he happened to read a magazine article about the navy's counterintelligence teams, the SEALs. The training, potential for excitement, and physical challenge all appealed to Norris. His application to the Underwater Demolition School was accepted.

Nearly a year of rugged training followed. In addition to diving school and parachute training, Norris also attended the army's Ranger school, Special Forces officer school, and the Special Forces demolition school.

Norris's schedule called for him to begin language training in January 1970. Instead, he went to South Vietnam because another SEAL team had been badly chewed up; replacements were desperately needed.

After an eight-month tour, Norris came back to the States to attend language school. Then in March 1971, he returned to the war zone.

Norris spent most of his second tour in the Mekong River Delta, where he ran clandestine operations designed to rupture the enemy's supply lines. Then came North Vietnam's Easter Offensive and the loss of Hambleton and Clark. Norris was ordered north.

On the night of April 10, 1972, after being briefed on the situation, Norris and his team of South Vietnamese SEALs moved to the ARVN's forward-most outpost just a few miles from the downed airmen. By radio message, Lieutenant Clark was told to move after dark from his hiding place to the river. He would then float downstream to where Norris and his team waited. Clark did as he was told, but just as he reached Norris's position, an NVA patrol appeared out of the darkness just feet from where the rescuers lay hidden. Norris had to let Clark float by.

When the NVA left, Norris took his team into the water. Cautiously making their way downriver, they finally found an exhausted Clark huddled alongside the riverbank. They retrieved him and brought him back to the ARVN outpost near Cam Lo.

One down and one to go.

The next night Norris and his team headed out for their rendezvous with Hambleton. As the four men stealthily moved deeper into enemy-controlled territory, two of the South Vietnamese balked. They did not want to risk their lives to save an American. Norris sent them back. He and Petty Officer Nguyen Van Kiet continued on. The intrepid pair, disguised as fishermen, boarded an abandoned sampan and paddled upstream.

In the meantime, Hambleton had been told to move to the river. Nearly spent, Hambleton staggered and stumbled to the riverbank, miraculously avoiding the NVA. The air force officer rolled into the water and hid under some brush. There he awaited Norris.

Because a fog bank had developed, Norris and Kiet paddled right past Hambleton's position. They realized their error when they passed under a bridge filled with enemy soldiers and vehicles. Quietly, barely breathing, the two reversed direction and headed downstream.

Less than one-half mile away, Norris spotted Hambleton.

The airman was nearly delirious from hunger and hypothermia. Norris and Kiet pulled Hambleton into their boat, covered him with leaves, and began to paddle away from the riverbank. As they glided along, they were challenged several times by NVA sentries. Norris ignored their shouts.

A short distance farther, another sentry issued a challenge. Norris and Kiet again ignored the soldier. This time the enemy greeted the silence with several bursts from his machine gun. Norris directed the sampan to the opposite bank, where he took cover. From there he called in an air strike on the enemy position. When it was destroyed, Norris and Kiet resumed their journey.

Just after dawn, Norris arrived back at his starting point. Eager hands hurried Hambleton to a waiting medevac helicopter.

For his role in the unprecedented rescue of the two American aviators, Norris was recommended for the Medal of Honor. To the surprise of his superiors, Norris declined to help prepare the paperwork. He did not think his actions warranted the country's highest award. He did support the award of the Navy Cross to Kiet, the only time the navy's highest award was ever granted to a member of a foreign country's military.

Norris returned to his regular assignment and remained in South Vietnam until the end of October.

By early May 1972 the South Vietnamese military had reorganized its forces and was ready to go on the offensive to recover lost territory. On May 12, units of the Vietnamese Marine Corps caught an unsuspecting NVA regiment in a pincer movement south of Quang Tri city. Buoyed by this success, the ARVN commanders launched a major drive to recapture Quang Tri city. On June 8, four ARVN battalions began the attack. Enemy resistance was strong, but the ARVNs fought well and within forty-eight hours were established in Quang Tri Province. By June 28 the South Vietnamese had closed on Quang Tri city and were ready to begin their final push.

Restricted by a war-weary Congress from introducing

ground troops into South Vietnam, the U.S. military was limited to providing logistical support and aerial and naval bombardment. Naval gunfire coordinators traveled with the ARVN ground forces and flew over the battlefield in aircraft based at Da Nang.

STEVEN L. BENNETT

On the afternoon of June 29, 1972, U.S. Air Force *Capt. Steven L. Bennett* was piloting an OV-10 Bronco on a naval gunfire coordination mission in support of the ARVN Marines moving on Quang Tri city. His airborne observer was Marine Capt. Michael Brown. Bennett, a twenty-six-year-old native of Palestine, Texas, had been commissioned in the air force after his graduation from the University of Southwestern Louisiana in 1968. After four years of flight training, B-52 crew school, and forward air controller school, he arrived in South Vietnam in April 1972.

The NVA's Easter Offensive was well under way when Bennett reported in to the 20th Tactical Air Support Squadron at Da Nang. There was little time for any serious indoctrination, so Bennett began to fly missions as a forward air controller almost immediately. He performed exceptionally well. In the next sixty days he earned four Air Medals.

Three hours after Bennett arrived at his assigned area on the afternoon of June 29, he spotted a force of North Vietnamese regulars in a tree line. He called for an air strike, then circled above the enemy's position. When the fighters arrived, Bennett swooped down, marked the target with a smoke rocket, then directed the fighters on their bombing runs.

By the time the fighters had finished, the target area was devastated. Normally Bennett would have flown a damage assessment run over the target, but he picked up an urgent call for help from a nearby friendly unit.

The ARVN unit's American adviser radioed Bennett that they were under attack by a superior enemy force. If they did not get immediate help, they would be overrun.

Bennett called for air support, but was told that no planes were available. Captain Brown tried to get a naval gunfire mission. He was told that the friendly troops were too close to the enemy. No help was available. Even though his aircraft was not designed for a strafing mission, Bennett decided to go in himself and help.

Alone and unaided, Bennett roared down on the enemy force. Four times he strafed the enemy positions. After the last pass he could see that the NVA had begun to withdraw. The gutsy pilot elected to make one final pass. As he pulled up after that run and banked left, a surface-to-air missile flared out of a nearby tree line. The missile came straight at Bennett's low and slow Bronco. It exploded at the left wing, nearly flipping the plane on its back. Bennett used all of his piloting skills to right the aircraft. Shrapnel had peppered the airplane, but fortunately neither Bennett nor Brown was hit. However, the left engine was on fire and the left main landing gear had dropped down, creating additional drag, which made the plane hard to control.

Bennett set a course for the Gulf of Tonkin. He did not want himself or Brown to bail out over land where they might be captured. Fighting a serious yaw to the left, Bennett guided the dying aircraft to the sea.

As Bennett neared the coast, another OV-10 pulled up alongside. That pilot advised Bennett that the engine fire was more serious than Bennett had thought. He advised Bennett to eject immediately. Bennett ordered Brown to prepare to bail out.

Only then did Brown realize that shrapnel had damaged his ejection system. He could not bail out.

Bennett faced a dilemma. There was no way he could keep his damaged plane in the air long enough to reach a friendly air base. His observer could not leave the plane; he could not abandon him. He could not risk turning back to land; he did not think his plane would make it. Even though he knew that no pilot had ever survived a water ditching of a Bronco, Bennett elected to put the plane down at sea. He set up for a water landing.

Bennett brought the plane in low, just skimming above the

waves. Then the hanging left gear caught the water. The
Bronco veered violently left, then began to cartwheel. Once.
Twice. Then it settled in the water. The front cockpit area
was crushed by the impact.

In the rear, however, Brown was able to break out of the
wreckage. He struggled to free Bennett from the twisted
front cockpit but could not. In seconds the plane sank.

A short time later a destroyer rescued Brown. The next day
navy divers recovered Bennett's body.

Bennett's widow Linda and their five-year-old daughter
Angela received his posthumous Medal of Honor from President Gerald R. Ford in White House ceremonies on August
8, 1974. Linda later said of her husband, "His nature required this behavior. He couldn't have lived with himself if
he'd made another choice. He was aware he was going to die
when he did it. Being the kind of person he was, I think he
would have suffered worse if he had [bailed out] and lived."

By the end of August 1972, all U.S. ground forces had departed South Vietnam. The last unit to withdraw was the 7th
Cavalry Regiment's 1st Battalion. It had served just under
seven years in the war zone.

During September 1972, ARVN Airborne and Marine
units recaptured Quang Tri city after weeks of bitter fighting.
Most of the province, though, still remained in enemy hands.
In order to learn more about the NVA's strength there, the
Strategic Technical Directorate routinely sent its men behind
enemy lines. One such mission was planned for Halloween
night. Intelligence headquarters wanted information on a former South Vietnamese naval base located at the mouth of the
Cua Viet River, a few miles south of the DMZ along the coast
of Quang Tri Province. The capture of a prisoner or two
would help a great deal. A five-man joint American–South
Vietnamese commando team prepared for the mission.

MICHAEL E. THORNTON

The assistant U.S. Navy adviser to the three South Vietnamese commandos was twenty-three-year-old engineman second class *Michael E. Thornton*. He had enlisted in the navy in the fall of 1967 after graduating from high school in his hometown of Spartanburg, South Carolina.

After one and one-half years of service aboard destroyers, the ruggedly built Thornton volunteered for SEAL training. Almost immediately upon graduating from that rigorous training, Thornton shipped overseas to South Vietnam. He served there from January 1970 through January 1973.

At dusk on October 31, 1972, Thornton, a navy lieutenant serving as the senior adviser, and three South Vietnamese, set out in a junk for their target. The skipper of the junk assured them that he would insert them about five miles south of the Cua Viet.

Once in the vicinity of the naval base, the commandos boarded rubber boats and rowed toward shore. They reached the beach about 4:00 A.M. After they concealed the boats, the team lay low for several minutes. There was no sign that they had been detected. Using prearranged hand signals, the five men carefully proceeded by foot through the sand dunes toward the base.

Along the way they passed numerous caches of supplies and encampments of enemy soldiers. Thornton could not believe the quantities of matériel and men. He frequently conferred in frantic whispers with the team leader, confirming what he had seen.

After more than an hour of patrolling north, Thornton and the team leader began to realize that something was wrong. They should have already reached the naval base. The two sailors conferred. They concluded that the junk skipper had taken them five miles *north* of the Cua Viet River. By now they were nearly to the Ben Hai River and the DMZ. The team hastily reversed direction.

The five men had almost returned to their starting point when they spotted a two-man NVA patrol. The enemy soldiers appeared to be following the SEAL team's tracks. Thornton and the others scurried to find cover. They all held their breath as the enemy soldiers approached.

At first it seemed as if the commandos might escape detection in the dim light of dawn. The two NVA soldiers had nearly passed by when one of the South Vietnamese panicked. He jumped from cover and called for the NVA to come to him.

Thornton reacted instantly. Because he wanted to avoid any gunfire that would alert the rest of the enemy, he charged the closest NVA and knocked him cold with a butt stroke from his rifle.

The other enemy soldier let loose with a wild burst from his AK-47, threw the weapon aside, then took off running for his life. Thornton and one of the South Vietnamese commandos gave chase, but it was too late. The gunfire had alerted the other NVA. A squad of them came running around a nearby sand dune.

Thornton and his companion hightailed it back to the rest of the team. While they set up a hasty defensive perimeter and engaged the onrushing enemy, the team leader radioed for help.

A fierce firefight raged for the next forty-five minutes as the enemy closed on the team. Despite the valiant effort of the men, the NVA were soon within hand grenade range. One exploding missile wounded Thornton and a South Vietnamese. Another grenade sailed over the top of the dune that protected Thornton. He picked it up and threw it back. It came flying back over the dune. Thornton returned it again. It came back again. This time it blew up behind Thornton, sending razor-sharp pieces of red-hot shrapnel into his back. He moaned in pain but answered the team leader's question with a brisk, "I'm okay."

By this time the situation was desperate. The team leader, in contact with the cruiser *Newport News,* told them to wait five minutes, then obliterate the team's position with 5-inch shells. The team would pull out just before the time limit expired.

Maneuvering carefully, firing their weapons as they

moved, the team pulled back to the last dune before the open beach and the ocean. While Thornton and two South Vietnamese broke for the water, the team leader and the other commando remained behind to provide covering fire. Thornton had nearly entered the surf when a furious exchange of fire broke out behind the dune. Before long the commando raced alone across the beach toward Thornton.

When he reached his waiting team members, the South Vietnamese told Thornton that the lieutenant had been hit in the face and killed. Thornton accepted the news, but did not want to leave the lieutenant's body behind for the enemy to find and use for propaganda purposes. He immediately sprinted back across the beach to the dune.

As Thornton reached the lieutenant, two NVA soldiers came at him. Thornton immediately charged and killed them both in hand-to-hand combat. Then he returned to the lieutenant. To Thornton's amazement, the officer was alive, but just barely. He was drifting in and out of consciousness.

Undaunted by the fire directed at him, Thornton hoisted the limp form across his broad shoulder and ran back across the beach to his comrades. "Come on," he yelled, "we're swimming for it."

The four dashed into the surf as enemy bullets splashed all around them. Thornton inflated his and the wounded officers' life jackets, pushed the casualty ahead of him, then used the breaststroke to swim out to sea. Behind the men, NVA soldiers ran across the sand firing their weapons. One round struck a commando in the leg. He grabbed on to Thornton. With him in tow and pushing the officer in front of him, Thornton used powerful strokes to cross the breakers. By now several NVA had waded out into the water after the escaping men, but the rising and falling waves made it hard for them to take accurate aim.

Then a thundering crash of high-explosive shells from the *Newport News* erupted along the dunes and the beach. The NVA scattered as the 5-inch shells blew huge columns of sand into the air.

Thornton and his teammates swam for more than two hours. Unknown to them, they had been given up for dead by their commanders. A few SEALs, however, refused to accept that. One commandeered the junk that had dropped off the team and ordered it to head toward shore.

At about 11:30 A.M. the swimming SEALs were spotted by teammates on the junk. A short time later all were aboard the *Newport News* receiving medical treatment.

Thornton's Medal of Honor was presented by President Nixon on October 15, 1973. He remained in the navy, served with SEAL Team Six, the navy's Delta Force, was commissioned, saw action during the First Gulf War, and retired as a lieutenant commander.

And what of the navy lieutenant Thornton had rescued? In a remarkable twist of fate, unique in Medal of Honor history, the man Thornton risked his own life to save was Lt. Tom Norris, the SEAL who had rescued the two air force men from behind enemy lines five months earlier.

The gruesome injuries from that night cost Norris his left eye and two years in the hospital to recover from his wounds. He was medically discharged in 1975.

When Norris learned that a Medal of Honor recommendation had been submitted despite his protests, he relented. He was presented his decoration by President Ford on March 4, 1976. He later joined the FBI and worked as an undercover agent for many years before retiring.

Thornton's award was the last one earned by a member of the U.S. Navy and the last one earned overall during the Vietnam War.

On January 27, 1973, the Paris Peace Agreement was signed, ending the war in Vietnam. Two years later a North Vietnamese offensive easily overwhelmed the South. The Republic of Vietnam disappeared as a separate nation on April 30, 1975.

CHAPTER ELEVEN

Troubled Heroes

On the dark, drizzly evening of April 30, 1971, a Detroit, Michigan, liquor store clerk shot and killed a would-be robber. The incident would have been unremarkable, except that the dead man was an active duty army sergeant—and a recipient of the Medal of Honor.

It was a tragic story that shocked America, rocked the Pentagon, and proved how difficult it can be to be a hero of an unpopular war.

DWIGHT H. JOHNSON

When *Dwight H. Johnson* came home from the army in July 1968, he tried to find work. He visited one employment office after another, but it was a futile search. No companies were interested in hiring a black Vietnam veteran from Detroit's worst ghetto.

Until November 19, 1968.

On that day President Johnson presented the twenty-one-year-old with the Medal of Honor for a remarkable display of gallantry in South Vietnam eleven months earlier.

As a tank driver, Johnson had served with the same crew since his arrival in South Vietnam in February 1967. Remarkably, in all that time neither Johnson nor his crew had experienced any enemy action. They considered themselves very lucky. Then, on the night of January 14, 1968, Johnson's platoon commander assigned him to a different M-48 tank. A sick driver prompted the move. Johnson took the change in stride. He already had his orders back to the States. In less than one week he would be back in "the World."

The next morning the four tanks of Company B, 1st Battalion, 69th Armor, 4th Infantry Division, raced down a road toward Dak To in Kontum Province. Without warning, enemy rocket-propelled grenades flashed through the air. Two tanks spun out of control; waves of North Vietnamese soldiers poured out of the nearby jungle.

Johnson watched in horror as his old tank burst into flames. Stan Enders, the gunner in Johnson's new tank and a close friend, remembered, "He was really close to those guys in that tank. He just couldn't sit still and watch it burn with them inside."

Johnson moved to climb out of his tank. Enders grabbed him. "Don't go out there," he told Johnson. "There must be five hundred of them. You're okay if you stay inside. Don't be crazy . . ."

But there was no stopping Johnson. Out of the hatch he went, through the deadly cross fire to his buddies' aid.

Johnson got the first man out, burned but still alive. Johnson had the man on the ground when the tank's artillery shells blew up and killed those left inside.

"When the tank blew and Dwight saw the bodies all burned and black, he sort of cracked up," Enders recalled.

For the next thirty minutes, first with a .45-caliber pistol and later with a submachine gun, Johnson vented his rage on the North Vietnamese. He charged right into the midst of the ambush, guns blazing. When he ran out of ammunition, he beat one enemy soldier to death with the stock of his empty machine gun.

At one point in the fight, an NVA soldier rushed up to Johnson, put his rifle in his face, and pulled the trigger. The weapon misfired. Johnson killed the man with one shot.

Nobody knew for sure how many NVA Johnson killed.

Some said five, others said twenty. What they did know for sure was that Johnson had done rather well for his first time in combat.

"When it was all over," Enders said, "it took three men and three shots of morphine to hold Dwight down. He was raving. He tried to kill the prisoners we had rounded up. They took him to the hospital in Pleiku in a straitjacket."

Johnson lay unconscious for ten hours. Enders saw him in camp the next day. He had been released from the hospital; he was going home. He had only come back to the tent to pick up his gear and say good-bye to his buddies.

Johnson finished his two-year active duty commitment at Fort Carson, Colorado, then returned to the Detroit tenement where he had been born out of wedlock. Johnson had a stepfather, but ten years earlier the Jamaican had been deported as an illegal alien.

Raised by a strict mother in the dreary projects, Johnson had been a good kid. An altar boy and Explorer Scout, he avoided the street gangs, did not hang out on the corner, did not do drugs, and did not get into trouble. He graduated from high school in June 1965 and was drafted the following year.

When Johnson returned home from the war, his friends noticed very little difference in him. Some thought he "was a little quiet," others said he seemed "jumpy and nervous," but to most he was the same Dwight Johnson they had known before.

Then began the seemingly endless search for a job. A friend remembered, "We went lots of places looking for work, but it was no use." At the time, Detroit's unemployment rate stood at 13 percent. Among young blacks it was at least twice that.

Johnson almost secured a job with the post office, but it never came through. He made the rounds of dozens of small factories, but the answer was always the same: No work.

Johnson's friend recalled, "Dwight took the test to be a lineman for the phone company. They told him he had passed but they never called him. He later found out three white guys had been hired ahead of him."

Then came the medal.

Companies that could not find work for Dwight Johnson, unemployed black Vietnam veteran, suddenly found plenty of room for Dwight Johnson, Medal of Honor hero.

The irony did not escape Johnson.

Among those who wanted Johnson on their payroll was the U.S. Army. The army's motives were just as obvious. Having a black war hero as a recruiter in a largely black city had its advantages.

Johnson elected to return to the army. The camaraderie and fellowship he had enjoyed during his two years of service remained as fond memories.

As soon as he put his uniform back on, Johnson became a hot property. He spent very little time as a recruiter. Most of the time he was in a public relations role. He attended dozens of lunches and dinners for civic organizations. Johnson lived a frantic schedule.

A friend who knew Johnson observed, "He didn't know how to handle all the attention he got. Events half a world away had propelled him into an alien culture. He was forced to play a role for which he had no training."

To add to Johnson's worries, he found that his army paycheck barely covered his expenses. He and his wife Katrina, whom he had married in January 1969, had trouble making the payments on their modest house.

In the spring of 1970, Johnson wrote a bad check for less than fifty dollars. One of Detroit's black leaders made it good. The man did not want any adverse publicity for Detroit's black hero. Unfortunately, it would not be the last bad check.

Guilt over the events in South Vietnam—over his survival—also bothered Johnson. He could not understand why he had been ordered to switch tanks. He was haunted by the image of that AK-47 barrel pointed right at his face. He could still hear the *click* of the misfire. Why had fate spared him? This question-with-no-answer plagued him.

Johnson began to stay away from his job as a recruiter, missed appointments, and did not show up for several speaking engagements. He complained of stomach pains. In the summer of 1970 the army sent him to the hospital at Selfridge Air Force Base near Detroit for treatment. From there he went to Valley Forge Hospital in Pennsylvania.

At Valley Forge the doctors found no physical basis for Johnson's ailment. He agreed to a psychiatric evaluation. In the meantime he received a thirty-day convalescent leave— until October 16, 1970. Johnson did not return on time. He stayed absent without leave until January 21, 1971, when he voluntarily returned to Valley Forge.

While AWOL, Johnson spent time with his wife, pregnant with their second child, and with the kids at his old grade school. To those youngsters, Johnson was something special. He had made it. They were proud of him and his medal.

To Johnson, the children posed no threats. They made no promises that could not be kept. They placed no demands on him as a war hero. To them he was just Dwight Johnson.

Back at Valley Forge, Johnson began his psychiatric analysis. For the first time he revealed his anxieties. He talked of how inadequate he felt; how guilty he was over his survival; he expressed doubts about his decision to reenter the army. He felt the military had lied to him about the role they had for him.

Johnson said he felt exploited by the army. He told of how upset he had been when one of his talks at a black Detroit high school had been picketed by protesters who called him an "electronic nigger," a machine that the army used to enlist blacks to fight in Vietnam. His whole role in the army confused him.

On March 28, 1971 the hospital gave Johnson a three-day pass. He never returned.

By April, Johnson's mortgage payments were nine months in arrears and foreclosure proceedings had begun. His car needed seventy dollars in repairs; Johnson could not afford them. On April 28, Katrina entered the hospital for minor surgery. Johnson promised the admitting clerk he would pay the twenty-five-dollar processing fee the next day.

On April 30, Johnson took his eighteen-month-old son to see Katrina in the hospital. She told Dwight that the hospital was pressuring her for the twenty-five dollars. He left, promising to be back with the money that evening.

At nine that night Johnson telephoned a friend. He needed a ride to pick up some money from another friend, Johnson said. Would he drive Johnson to meet the man?

Just after 11:00 P.M. the friend and two others picked Johnson up. He directed them to an unfamiliar white neighborhood.

"Stop here," Johnson told them. "This guy lives down the street and I don't want him to see me coming."

Twenty minutes later Johnson lay dying on the floor of the liquor store.

According to the clerk, Johnson entered the store and asked for a pack of cigarettes. When he opened the register for change, Johnson pushed him aside, a gun in his hand.

The two men fought. Johnson fired. A bullet lodged in the clerk's shoulder. The clerk grabbed his own revolver. He shot Johnson twice.

"But he just stood there," the clerk later told reporters, "with the gun in his hand and said, 'I'm going to kill you!' I kept pulling the trigger until my gun was empty."

At the funeral at Arlington National Cemetery, Katrina Johnson said, "They kept pushing him to be some kind of a monument. And they never let up. They never came near him to help. They just wanted a hero to sit at the head table."

While drug abuse proved to be a serious problem for many men assigned to South Vietnam, especially after 1968, far more turned to alcohol to block the moral and political dilemmas of the war. The military had always had a lax attitude toward liquor. The Vietnam War was no different. Clubs for enlisted men, NCOs, and officers could be found on every base in the war zone. Escape from the war was never more than a quick walk from one's quarters.

RAYMOND M. CLAUSEN

When *Raymond M. "Mike" Clausen* returned to South Vietnam for a second tour in November 1969, he no longer entertained any illusions about the U.S. war effort. When he first went overseas in late 1967, he had believed in his country's commitment to aid the South Vietnamese in their struggle against communism. Eighteen months in-country had changed his mind.

In spite of his misgivings, though, Clausen volunteered to return. No patriotic motivations stood behind his decision. "There was a whole lot less bullshit in Vietnam than there was in the States," he said.

Raised in Hammond, Louisiana, Clausen left Southeastern Louisiana University in March 1966 to enlist in the Marine Corps "to help win the war."

Training as a helicopter mechanic came first. It was not until December 1967 that Clausen finally was posted to South Vietnam. He spent eighteen months with Marine Air Group 16 before returning to the States in August 1969.

Clausen's disillusionment began late in his first tour—after Vietnamization had begun. Clausen was torn by ambivalent feelings. He could not see any purpose to America's involvement if there was not going to be an all-out effort to win. At the same time, he felt his role as a helicopter crew chief was important.

After becoming a senior crew chief, Clausen could handpick his missions. Invariably he chose medevac missions; if there were wounded men involved, Clausen wanted to help. He did not want to hurt anyone anymore, only help them.

Clausen battled his inner turmoil with alcohol. He drank heavily and earned several captain's masts (nonjudicial punishment) and a summary court-martial as a result. He spent more time as a buck private than in any other rank.

Even after he rotated back to the States the first time, he continued to drink. He quickly found the Stateside Marine Corps much less tolerant of his behavior. The "spit-and-polish" Marine Corps was not for him. After three months of Stateside duty, he put in for a transfer.

Fortune placed Clausen back in the same squadron with which he had served during his first tour. He was back in familiar territory at the Marine Air facility at Marble Mountain, outside Da Nang.

Clausen still drank to mask his frustrations, but at least he felt he could help people.

. That is why Clausen volunteered on January 31, 1970 to rescue a platoon of Marines trapped in a minefield outside Da Nang. While in pursuit of a small NVA force, the twenty Marines had stumbled into an abandoned American minefield. One Marine was dead, eleven were wounded, and the others were too scared to move. Only a chopper could save them.

Clausen jumped aboard a CH-47 twin-rotor helicopter piloted by Lt. Col. Walter Leadbetter. A few minutes later they were hovering above the trapped men.

By leaning out of the aircraft's open door, Clausen could spot areas in the tall grass where mines had already detonated. Assuming that such areas were safe, Clausen directed Leadbetter to a landing. "Put her down there," Clausen told the colonel. A miscalculation of a few inches could spell disaster. The chopper landed safely.

Clausen disregarded Leadbetter's command to remain on the chopper. He leaped out the door, intent on rescuing the wounded. Clausen ignored the danger from the hidden mines and walked carefully to a casualty, picked him up, then carried him back to the chopper. Nearby Marines followed Clausen's footprints to the helicopter.

After Clausen got all of the Marines in one area safely aboard, he directed the CH-47 to another site. Again he calmly walked into the minefield to retrieve wounded men. Even when a mine exploded nearby, killing one and wounding three others, Clausen never hesitated on his mission of mercy. He simply guided Leadbetter to the site of the explosion, loaded up the three wounded, then pulled aboard the dead man.

In all Clausen made six trips into the hazardous minefield and saved eighteen men. Colonel Leadbetter recognized Clausen's courage by recommending him for the Medal of Honor.

Clausen had eight months remaining on his tour at the time of his daring rescue. They were not easy months. The heavy drinking continued and brought repeated clashes with his superiors.

Shortly after Colonel Leadbetter left the unit, Clausen's new CO ordered him to fly a particular mission. Clausen refused. It was not a rescue mission, so he did not want to go. The CO prepared court-martial charges against Clausen, but Colonel Leadbetter intervened. Clausen received another captain's mast and was busted back to private. He stayed a private through his discharge in August 1970. He was the only buck private to earn the Medal of Honor in the Vietnam War.

Civilian life did not bring an end to Clausen's problems. Still unable to reconcile his confusion over his role in the war, Clausen kept up his heavy drinking. As a result, he found it hard to hold a job. A severe automobile accident nearly cost him his life; he lay unconscious for two months. The recuperation period delayed the Medal of Honor presentation ceremony until June 15, 1971.

Holding the Medal of Honor did not make life any easier for Clausen. If anything, his mental turmoil increased. Now he not only had to deal with problems related to his war experience, he also had to try to live up to other people's expectations. It was nearly more than he could handle.

"I could not find a reason for my existence," Clausen explained. "I was confused about my role in life."

Then in 1984, Clausen's life changed. "I was watching TV late one night, drunk as usual," he recalled. "Because there wasn't anything else on, I tuned in a religious program. What I heard made me sit up. For the first time in years things made sense."

Clausen bought a Bible the next day. He read it thoroughly.

A few weeks later he joined a church. The Bible gave Clausen a completely new perspective on his life.

Although the road was not smooth after his conversion, Clausen said, "Studying the Bible helped me understand myself. I've found answers to a lot of questions that had been bothering me. My life is now devoted to God."

Eventually, chronic liver problems cost Clausen his life. He died on May 30, 2004 while awaiting a liver transplant.

Morale and discipline problems abounded in the latter years of America's involvement in South Vietnam. Not only had antiwar sentiments spread to the war zone, but the advent of Vietnamization made it difficult to motivate the troops. In several well-publicized cases, combat troops refused to carry out their leaders' orders.

Some soldiers expressed their dissatisfaction with gung-ho superiors by "fragging" them. With this technique, an anonymous hand grenade would be tossed into a hated officer's or NCO's quarters. If the explosion did not kill or wound the target, at least the message was clear.

Besides the more violent, overt actions against the war, instances of racial violence, black market activities, and crime soared. The lessening of combat resulted in considerable free time for frontline troops. To combat the boredom, more and more men turned to drugs.

In 1965 less than fifty cases of drug abuse were reported by the army. In 1970 over *eleven thousand* soldiers were apprehended on drug-related charges. By 1971, drug use had reached epidemic proportions. MACV implemented a "drug abuse counteroffensive" to fight the problem.

President Nixon announced in early June 1971 that his new antidrug campaign would include the identification of heroin users in Vietnam. Henceforth, troops departing the war zone would be required to submit to urinalysis. Those identified as drug users would be placed in drug treatment centers before they rotated home.

On June 15, 1971, Nixon presented Medals of Honor to

several Vietnam War heroes; among them were *Peter C. Lemon* of Tawas City, Michigan, and *Richard A. Penry* of Petaluma, California. Nixon's remarks at the ceremony heralded the young men as "champions of democracy" who saw their duty and did it "above and beyond the call of duty." He made a not-too-subtle distinction between the heroes standing before him and the malcontents, dissenters, and deserters who were working against his patriotic policies.

Irony was at work, however, for both Richard Nixon and these two heroes, at that point standing high on a national pedestal, soon fell with a resounding thud. America had erred in believing that its leaders and heroes existed without human frailties.

On June 21, 1971 newspapers across the country reported that Peter Lemon had been "stoned on pot" the night he earned his medal.

PETER C. LEMON

Born in Canada on June 5, 1950, Peter C. Lemon became a U.S. citizen at age twelve. Like many naturalized citizens, Lemon felt strong ties to his new country. When the United States decided to support South Vietnam in its struggle against communism, Lemon did not hesitate to get involved. He enlisted in February 1969 when he was eighteen.

To fully prepare himself for combat, Lemon volunteered for Recondo (reconnaissance/commando) training after he arrived in-country in July 1969. When he completed the grueling course, he joined the 1st Infantry Division's Ranger Company.

Lemon transferred to the Ranger Company of the 1st Cavalry Division (Airmobile) in March 1970 after the 1st Infantry Division went home. Over the next few weeks Lemon became acquainted with the other eighteen men of his platoon on recon patrols conducted deep within enemy territory. The teams crossed into Cambodia several times in their search for the enemy.

Early on the morning of April 1, Lemon returned from a patrol to his base camp at Fire Support Base Illingsworth. This FSB was one of five ringing the city of Tay Ninh, fifty miles northwest of Saigon. During the previous few weeks several of the other FSBs had been attacked by the NVA.

"We knew our turn was coming," Lemon said. "Our recon patrols had seen too many signs of the NVA around the base. Everybody was on alert."

The NVA came that night. Between 300 and 400 hard-core enemy soldiers hit FSB Illingsworth. Lemon took up a defensive position along the perimeter's berm and fired into the enemy hordes pouring out of the nearby jungle. Soon after the attack began, Lemon's commanding officer, Lt. Greg Peters, ordered him and another soldier to man an abandoned .50-caliber machine gun.

"We couldn't get the darn machine gun to work," Lemon recalled. "We tried desperately for at least five or ten minutes to open fire on the enemy. Then a mortar shell went off by us, wounding me and totally destroying my buddy."

Badly shaken, Lemon went back to his bunker. From an open container he scooped up grenades and threw them as rapidly as he could into the ranks of the swarming NVA. When another buddy went down, Lemon carried him through the enemy fire to the aid station. He was wounded again while returning to his bunker.

Undeterred, Lemon ignored the pain to continue to battle the attackers. When an NVA RPG gunner sent repeated accurate rounds into the perimeter, Lemon crawled atop his exposed bunker to spot the weapon. He knocked it out with a well-aimed burst from an M-60 machine gun.

After an hour of heavy fighting, the enemy attack abated. Lemon, bleeding from wounds in the head, neck, leg, and arm, moved to a fortified bunker where he discovered a wounded ARVN soldier he knew. For some reason the man's wounds had not been tended. Lemon comforted the man, and then, when the medics arrived, refused aid for his own serious wounds until his friend was treated.

"I didn't think I was hit that badly, and here was this

ARVN bleeding to death. I told the medics to take care of him first," Lemon said.

Lemon himself was evacuated later that night. He spent a month in the hospital before being reassigned to a support unit. On December 4, 1970 he was honorably discharged.

Lemon returned to his parents' home, where he spent long hours wandering the nearby woods, deep in thought about his war service, trying to overcome his feelings of survivor's guilt. He had lost many friends in the war, including three good buddies that night at Illingsworth. His grief was nearly overwhelming.

When word of the Medal of Honor came, Lemon thought about refusing it. "I didn't think what I'd done was out of the ordinary. But I guess you can't split the medal up among twelve guys. That's who it really belonged to."

A week after the presentation ceremony, reporters from the *Detroit Free Press* interviewed the new hero.

"It was the only time I ever went into combat stoned," they quoted Lemon as telling them. "We were all partying the night before. We weren't expecting any action because we were in a support group.

"All the guys were heads. We'd sit around smoking grass and getting stoned and talking about when we'd get to go home."

The newspaper article shocked America.

Lemon says that the reporters took his comments out of context. According to him, he was misquoted.

"I was a young kid, just back from Washington where I'd met the president," Lemon said. "I was a little cocky, a little overconfident, when these two hotshot reporters from the *Free Press,* long-haired hippie types, interviewed me. We talked about drug use in Vietnam, but I never said I used drugs in combat, because I didn't."

Even though the story received national exposure, vilifying Lemon, he never bothered to dispute it. He did not think his protests would be heard. "What would they do?" he asked rhetorically. "Put a retraction on page thirty?"

The newfound notoriety coupled with his anxieties over his role in the war were more than Lemon could handle. He left his family in Michigan and set out for Colorado. In the tranquility of the Rocky Mountains he hoped to reconcile his tortured emotions about the war.

"I had deep guilt feelings over the loss of my friends. I wasn't sure if I had done enough to keep them alive."

Lemon dropped out of society for the next five years. He found anonymity working as a carpenter on construction projects throughout Colorado, an anonymity that allowed him to deal with his confused feelings. Eventually he came to terms with his guilt. He became determined to get on with his life.

In 1976, Lemon used his GI Bill benefits to enroll in college. In the next four years he earned not only his bachelor's degree, but a master of science in business as well. He then started a successful specialized insurance brokerage firm that he headed for four years before selling out. He then opened another agency.

Today Lemon enjoys a level of success that eludes most men. He has authored a book offering the reflections of a number of other Medal of Honor recipients. He has taken a major role in developing an Internet site devoted to the Medal of Honor and its recipients. Yet, the fight at Illingsworth continues to bother him.

"There isn't a day goes by," he said, "that I don't think about that night and getting the Medal of Honor."

The medal reminds him of a past he would like to forget.

"I'd trade the medal in an instant if it would bring back my three buddies who were killed that night," he said.

RICHARD A. PENRY

When twenty-one-year-old "Butch" Penry came home from South Vietnam in August 1970 he told his mother, "I'm not running anymore, Mom. From now on, all I'm going to do is walk."

It was years before Mrs. Penry understood what her son meant.

Born and raised in Petaluma, California, Richard A. "Butch" Penry went to work as a dishwasher in a local restaurant after graduating from high school in 1966. He had worked his way up to chef when he was drafted in March 1969. Six months later he went to South Vietnam as an infantry replacement for Company C, 4th Battalion, 12th Regiment, 199th Light Infantry Brigade.

In Binh Thuy Province, sixty miles northeast of Saigon, on the night of January 31, 1970, Penry's platoon worked silently to set up a night ambush. In the waning daylight the NVA launched an ambush of their own. The opening fusillade of mortars, rockets, and automatic weapons fire seriously wounded the company commander and dozens of others. Small pockets of wounded Americans lay isolated throughout the site, vulnerable to the enemy.

Penry reacted with incredible courage to the dire situation. He gave first aid to the wounded CO, then moved the command post to a more secure area. After that he made three trips outside the perimeter to retrieve radios. All proved defective.

When thirty NVA charged into a group of wounded men, Penry single-handedly drove them off with machine gun fire and grenades. With that threat over, he went after another radio. At last, he found one that worked. With it he called for medevac choppers.

Word reached Penry that five wounded men lay isolated close to an enemy bunker. He ignored the threat of death and crawled through the gunfire to them. He administered first aid, then led them all back to safety.

In the inky blackness Penry had to use a strobe light to guide the helicopters into the LZ. As one of the few men left unwounded, he personally carried eighteen casualties to the helicopter. After all the wounded were evacuated, Penry joined the relief platoon and led them in pursuit of the enemy.

It was quite a night for the husky soldier.

After he received his Medal of Honor, Penry talked about the war and what he had seen. "In Vietnam," he said, "you have no way of knowing who the enemy is. A fellow will sell you a soft drink in the daytime and while doing so be your friend. The same fellow will try to kill you the same night."

On the matter of drugs in South Vietnam, Penry spoke candidly. "Marijuana grows there like trees grow in the United States. When one runs out of tobacco, he can pick a twig and smoke it, and if he has to pay for it the price is really cheap. Many American soldiers were smoking marijuana. When caught, these soldiers were either restricted or lost some of their pay. The army used more drastic methods against those caught with any hard stuff."

So did the civilian police in the United States, as Penry learned.

Late on the morning of October 4, 1973, Richard Penry was arrested by Petaluma police and the Sonoma County Sheriff's Office on charges of selling cocaine to an undercover officer. The crimes occurred on September 21 and 24, 1973, when Penry allegedly sold a total of $950 worth of cocaine to the narcotics agent.

"With that amount," said one officer, "a guy has to be considered a distributor—in effect, one who sells the stuff to 'retailers,' who in turn sell to users."

Penry's mother disagreed. "If he didn't have the Medal of Honor, they wouldn't have arrested him," she said at the time. "They just want to get their names in the paper for arresting a war hero."

Penry's attorney agreed. Robert Mackey stated in a motion seeking dismissal of the case that Penry had been "entrapped into committing an offense."

In the end Mackey's argument made no difference. Penry pleaded guilty. He was sentenced to three years' probation. He violated the terms of his probation and spent seven months in jail. In 1984 he was arrested again on drug and weapons charges. In 1986 he was put on probation for possession of an AK-47 assault rifle.

Penry dropped out of society about that time. He left his wife and son and moved into a cabin behind an elderly woman's house. He maintained the property in exchange for rent. He worked sporadically as a tile-setter. Most of the time, though, he lived off of his monthly Medal of Honor stipend.

Penry generally shunned the press but did grant an occasional interview. In 1986 he explained his heroics with a casual, "It was either that or die." But he admitted that January 31 was a fearful night. "I was scared so bad. I talked to God and everything," he said.

About the Medal of Honor, Penry commented, "I feel proud I got it. But realistically it don't mean shit."

Soon after Penry's discharge from the army, he was diagnosed with the chronic skin disorder lupus. Complications from that disease caused his death on May 5, 1994.

For many young men who wished to avoid military service during the Vietnam War years, Canada loomed as a safe haven. Because Canadian-American treaties did not allow for the extradition of war protestors, escape to Canada offered an easy alternative to those who did not want to serve their country.

Thousands of draft-age men fled to Canada, particularly during the later years of the war. Most draft evaders remained in Canada, enjoying their lives, until President Carter offered them a general pardon in 1976.

A handful of those who evaded the draft later regretted their decision. They returned to the United States to face the consequences of their actions. Most ended up serving in the military. Some went to South Vietnam. At least one found the decision to return to his homeland the beginning of a personal hell.

KENNETH M. KAYS

When *Kenneth M. Kays*'s draft notice arrived at his parents' home in Fairfield, Illinois, the nineteen-year-old took off for Canada. His application for status as a conscientious objector had recently been turned down, leading to the induction notice. He seemed content to sit the war out, to let others do the fighting.

After thirty days Kays had a change of heart.

"I decided to come home and go into the army," Kays recalled. "I thought I could become a medic and help people."

Kays arranged a deal with the authorities: He would report for induction if guaranteed service as a medic. The army agreed. Kays reported for induction on September 24, 1969. After basic training, he went to Fort Sam Houston, Texas, for specialized training as a medic. In the last week of April 1970 he arrived in South Vietnam, where he joined the 101st Airborne Division's 1st Battalion, 506th Infantry.

Two weeks later, as a patient at Fitzsimmons General Hospital in Denver, Colorado, minus the lower half of his left leg, Kays was a candidate for the Medal of Honor.

Fire Support Base Maureen was one of several similar outposts manned by elements of the 101st Airborne in the wild western half of Thua Thien Province. Beginning in early April the NVA had been attacking different FSBs in an attempt to break the pressure on their movements in the nearby A Shau Valley. They hit Maureen on May 1, 1970.

Kays was assigned to Company D that night. He was still getting accustomed to the routines of duty at a fire support base when the 803d NVA Regiment struck. Assault rifle fire, RPGs, and satchel charges killed and wounded a number of infantrymen in the opening moments of the attack.

Kays disregarded the heavy fire and the NVA sappers stealing through the night and left the safety of his bunker to help his wounded comrades. In the darkness he heard something fall alongside him. To his horror he realized it was a satchel charge. Before he could react the device exploded. The blast blew off the lower portion of his left leg.

With a veritable hell raging around him, Kays calmly and expertly affixed a tourniquet to his bloody stump. With that in place, Kays continued to crawl to the wounded. He found one man, patched him up, then dragged him to the aid station.

Rather than have his own wound treated, Kays went back into the carnage to look for more wounded. He ignored his intense pain and moved about the perimeter, treating the injured and using his own body to shield them. At one point he actually crawled outside the perimeter to treat one wounded American and pull him back inside the wire.

After several hours of savage fighting the NVA were beaten back. When the company commander made his rounds of the perimeter, he found Kays crawling to aid yet another casualty. The onetime draft evader refused treatment until all the other wounded men had been evacuated. He finally collapsed from loss of blood and was medevacked out.

The army discharged Kays on December 28, 1970. He returned to Fairfield.

"When he got back from the service," his father said, "he seemed normal enough, but I guess the thought that he had lost part of his leg hadn't hit him. Like, he'd go to dances and run around just as if nothing had happened.

"Then, all of a sudden, about the time he got that medal, he stopped talking to me and his mother. He started raising hell and smoking grass."

Kays was one of nine Vietnam War veterans who received the medal from President Nixon on October 15, 1973. Kays was nonchalant about the whole ceremony, according to his father. "He acted like the whole thing was a joke," Mr. Kays said.

Kays refused to cut his long hair and beard for the presentation. As a result, the army refused to let him wear a uniform.

The reason Kays even went to the ceremony, he later said, was to "look Nixon in the eye." When the president entered the room, Kays alone remained seated. Everyone thought it was because of his leg. But when the president approached him to hang the medal around his neck, Kays stood up. "No one caught on," he said.

Right from the start Kays had trouble handling being a hero. He refused a parade in his hometown. He ran away from the press and hid for three weeks in a cabin in the woods.

"I can't handle being a hero," he said then. "I just don't think I've been that brave. Besides, being a Medal of Honor man doesn't make me any better than anyone else."

On April 4, 1974 the local police arrested Kays for growing marijuana in his parents' greenhouse. On April 23 the court fined him and gave him one year probation. Two weeks later the Fairfield police arrested him again on the same charge.

In an interview given at that time, Kays said, "I believe a man must be true to himself, must do what he thinks is right. But first, he must be free to find himself so that he'll know what is right. Marijuana is a tool in that quest."

Kays refused to participate in a system that obstructed his search.

"They [the authorities] see my adherence to responsibility as irresponsibility," Kays further stated. "All they are is what they've been told. What purpose is served by restricting freedom?"

On May 31, 1974, Kays was arrested by Fairfield police on charges of reckless driving after he made half a dozen loops through the little town at sixty miles an hour, honking his horn. "I was trying to wake the dead," he explained.

One week later, Kays's father had him committed to the Chester Mental Health Center in Chester, Illinois. According to the petition, Kays was "yelling and screaming and was irrational" when the elder Kays visited his son's trailer that morning.

"I'm just concerned about my son's welfare," Mr. Kays told reporters.

On June 10, 1974, Kays voluntarily committed himself to the state mental institution in Anna, Illinois.

Kays could not be held in any of the institutions unless so committed by a court of law. After a few weeks of care, he was released. For the next five years Kays wrestled with what experts call "survivor's guilt," an inability to cope with his own survival while those around him had died.

Mrs. Kays found notes that her son had written to dead comrades—apologizing for not having reached them quickly enough on the battlefield to save them. "Listen,"

Kays said, "that survivor's guilt was worse than any pain I felt from my leg."

In August 1979 the police arrested Kays on charges that he had terrorized two of his neighbors. He yelled at them, chased them to another neighbor's house, then threw a flowerpot through a glass door. He then took the couple's car for a wild ride through the streets of his hometown.

Like most residents of Fairfield, Kays's parents were extremely concerned about his mental health. That is why his father refused to bail him out of jail.

"Why should I?" he asked. "If Kenny gets out, he'll just do the same thing over."

On August 14, 1979 a circuit court judge sent Kays to the Chester Mental Health Center "until such time as he is able to understand the charges brought against him." For the next six years Kays remained in treatment. In 1985 he was released to his father's care.

Those who knew him were glad to see Kays return home. "No one ever wished him ill," said one resident. "We just wanted to see him helped."

For the next few years Kays did well. Then his mother died. Soon afterward so did his father. Without them to care for him, Kays returned to drugs and drinking. He began to hang around with a much younger crowd—the undesirable element from the local high school. They took advantage of Kays's diminished capacity, setting up residence in his parents' house, stealing from him (they even took his Medal of Honor), and encouraging his drug use.

The devils inside Kays's mind continued to plague him. He had several more less-well-publicized run-ins with the authorities. Eventually life became too much for Kays. On November 29, 1991 he was found hanging from a light fixture in the living room of his parents' house, yet another casualty of the Vietnam War.

CHAPTER TWELVE

The Unknown Soldier

Soon after the Vietnam War ended, its veterans began to clamor for an Unknown Soldier of their own to be laid to rest alongside the Unknowns from World War I, World War II, and the Korean War in Arlington National Cemetery. Because the media and Hollywood were already portraying the war and its participants as losers, Vietnam War veterans viewed their war's Unknown as an inspirational symbol that would legitimize and validate their sacrifices.

Sensitive to the issue, Congress in 1973 authorized the selection and burial of a Vietnam War Unknown. But like so many issues relating to this war, the search for an unidentified American serviceman would prove difficult, controversial, and ultimately result in a decision based on lies.

The nature of the war in Vietnam and the advances made in forensic medicine made it extremely difficult to designate a Vietnam Unknown.

Unlike earlier wars, where the battle dead might lie unattended for weeks, medical evacuation teams in South Vietnam were often on the battlefield while the fighting still raged. In addition, because most firefights were limited to units of company size or smaller and were contained in small geographical areas, identification of the dead was relatively easier than before.

In World War II, 75 percent of American casualties were caused by the more destructive forces of artillery shells and mortars; only 10 percent of all casualties were hit by gunfire.

Gunshot wounds, by comparison, accounted for 40 percent of the casualties in South Vietnam, with enemy mortars or artillery responsible for only 21 percent. These factors also helped in identifying casualties.

Technical advances along with detailed military and medical records enabled the medical scientists to identify nearly all of the remains of the war's dead, including those returned after the hostilities had ceased. In those days, before the advent of sophisticated DNA analysis, the Army's Central Identification Laboratory in Honolulu, Hawaii, used a technique known as "photo superimposition" to identify remains. Using this technique, computers would generate likely facial features over a skull so that the image could be compared with photographs of still-missing servicemen.

The emotional stress on those whose loved ones were still unaccounted for in Southeast Asia also played a role in delaying the designation of a Vietnam Unknown. The National League of POW-MIA Families opposed the entombment of an Unknown because they feared it meant an end to the efforts to locate their family member. A spokesperson for that organization presciently told a reporter, "The major problem is that they could be interring somebody who might eventually be identified."

But in the late 1970s, Vietnam veterans increased the pressure on Congress to expedite the designation of an Unknown. The veterans saw the delay as further evidence of the country's rejection of their service and sacrifices. Support for their cause even came from the American Legion, which also began to push the issue.

But the government would not be hurried. In response to critics, the Carter White House said, "We have resisted congressional and veterans groups pressure to rush the process, thus ensuring integrity for the families. The burial will be an act of national unity that will spark greater public awareness that the Vietnam War is not behind us . . ."

By 1982 only four sets of unidentified remains were held at the army laboratory. While this was an obvious relief for the families of the missing, it also posed a further dilemma for those campaigning for an Unknown. There was a strong possibility that the remains would eventually be identified.

That's exactly what happened to two of them.

Then, the third set was thought to "possibly not be American," according to the army. Chances were good that the body was that of a Southeast Asian.

That left one set of remains. An army spokesman said, "Information we have on this individual does not match anything we've got."

Though it happened by default, an Unknown from the Vietnam War finally existed.

To preserve the casualty's anonymity, the army ordered that all of the records pertaining to the case be destroyed. Personnel at the Hawaii laboratory were told to not discuss any aspect of the investigation. The army said, "He's an American. We know he died in the conflict, but we just don't know who it is. We used every trick, but we cannot match him to any known missing soldier. We think we can say that this is a true Unknown Soldier from the Vietnam War."

Official designation of the remains took place on May 17, 1984. In a dockside ceremony at the Pearl Harbor Naval Base, Marine Corps Sgt. Maj. Allan J. Kellogg, who had earned a Medal of Honor in South Vietnam in 1970 by throwing himself on an enemy hand grenade, placed a wreath at the foot of the casket.

Pallbearers then placed the casket aboard the USS *Brewton* to commence the long journey to Washington, DC. Once there, the casket lay in state in the Capitol Building's Rotunda. Over the next few days, thousands of people filed past the casket to pay their respects to America's latest hero.

At noon on Memorial Day, May 28, a military funeral procession carried the casket to Arlington National Cemetery.

In the cemetery's amphitheater, hundreds of invited guests,

including over one hundred Medal of Honor recipients from all wars, joined tens of thousands of spectators in viewing the ceremonies on national television. The honorary pall-bearers were Vietnam War medal recipients from each military branch: Walter J. Marm and Jon R. Cavaiani, U.S. Army; Jay Vargas and Allan J. Kellogg, U.S. Marine Corps; James E. Williams and Michael E. Thornton, U.S. Navy; and George E. Day and James P. Fleming, U.S. Air Force. President Ronald Reagan gave an emotionally charged speech during the somber funeral services.

"Today we pause to embrace him and all who served so well in a war whose end offered no parades, no flags, and so little thanks. About him we may well wonder as others have: As a child, did he play on some street in a great American city? Did he work beside his father on a farm in America's heartland? Did he marry? Did he have children? Did he look expectantly to return to a bride?

"We will never know the answers to those questions about his life. We do know, though, why he died. He saw the horrors of war but bravely faced them, certain his own cause and his country's cause was a noble one, that he was fighting for free men everywhere."

President Reagan then assured the families of the MIAs that the quest for their loved ones was not over. "We write no last chapters," he said. "We close no books. We put away no final memories."

The president then presented the Medal of Honor by stating that America should "debate the lessons learned at some other time: Today we simply say with pride, 'Thank you, dear son. May God cradle you in His loving arms.' We present to you our nation's highest award, the Medal of Honor, for service above and beyond the call of duty in action with the enemy during the Vietnam Era."

And there the matter rested for thirteen years. Then, in 1997, acting on rumors that had floated around since 1984, CBS TV news reporter Vince Gonzales began an investigation of the Vietnam War Unknown. What he found was shocking.

Gonzales uncovered a memo written in 1984 by the head of the army's Hawaii lab in which the man admitted he had been pressured to destroy all evidence relating to the identification of the remains and redesignate them as unidentifiable. The remains that comprised the Unknown, six bone fragments, were long believed to be those of air force *1st Lt. Michael J. Blassie.* The twenty-four-year-old St. Louis, Missouri, native had been killed in May 1972 when his A-37 attack plane was shot down near An Loc, about sixty miles north of Saigon, during North Vietnam's spring offensive.

Fierce fighting in the area prevented a recovery team from reaching the crash site for five months. What the team found then included a pilot's flight suit, Blassie's military ID card, a handful of bones, one thousand dollars in South Vietnamese currency, and a number of miscellaneous items. The team bagged the remains and sent everything to the mortuary in Saigon. Somewhere in between, the currency and ID card disappeared. The three Americans who had been at the scene signed affidavits that the ID had been Blassie's.

However, military policy kept that information from Blassie's family. Without dental records or fingerprint identification, the military would not reveal the identity of a body to the family. As far as the Blassies were concerned, Michael was "killed in action, body not recovered."

But, to those at the Hawaii lab, the remains continued to be classified as "believed to be" Blassie's.

The remains were held by the laboratory for eight years. During that time the pressure mounted to designate a Vietnam War Unknown. Then in 1980, an army review board suddenly declared that the bone fragments long thought to be Blassie's were not his. The bones were redesignated "X-26." All documents relating to the lab's efforts to confirm that the bones were Blassie's were ordered destroyed.

Just like that, the country had a Vietnam War Unknown.

As a result of Gonzales's investigation, Blassie's family, spearheaded by Michael's sister Patricia, urged the Pentagon to exhume the Vietnam War Unknown and conduct DNA testing. Although Defense Secretary William Cohen initially expressed reluctance to "disturb this hallowed ground," he finally agreed to the exhumation.

On May 14, 1998, the crypt of the Vietnam War Unknown was opened. The Central Identification Laboratory ran tests that utilized a new technology called mitochondrial DNA. On June 30, 1998 the expected announcement was made: the bone fragments were indeed Michael J. Blassie's. The family accepted the remains for reinterment in St. Louis.

Then, just when it seemed the matter was being put to rest, the Blassie family startled the government and the public when they demanded that the Medal of Honor that had been presented to the Unknown be given to them.

"I understand the medal is symbolic," said Patricia, "but it was Michael who served as that symbol for fourteen years and it should stay with him."

Undersecretary of Defense Rudy de Leon told the family on August 20, 1998 that the medal would not be transferred to them. The medal, de Leon told them, had indeed been a symbolic award to all service members who had lost their lives in the conflict and had not been given to any specific individual. The medal would remain in the museum adjacent to the Unknowns' Tomb.

Although disappointed, the Blassie family accepted the decision.

On June 17, 1999, Secretary Cohen announced that no remains of an American serviceman would be placed in the crypt at Arlington unless "it can be unequivocally assured, in perpetuity, that the remains . . . would be forever unidentifiable." Forensic experts at the Army Central Identification Laboratory said they had no remains that would meet that standard.

Secretary Cohen, after consulting with Vietnam War veterans groups, families of those listed as missing in action, and members of Congress, rededicated the empty crypt on September 17, 1999. An inscription on the tomb reads: HON-ORING AND KEEPING FAITH WITH AMERICA'S MISSING SER-VICEMEN, 1958–1975.

CHAPTER THIRTEEN

Final Heroes

President Ronald Reagan stepped to the podium in front of several hundred people gathered in the Pentagon's inner courtyard. It was February 21, 1981. Speaking solemnly, the president said, "Several years ago we brought home a group of Americans who obeyed their country's call and fought as bravely and well as any Americans in history.

"They came home without a victory not because they had been defeated but because they had been denied permission to win."

President Reagan then called forward a forty-five-year-old retired Green Beret. In the terse words of the official citation, President Reagan told of the nearly overlooked heroism of the stocky Texan—thirteen years earlier.

ROY P. BENAVIDEZ

As *S.Sgt. Roy P. Benavidez* passed the command shack on his way back from Mass at the Special Forces encampment at Loc Ninh, seventy-five miles north of Saigon on the Cambodian border, on May 2, 1968, he heard yelling over the radio. In the background was noise he later described as a "popcorn machine gone wild."

Three Green Berets—SFC Leroy Wright, S.Sgt. Floyd Mousseau, and Sp4. Brian T. O'Connor—and nine Montagnards were on a secret mission about twenty-five miles west of Loc Ninh, ten miles inside Cambodia. They had walked into a clearing and suddenly found themselves face-to-face with an NVA patrol. Although the Americans and Montagnards were dressed in North Vietnamese Army uniforms, the disguises did not work. The NVA opened fire. Their rifle fire was soon followed by mortar shells and grenades.

Wright, who carried secret documents, died in the initial exchange of fire. All the others fell to the ground, wounded. Still, they sent out a blistering hail of their own fire that momentarily stopped the NVA. At Loc Ninh, Benavidez heard O'Connor's frantic calls for help over the radio.

Benavidez knew that immediate action had to be taken. Quickly, he ran to the airfield. There he encountered WO Larry McKibben, a chopper pilot. Benavidez explained the situation. "Let's go," McKibben said.

"McKibben was in a unit nicknamed 'the Greyhounds,'" Benavidez later said. "All of their pilots had vowed never to leave a Special Forces member behind. They knew what we were up against."

McKibben took off. First he stopped to rescue the crew of a gunship that had been shot down near the isolated patrol. McKibben's Huey took several hits during this rescue mission. He flew back to Loc Ninh, dropped off the crew, had some quick repairs made to his Huey, then headed back into Cambodia.

The enemy fire was so heavy, McKibben could get no closer than fifty yards to the stranded team. He hovered there inches above the ground.

"I made the sign of the cross, then jumped out," Benavidez recalled. "I was running like hell. The men were about one hundred feet away from me when suddenly something blew up behind me. It knocked me down. My right leg was stinging and bleeding, and blood was running down my face.

"I was scared. I shouted, 'Hail Mary full of grace, help me,' and kept running."

Benavidez made it to O'Connor. The spec four was still fighting. Benavidez looked around for a radio—his had been smashed when he was knocked to the ground. O'Connor gave him his. Benavidez instructed McKibben to make strafing runs on the NVA. After three such passes, McKibben brought the Huey in for a landing.

Benavidez lifted Wright's body to his shoulder, then ran through a fusillade of fire. He put the body with its secret documents aboard the helicopter, then helped two of the wounded Montagnards aboard. Determined to rescue the others, Benavidez guided McKibben forward by holding the front of the chopper's strut and using hand signals.

Enemy rounds continued to slam into the chopper's thin aluminum skin. Suddenly an AK-47 round hit Benavidez in the back. He dropped to the ground. An instant later the Huey exploded.

McKibben was dead. The copilot sat stunned, a piece of wood embedded in his head.

"Hell was in session," Benavidez later said. "Sergeant Mousseau's head was half blown off, from his left ear to his left eye. I started dragging the wounded to cover."

Benavidez called for air support. Soon helicopters and jets were crisscrossing the sky and zooming down on the enemy. Their fire kept the enemy at bay.

On the ground, Benavidez organized the survivors into a tight defense. He passed out ammunition, distributed water, and inspired the men to hold on.

After three hours and three unsuccessful rescue attempts, another chopper finally landed. Benavidez got the wounded men aboard. He was on his way to retrieve Wright's body from the wrecked Huey when an NVA soldier, bayonet gleaming at the end of his rifle, charged him. The blade slid into Benavidez's back and right arm.

"He gave me a rifle butt to the jaw and knocked me down," Benavidez said. "I was yelling at O'Connor to shoot, but I had my back to the chopper. The guy got me again in the left arm."

The thickset Green Beret sergeant threw the enemy soldier to the ground. He pulled his own knife and buried it in the man's chest.

Covered with blood from over a dozen wounds, Benavidez pulled Wright's body to the Huey. He had to hold his intestines in with one hand while pulling Wright with the other. Once at the chopper, eager hands pulled the corpse aboard.

As Benavidez threw his leg up to board the chopper, thirty North Vietnamese soldiers burst from the nearby trees. Benavidez grabbed a machine gun from the floor of the chopper, turned, and fired. He killed two enemy soldiers trying to crawl under the Huey and two others charging the cockpit.

So much blood ran down Benavidez's face that he had to shake his head back and forth to keep his eyes clear. The helicopter crew thought he was signaling that he did not want to go. Two of them grabbed Benavidez and forcibly pulled him aboard.

"Me and Mousseau were holding hands on the flight to the hospital. He died on me. I cried like a baby," Benavidez said.

When the Huey landed, a doctor took one look at Benavidez, said he would not make it, and ordered him placed with the dead. With a mouth so badly injured he could not talk, Benavidez communicated the only way he could—he spit in the doctor's face. The medics hustled him into surgery.

The surgeons cut Benavidez open from the middle of his back to the front of his left lung. Almost all of his major organs required repair. Half of his left lung was removed; two pieces of shrapnel were left in his heart. From Saigon, Benavidez went to a hospital in Japan. A few weeks later he was transferred to Fort Sam Houston Hospital. It was like old home week. Benavidez had been sent there previously to recover from wounds he had received on his first tour in South Vietnam.

Born on August 5, 1935 in Cuero, Texas, Benavidez had been orphaned at age eight. He and his brother went to live with an uncle in El Campo, Texas.

Life was hard. For six months each year the youngster

picked crops with the rest of his new family. Benavidez had to leave school after the seventh grade to work full-time. At seventeen he enlisted in the Texas National Guard for the extra money.

A few years later Benavidez realized that the army could be an avenue for improving his life. Through the army he could earn a high school diploma. He enlisted. He served in South Korea and Germany before being accepted into Airborne training.

Benavidez went to South Vietnam in 1964 as an adviser. He had nearly completed his tour when he had a disastrous encounter with a land mine. "I was paralyzed from the waist down. The doctors told me I'd never walk again," he recalled.

Benavidez proved them wrong. He began to exercise by crawling out of bed and pulling himself up the wall. He then just stood there, building up his weakened muscles. He eventually took a few cautious steps. Gradually Benavidez rebuilt his shattered limbs. He walked, slowly and painfully, but he walked. That goal reached, he took up running.

Less than a year after he was told that he would never walk again, the Special Forces accepted Benavidez for training. In April 1968 he returned to South Vietnam, this time wearing a green beret.

For his incredible display of raw courage that bloody day in May 1968, Benavidez's commanding officer, Lt. Col. Ralph Drake, recommended him for the Distinguished Service Cross. It was awarded in September 1968.

Six years later, at Benavidez's urging, Colonel Drake reexamined the events of that frightful May day. He developed more information on the sustained nature of Benavidez's heroism and the fact that his presence at the battle site was completely voluntary. Drake recommended the DSC be upgraded to the Medal of Honor. Unfortunately, the legal time limit for submitting the recommendation had expired. The award could not be processed.

Late in 1974, Congress passed a law extending the time

limit for awards for the Vietnam War. Colonel Drake resubmitted the Medal of Honor paperwork.

The Army Decorations Board acknowledged Benavidez's bravery but could not find the necessary second witness. Without him, they had no choice but to disapprove the award.

But Benavidez would not be dissuaded. He believed that his actions warranted the Medal of Honor. Undaunted by the rejections, he persisted in his quest for the nation's highest award. Twice more the recommendation was submitted. Twice more the board rejected it. The regulations were clear: There had to be two corroborating witnesses.

Then in 1980 the army found the missing eyewitness.

Benavidez had thought that Brian O'Connor was dead. Brian O'Connor thought that Benavidez was dead.

"The last time I saw him, he was floating in his own blood," O'Connor said about Benavidez, when he was found living in the Fiji Islands.

In testimony before the Decorations Board, O'Connor said, "I was ready to die, and I'm sure the other team members realized the futility of continuing on against such odds. It was Benavidez's indomitable spirit and courage that made us hold on for the extra five or ten minutes that dragged into hours."

With O'Connor's statement, the Decorations Board unanimously approved Benavidez's Medal of Honor.

Once he received the Medal of Honor, Benavidez, who had retired in 1976 as a master sergeant, became a champion of Vietnam War veterans. He devoted most of his time to speaking about the war and his medal. He authored three books about his experiences. He wore his medal and his old uniform constantly. He even appeared before Congress to testify in favor of Social Security disability payments. He rarely passed up an opportunity to tell his story.

Roy Benavidez died on November 29, 1998.

The upgrade of Benavidez's Distinguished Service Cross opened the door for other veterans to be considered for the

Medal of Honor. Over the next two decades, dozens of veterans or their former comrades submitted recommendations for the Medal of Honor. Most were rejected for various reasons. However, the actions of six men were considered to be so gallant that Congress waived the regulatory time restrictions to make it possible for the military branches to grant these veterans the Medal of Honor.

In an unplanned testament to the day-to-day heroics of field medical personnel, three of these awards went to those brave men whose battlefield job was to save lives, not take them.

ALFRED V. RASCON

When the 173d Airborne Brigade (Separate) deployed to South Vietnam from Okinawa in May 1965, one of its members was twenty-year-old *Alfred V. Rascon*. A Mexican citizen by birth, Rascon was brought to the United States at a young age by his parents. The family settled in Oxnard, California, where Rascon graduated from high school in June 1963. Deeply committed to his new home country, Rascon enlisted in the army two months later. After basic and medical training, Rascon volunteered for jump school. He joined the 1st Battalion, 503d Infantry (Airborne), on Okinawa in February 1964.

By March 1966, Rascon was a highly experienced combat veteran who had already been wounded in action. On March 16 his unit, the battalion reconnaissance platoon, was moving through the thick jungle north of Saigon on its way to reinforce the brigade's 2d Battalion. That unit had come under heavy enemy fire and had called for help. The 1st Battalion sent its recon platoon to flank the enemy positions. The Viet Cong were waiting.

The opening blast of enemy crew-served weapons, small-arms fire, and grenades felled several members of the point squad. Although ordered to remain with the command group, Rascon could not ignore the frantic calls of the wounded. He dashed forward through the jungle. Heavy enemy fire drove Rascon to cover several times, but he persisted in his mission. He had to reach the wounded.

Rascon suddenly burst from cover and ran to the side of a badly wounded machine gunner, PFC Neil Haffey. With enemy riflemen zeroing in on him and hand grenades exploding all around, Rascon deliberately placed himself between the enemy and Haffey. Shrapnel tore into Rascon's body in several places and a slug ripped into his hip, causing serious injury and severe pain.

Rascon overcame the pain and dragged the much heavier Haffey back to a position of relative safety. After he had patched up Haffey, Rascon heard a second machine gunner call out that he needed ammunition. Rascon pulled several bandoliers off of Haffey, then ran through the enemy fire to give the rounds to the second gunner.

About this time, Rascon realized that Haffey's M-60 still lay outside the lines in the jungle. Determined to keep the weapon from the VC, Rascon made his way forward of the friendly perimeter. He was hit again by shrapnel before reaching the weapon, but retrieved it, several spare barrels, and a number of ammunition bandoliers, and brought them all back into the lines. Soon the rescued weapon's heavy bark was added to the din of the fight.

By this time Rascon was weak from loss of blood and the exertion of the battle, but he did not stop. When he saw that the wounded point grenadier was the target of the VC, he rushed to the man's side. Determined to save him, Rascon lay on top of the casualty and absorbed several more enemy slugs.

After the grenadier was pulled to safety, Rascon repeated his selfless act by shielding the point squad leader from the blasts of several enemy grenades. Even after his battered and bleeding body had absorbed the full force of the explosions, Rascon managed to help the squad leader to cover.

Throughout the rest of the fight, Rascon declined treatment for his many wounds. Although suffering incredible pain, Rascon did not want a shot of morphine to slow him down. When the VC broke contact, he continued to refuse aid and personally directed the evacuation of the other casualties. Only then did the exhausted paratrooper allow himself to be helped to a medevac helicopter.

Rascon was medically evacuated from South Vietnam. A few months later he received a Silver Star, but the accompanying citation did not do justice to the medic's incredible conduct. But Rascon paid little attention to the award. He had a life to live.

Discharged in May 1966, Rascon entered college. In 1967 he became a United States citizen. In August 1968 he graduated from college. Although he had experienced enough war to last most men a lifetime, he still felt an obligation to his new country. Rascon reenlisted, completed Infantry Officer Candidate school, was commissioned a second lieutenant, and went back to South Vietnam.

After completing another full combat tour as an adviser to the ARVN, Rascon continued his army career until 1976, when complications from his 1966 wounds forced him to take an honorable discharge from active duty. However, late in 1976 he was appointed as the U.S. Army's liaison to the Republic of Panama.

Rascon's subsequent career included assignments with the Drug Enforcement Agency, INTERPOL, and the Immigration and Naturalization Service. He later became inspector general of the U.S. Selective Service System.

In 1992, veterans of the 173d Airborne Brigade were surprised to learn that Rascon's actions had not been recognized by an award of the Medal of Honor. Determined to reverse this oversight, Rascon's former comrades began an eight-year campaign. Although they were rebuffed several times, the Sky Soldiers, as they had many times in the war, refused to give up. They kept on collecting statements from witnesses and researching contemporary documents until they had a case so strong that the army could no longer refuse the award.

On February 8, 2000, President William J. Clinton presented the Medal of Honor to Alfred Rascon. The White

House ceremony featured survivors of that long-ago battle as well as Rascon's friends and family members. The president said, "This man gave everything he had, utterly and selflessly."

Rascon, the pale blue ribbon holding the medal draped around his neck, wiped away a tear as he told the president, "The honor is not really mine. It ends up being the honor of those who were with me that day."

In 2002, Rascon accepted a presidential appointment to head the Selective Service System.

Less than two weeks after Rascon's heroic actions, a navy corpsman also ignored several painful wounds in order to continue treating his wounded Marine buddies. A member of Company C, 1st Battalion, 7th Marines, twenty-one-year-old *Robert R. Ingram* had earned a reputation during nine months of combat as a near-fearless man. Unlike some field medical personnel, Ingram carried an M-14. He was not leaving anything to chance.

On March 28, 1966, Ingram's platoon prematurely triggered an enemy ambush while on patrol in Quang Ngai Province. The opening burst of Viet Cong rifle fire was so intense, thirteen of the twenty-three men in the platoon were hit. "How I was not hit in the initial barrage, I have no idea," Ingram said.

For more than three hours, until dusk, Ingram administered lifesaving treatment to the other wounded. Even after he was shot five times, Ingram did not give up. Over and over he risked his life to save others. Not until the enemy pulled back and the medevac helicopters came in did Ingram relinquish his role.

Of the 114 men from Company C on the patrol that day, 44 were wounded and 11 were killed. The count was nearly 12 dead, because when Ingram reached the aid station his vital signs were so low that he was placed in the stack of dead Marines. Not until someone saw him move a few hours later did his medical treatment start. It would be eight months before his hospitalization ended.

Ingram was recommended for the Medal of Honor immediately after the action. Somehow the paperwork was lost at 3d Marine Division headquarters. The recommendation was never acted on. When Ingram's former company commander learned in 1995 that the award was never processed, he set out to make it right. The well-deserved award was finally made on July 10, 1998.

On April 11, 1966, as the grunts of Company C, 1st Battalion, 16th Infantry, 1st Infantry Division, were fighting for their lives in the jungle east of Saigon, and Sgt. James W. Robinson lost his life earning his Medal of Honor, another heroic drama was occurring that would take more than thirty-four years to conclude.

WILLIAM H. PITSENBARGER

William H. Pitsenbarger was known as a daredevil in his hometown of Piqua, Ohio. As a youngster Pitsenbarger was always the one to climb the tallest tree or scurry around the ledges of the highest building in town. The scarier the dare, the more willing he was to accept the challenge. "Nothing scared him," said his father William.

Less than a year after Pitsenbarger graduated from high school in June 1961, he enlisted in the air force. He had earlier tried to gain his parents' permission to join the army, but they declined; he was only seventeen at the time and they wanted him to complete high school.

When Pitsenbarger completed basic training a few months later, he volunteered to enter the program for pararescuemen, known as "PJs." Nearly a year of intense additional training lay ahead of him. First, there was Airborne training at the U.S. Army's Parachute School at Fort Benning, Georgia. That was followed by the U.S. Navy's underwater swimmers' school. After that, Pitsenbarger completed the U.S. Air Force's tough rescue-and-survival medical course. More training came at the combat survival course at Stead Air

Force Base, Nevada. Then came the Tropical Survival
School at Eglin Air Force Base, Florida. All of that was
capped off by graduation from the firefighters course for the
HH-43 helicopter at Albrook Air Force Base in what was
then the Canal Zone in Panama.

Successful completion of all of this difficult training allowed Pitsenbarger to join the ranks of the air force's elite
pararescuemen. His early assignments included duty in Aus-
tralia as a member of the recovery team for the Gemini and
Mercury space program capsules.

In the summer of 1965, Pitsenberger received orders to
the 38th Air Rescue and Recovery Squadron based at Bien
Hoa Air Base outside Saigon. The unit was responsible for
a wide variety of rescue missions ranging from recovery of
downed aircrew members to evacuation of wounded
grunts. What made the air force unit different from other
medevac units was their aircraft, the twin-rotor Kaman
HH-43B "Huskie" helicopter. Unlike the ubiquitous Huey,
which at that time had to land to pick up casualties, the
Huskie could hover at the top of the jungle canopy and
winch a wire mesh litter basket to the ground. Once the casualty was securely strapped inside the litter basket, he
would be winched up into the Huskie, where a PJ waited to
give first aid.

On more than three hundred rescue missions during his
eight months in South Vietnam, Pitsenbarger earned a well-
deserved reputation for his coolness under fire and excep-
tional bravery. Time and again the twenty-one-year-old
volunteered to descend to the ground to help treat casualties.

When a South Vietnamese soldier stepped on a mine on
March 7, 1966, Pitsenbarger volunteered to attempt a rescue.
Because there were no maps of the old minefield available, a
plan had to be devised to extract the man without detonating
any more mines. Pitsenbarger had the answer: "Lower me
down on the jungle penetrator," he told the aircraft commander, "and I'll straddle the guy. Then I'll pick him up and
you can lift us up and out of there."

Pitsenbarger's plan worked exactly as he had described.

The ARVN soldier was successfully rescued, and Pitsenbarger received the Airman's Medal and was also decorated by the South Vietnamese government.

When Company C, 16th Infantry, was attacked on April 11, Airman Pitsenbarger was off duty. The call for the Huskies came about 3:00 P.M. that afternoon. The air force helicopters were needed because there was no LZ available for the medevac Hueys to use. Pitsenbarger immediately volunteered to go on the mission. As he donned his gear, the pararescueman commented to a friend, "I've got a bad feeling about this mission." It was the only time the man had heard Pitsenbarger voice any misgivings about a mission.

Pitsenbarger climbed aboard the Huskie, piloted by Capt. Harold Salem, call sign Pedro 73. By 3:30 P.M. it and another Huskie were in a hover above the jungle where Company C was fighting for its life. The other Huskie, Pedro 97, loaded aboard one casualty. Then Pedro 73 positioned itself to lower its litter. When it had recovered a wounded man, the two ships flew to a nearby village where an aid station had been set up.

In the meantime, the situation on the ground was deteriorating. Casualties mounted, and dead and wounded were lying everywhere. Sergeant Robinson was bleeding to death from his many wounds. Most of the officers and NCOs had been hit, as had the medics.

When Pedro 73 returned to the scene, Pitsenbarger lowered the litter. From his position he could see several grunts struggling to load a casualty into the wire-mesh basket. They needed help. "I'm going down," Pitsenbarger yelled over the intercom to Captain Salem. Salem nodded. Seconds later Pitsenbarger was headed earthward on the penetrator.

Those grunts who witnessed Pitsenbarger's descent were stunned. One platoon leader said later, "He must have been out of his mind to leave his helicopter."

Not out of his mind, just determined.

Once on the ground, Pitsenbarger helped load the casualty into the litter. When Pedro 73 flew off, Pedro 97 hovered into view. Completely oblivious to the crack of enemy rounds passing overhead, Pitsenbarger guided some grunts in loading up two more casualties. Pedro 97 headed off for the aid station.

While Pitsenbarger waited for the Huskies to return, he pitched in to help treat the numerous casualties. He repeatedly exposed himself to enemy small-arms fire to pull casualties off the line. Another platoon leader witnessed the airman's heroics: "While my own platoon medic lay frozen in fear, this air force guy was moving around and pulling wounded men out of the line of fire and then bandaging their wounds."

Pedro 73 returned a short time later. As it lowered its litter, a flurry of enemy AK-47 rounds erupted from the jungle. Dozens of bullets raked the helicopter as Captain Salem fought for control of his damaged aircraft. He had the crew chief cut the cable holding the litter, then flew off to safety.

Despite the continuing enemy fire, Pitsenbarger climbed into the trees and retrieved the litter. Back on the ground, he loaded a casualty into it and waited for the return of Pedro 97.

Unfortunately, by the time Pedro 97 did return, the NVA were lobbing mortar shells into the American perimeter. In addition, supporting American artillery rounds were dropping around Charlie Company. Pedro 97 had to leave.

On the ground, Pitsenbarger did what he could to comfort the many wounded. When the remnants of the company moved to consolidate their position, the airman cut tree branches to form litters so the wounded could be moved.

With that task completed, Pitsenbarger disappeared. When he reappeared about ten minutes later, he was carrying an M-16 and several dozen ammunition magazines. He had stripped the weapon and the magazines from the dead. Without hesitation, the pararescueman moved to the portion of the perimeter taking the heaviest enemy fire. He flopped down next to Sgt. Fred Navarro.

Navarro, wounded earlier but still in the fight, was surprised to see a member of the air force in the melee, but did not ask too many questions. He was just happy to have the additional firepower.

For the next thirty minutes, as night came, Pitsenbarger kept up his fire. At times his was the only M-16 answering the enemy's fire. Then, just after dark fell, Pitsenbarger's weapon fell silent. Navarro knew instinctively that the airman was dead.

The Viet Cong slipped away in the night. The next morning the rest of the wounded and the dead, including Pitsenbarger, were evacuated.

Sergeant Navarro was one of the Charlie Company survivors who submitted a statement in support of the Medal of Honor for Airman 1st Class Pitsenbarger. Unfortunately, because of the large number of casualties—only 14 men out of 134 were not hit—the soldiers had been widely dispersed to numerous hospitals in South Vietnam, Japan, and the United States. This meant that there was not enough information for the air force to approve the recommendation. Instead they awarded Pitsenbarger the Air Force Cross, that service's highest award. It was presented to the airman's parents on September 22, 1966.

Over the next three decades, Pitsenbarger's heroics were memorialized many times as a number of air force buildings were named for him. The Air Force Sergeants Association created an annual valor award named for the PJ. As time passed, though, knowledge of Pitsenbarger's heroics faded. Until the late 1990s.

Veterans of Company C had always assumed that Pitsenbarger had received a Medal of Honor. When they learned that he had not, they, along with a group of pararescuemen, other veterans, and private citizens from Piqua, went to work. By early 1999 they had gathered enough new information and interviewed enough additional eyewitnesses to petition the air force to review Pitsenbarger's actions. After a careful reevaluation of all the original paperwork and the new information, an air force board agreed that Pitsenbarger's actions warranted a Medal of Honor. It was presented to his parents at a ceremony at Wright-Patterson Air Force Base, Ohio, on December 8, 2000.

The withdrawal of U.S. forces from Cambodia following President Nixon's incursion in April 1970 did not mean the end to U.S. involvement in the war raging along that country's border with South Vietnam. Indeed, for several years afterward, U.S. troops repeatedly crossed the border in direct support of ARVN forces. One such mission resulted in a thirty-one-year wait for a burial and a Medal of Honor.

JON E. SWANSON

Jon E. Swanson was born in San Antonio, Texas, on May 1, 1942. He was raised in Denver, Colorado, and entered Colorado State University in Boulder after graduating from high school. Before earning his degree, he dropped out and enlisted in the army.

Swanson served a tour in South Vietnam in 1967 as a rifleman and was awarded a Purple Heart. During his weeklong R&R (rest and recuperation) midtour leave in Hawaii, he married his high school sweetheart, Sandie.

When Swanson returned to the United States after his tour, he decided he wanted to make the army a career. However, he did not want to be a grunt. He wanted to fly. So he applied to army aviation school. Swanson completed the demanding rotary wing pilot's course in 1969 and was commissioned a second lieutenant. Unfortunately, his new career meant a return to the war zone.

Just before he shipped out, Swanson took his wife and their two daughters on a trip to Washington, DC. After they visited the Tomb of the Unknown Soldier at Arlington National Cemetery, Swanson mentioned to Sandie that he would like to be buried there someday.

Upon his arrival in South Vietnam, Swanson was assigned to the 1st Cavalry Division's 5th Cavalry Regiment. He was flying Huey helicopters on a variety of missions. Just before the end of 1970, Swanson transferred to the 1st Battalion, 9th Cavalry. This unit served as the division's scout element. Using OH-3A light observation helicopters (LOHs, or "loaches"), the 9th's scout pilots would fly low in search of enemy troops. When the enemy was located, the LOH pilot would mark the spot with a colored smoke grenade. From a higher altitude a Cobra gunship would swoop down and engage the foe. If it was deemed necessary, a standby infantry unit would be air-assaulted into the area. The grunts would then either attack any remaining enemy or survey the damage caused by the gunships.

Jon Swanson flew the OH-3A, the most dangerous job in the 9th Cavalry.

On February 26, 1971, Captain Swanson and his observer, S.Sgt. Larry G. Harrison, were assigned to a close support reconnaissance mission for ARVN Task Force 333, which was operating well past the border of Cambodia. Two NVA regiments had been reported in the vicinity. Swanson's mission was to find them. To do so he would fly at treetop level at a reduced airspeed while Harrison searched the ground for any sign of the enemy. Low and slow, they would be a juicy target for the NVA.

As the ARVN troops advanced through the heavily forested terrain, they came under fire from NVA emplaced in bunkers in a tree line about one hundred meters to their front. Captain Swanson immediately responded to the ARVN call for help.

Swanson flew his helicopter just feet above the bunkers. While enemy automatic weapons fire sought out the little aircraft, Harrison dropped hand grenades on the bunkers and fired his M-60 machine gun at enemy soldiers who showed themselves. The pair destroyed five bunkers and killed a number of NVA as they darted back and forth above the trees. Then Swanson saw a .51-caliber antiaircraft machine gun hidden in the trees.

Since Swanson did not have sufficient explosives left to destroy the enemy position, he radioed for an overhead Cobra. The sleek attack helicopter swooped down, cannons blazing.

When the Cobra peeled off, Swanson returned. He saw that the position had not been destroyed. An enemy soldier was crawling through the undergrowth toward the weapon. Swanson immediately went into a hover and killed the NVA with his M-16.

Seconds later a second .51-caliber antiaircraft gun opened fire on the LOH. Several heavy slugs ripped into the aircraft but caused no serious damage. Swanson backed off and called in another Cobra.

Though low on fuel and ammunition, Swanson volunteered to remain on station and continue his mission. As he approached the second antiaircraft gun position to assess the damage, a third .51 opened fire.

Swanson could have evaded the fire and flown away. But he did not. Concerned about the damage that this new threat posed to the ARVN and the Cobras, Swanson flew right toward it, determined to mark the enemy position with a smoke grenade.

The LOH was struck several more times as it neared the enemy position. Swanson never wavered. He continued to head straight for the .51. Suddenly the little aircraft shuddered from a burst of heavy slugs. Then it exploded. The LOH fell to the jungle floor, a mass of twisted, smoking wreckage.

Another helicopter landed in a nearby clearing. Several of its crew members attempted to reach the crash site, but enemy small-arms fire drove them off. The helicopter took off.

The next day several U.S. helicopters flew over the wreckage. The pilots saw two bodies lying on the ground. Before any recovery attempt could be made, enemy fire drove off the helicopters. ARVN ground forces tried several times to reach and secure the crash site, but were unable to advance due to the heavy enemy fire. Eventually the attempts were halted.

As late as March 7, 1971, overflying helicopters reported

the remains were still at the crash site. Because the NVA often used the remains of aviators as bait, the decision was made not to launch any further recovery efforts.

Swanson and Harrison were listed as killed in action, remains not recovered. Sandie Swanson eventually remarried, to Jon's younger brother Tom. Together they raised Jon and Sandie's two daughters and their own children.

Outside of family members, very few people thought of Jon Swanson again. The U.S. government preferred not to discuss the case because that would require an admission that its forces had been operating in Cambodia in direct violation of a congressional prohibition. There the matter rested.

Then on December 28, 2001, President George W. Bush signed the 2002 Defense Authorization Act. Among the myriad provisions in the bill was a paragraph authorizing the Medal of Honor for Capt. Jon E. Swanson (Staff Sergeant Harrison was posthumously awarded a Distinguished Service Cross). The presentation ceremony was scheduled for May 1, 2002, Swanson's sixtieth birthday.

In February 2002, much to the family's surprise, they were advised that some bone fragments that had been recently turned over to U.S. representatives by the Cambodian government had been identified as Swanson's and Harrison's. Sandie Swanson could not help but wonder, "Why is all this coming together . . . after thirty-one years? What is he trying to tell us?"

Two days after the White House presentation ceremony, the Swanson and Harrison families traveled to Arlington National Cemetery for the burial services. Jon Swanson's youngest daughter Holly noted, "This has additional significance because of the war on terrorism. Before we commit troops to war, a lot of people say, 'Is it worth losing a son for?' I say, 'Is it worth losing a father for?' Every time we send troops in, that's what I ask."

Brigid Swanson Jones, the oldest daughter, said, "It's not really closure because he will always be with us. Instead, this means we're able to bring him home."

* * *

Unlike the other military branches, the U.S. Army refused for decades to award a Medal of Honor to a prisoner of war for heroism during captivity. That unofficial policy ended on July 8, 2002 when President Bush presented the award to the brother of one of the war's earliest prisoners.

HUMBERT R. VERSACE

Born July 2, 1937, *Humbert Roque "Rocky" Versace* was the oldest of five children of a career army officer and his wife. When he completed his senior year of high school in Alexandria, Virginia, Rocky struggled with two career choices: West Point or the priesthood.

Versace decided to follow his father and chose the army.

Upon graduation from West Point in 1959, Versace was posted to the Republic of Korea. During his tour there he became acquainted with the Maryknoll priests who operated a nearby orphanage. Soon he was spending most of his off-duty hours helping the priests. Doubts about his career choice began to grow.

In 1962, Rocky Versace was one of the first soldiers assigned duty as a military adviser to the fledgling Army of the Republic of Vietnam. At that time South Vietnam was just another country most Americans could not find on a map and did not care about. But not Rocky Versace. Almost immediately upon his arrival, he found himself taken in by the country, its culture, and its people, especially the children.

Versace became involved in a Maryknoll orphanage in the Mekong River Delta area, where he was assigned. Soon he was writing home to ask friends and family members to send him items ranging from food to sports equipment for the children. Nearly all of his free time was spent at the orphanage.

But there was still a war to fight. At that time in America's involvement in South Vietnam, advisers were training members of the ARVN in military tactics and modern weaponry. Although the Americans accompanied the ARVN on combat patrols, they rarely took an active role in the fighting. As did most Americans, the advisers believed they were helping a struggling democratic country resist communist-influenced insurgents. If the ARVN were made self-reliant, they could defeat the guerrillas and democracy would flourish.

Versace so sincerely believed in his country's and his mission that when his six-month tour ended, he volunteered for another. Before returning to Southeast Asia in February 1963, Versace had dinner with a boyhood friend, Michael Heisly. Heisly, who today owns the NBA Memphis Grizzlies, recalled that Rocky said, "This was going to be his last tour. He was going to talk to the Maryknolls about becoming a priest for the purpose of going back to run the orphanage."

Back in South Vietnam, Versace excelled at his duties of training the ARVN in intelligence gathering techniques. Though the six-foot-one officer towered over the diminutive South Vietnamese, they enjoyed his easy manner and his devotion to teaching them the ways of war. During his off-duty hours, Versace continued to help at the orphanage.

Because Versace planned to resign his commission when his service obligation expired, he volunteered to spend his last two months on active duty in South Vietnam rather than return to a brief billet in the United States. The extension was granted.

With less than three weeks to go before heading off to begin a new career, Rocky Versace volunteered to accompany a battalion of ARVN who were going to attack a suspected Viet Cong stronghold deep in the wilds of the U Minh Forest in the Mekong River Delta region. The ARVN troops marched out of their camp on October 29, 1963. Before they reached their objective, the VC ambushed them.

The withering fire scattered the ARVN. Versace and two other American soldiers, Dan Pitzer and James Rowe, held their ground. As the superior force of Viet Cong swarmed across the rice paddies, the three advisers returned fire and cut down many of the enemy.

But the VC fire was strong, too. Versace was hit three times in one leg, torn by red-hot shrapnel, and took a blow to his head. Finally the three Americans realized they could not hold out. They tossed their weapons aside, stood up, and raised their hands.

The three were bound and led deep into the swampy woods of the U Minh Forest. From that instant, Rocky Versace repeatedly and continuously demonstrated the highest level of courage in his defiance of his captors. Fluent in French and Vietnamese, he insisted that the three Americans be treated in accordance with the provisions of the Geneva Convention. The VC scoffed at his insolence. Versace did not relent in his demands for humane treatment.

Versace paid a heavy price for his defiance. He was denied even the meager rations Rowe and Pitzer received. For punishment his captors placed him in a bamboo cage just six feet long, two feet wide, and three feet high. Iron cuffs were clamped around his ankles.

During the frequent propaganda sessions, Versace would argue with the instructors, challenging their assumptions and ridiculing their statements. Beatings and torture followed each time, but Rocky Versace maintained his defiance.

Four times during the early months of his captivity Versace tried to escape. Though the odds of successfully navigating the vast swamplands were near zero, Versace persisted. Each time he was easily captured. Each time he was brutally tortured and beaten.

According to Rowe and Pitzer, Versace liked to torment the VC by singing patriotic American songs as loud as he could. The enemy would then throw Versace in the bamboo cage, slap on the leg irons, and stuff a filthy rag in his mouth.

"He told them to go to hell in Vietnamese, French, and English," Pitzer later said. "He got a lot of pressure and torture but he held his path."

Denied all but minimum nourishment, within months Versace's weight dropped in half, to about one hundred pounds. Dressed in tattered clothes, with no shoes, and suffering from malnutrition, jaundice, and covered with open sores that festered in the humid, mosquito-infested air, Rocky Versace could no longer attempt to escape. But his poor physical condition never weakened his spirit.

To dispel any myths the local Vietnamese villagers might have had regarding the invincibility of the Americans, the VC took to putting Versace on display. With a rope leash around his neck, his hair now whitened, and with bones protruding from his near-translucent skin, Versace would be paraded through a village. While his captors taunted him, Rocky Versace maintained his defiance. He shouted back at the VC, encouraged the villagers to resist, and challenged his captors every chance he had.

By September 1965, after nearly two years of captivity, Rocky Versace was a mere shell of his former self. Even though he was greatly weakened and forced to live in his own filth, Versace's stubbornness amazed Rowe and Pitzer. Whenever he could, Versace held his own against the Viet Cong.

Then on September 26, 1965, the VC came for Versace. As they led him off into the swamps, Rowe and Pitzer heard him break into song. He sang "God Bless America" as loud as he could. Soon his voice faded.

Later that day the VC announced that Rocky Versace had been executed. Their spokesman said the American had been killed in retaliation for the South Vietnamese government's execution of two Viet Cong sympathizers.

Until James Rowe escaped his captors in 1968, the world knew nothing of Versace's sustained heroism. Rowe made a vow to see that Versace would receive the Medal of Honor for his gallant conduct. In an audience with President Nixon in 1969, Rowe made his case. Nixon was so moved, he ordered his liaison officers "to make damn sure" Versace received the medal.

Unfortunately, due to the stigma in the army of being taken prisoner, the award was downgraded to a Silver Star.

Over the next twenty years Rowe and Pitzer, after his release, persisted in their efforts to bring the ultimate recognition to Rocky Versace. But to no avail. Then Rowe was killed by rebels in the Philippines in 1989. Pitzer died in 1995. It seemed there would be no one to advocate for Versace.

But in 1999 several of Rocky Versace's high school friends took up the cause. They were soon joined by a number of Versace's West Point classmates, some of whom held influential positions within the army. Then the army's Special Forces command became involved. A new recommendation for the Medal of Honor was submitted in January 2000. Although there continued to be resistance to the award among some senior army officers, it was eventually approved.

After the White House ceremony, Rocky Versace's family and friends attended a ceremony in Alexandria, Virginia, when a statue in his memory was dedicated. Versace's heroic conduct would always be remembered.

The Vietnam War was unlike any other war fought by the United States. With unclear political goals, no military objectives, and no victory, our involvement in South Vietnam produced only frustration and bitterness for the participants.

Yet despite all the problems associated with the war in Vietnam, there still existed a common thread with America's earlier conflicts—the role of the individual fighting man.

Whether they manned a picket line outside of Gettysburg in 1863 or stood guard at Khe Sanh in 1968, the men had much in common. The loneliness, the hardships, the dangers, and the fears of war never changed. And, though they existed one hundred years apart, both soldiers offered their lives in defense of their country's principles.

Many men went to South Vietnam with the hope that they could fulfill the promise they had made to defend their country. The adversities and discouragement that awaited them there made it difficult to keep that promise. Staying true to their commitment made them all heroes.

A handful of warriors went far above and beyond that commitment. Their heroic actions so impressed their comrades that they were selected to receive their country's highest honor. These gallant men must never be forgotten. For to forget them would mean that their sacrifices were made in vain.

Medal of Honor Distribution by Service Branch

SERVICE BRANCH	TOTAL AWARDS	POSTHUMOUS AWARDS	LIVING (AS OF 12/1/04)
U.S. Army	159	99	41
U.S. Marine Corps	57	44	10
U.S. Navy	15	6	7
U.S. Air Force	13	4	5
TOTAL	244	153	63

Medal of Honor Distribution by Year of Deed

YEAR	QUANTITY
1963	1
1964	2
1965	11
1966	28
1967	58
1968	58
1969	54
1970	22
1971	7
1972	3

Medal of Honor Distribution by Location of Deed

LOCATION	QUANTITY
SOUTH VIETNAM:	
An Xuyen Province	1
Bien Hoa Province	5
Binh Dinh Province	15
Binh Duong Province	10
Binh Long Province	9
Binh Tuy Province	1
Chau Doc Province	2
Dinh Tuong Province	4
Gia Dinh Province	2
Hau Nghia Province	7
Khanh Hoa Province	1
Kien Hoa Province	4
Kien Phong Province	3
Kien Tuong Province	1
Kontum Province	17
Long An Province	4
Long Khanh Province	2
Phuoc Long Province	6
Phuoc Tuy Province	3
Pleiku Province	11
Quang Nam Province	19
Quang Ngai Province	11
Quang Tin Province	21
Quang Tri Province	37
Tay Ninh Province	14
Thua Thien Province	13
Tuyen Duc Province	1
Vinh Long Province	1

LOCATION	QUANTITY
OTHER:	
Cambodia	4
Laos	7
North Vietnam	8

Medal of Honor
Distribution
by Unit

U.S. ARMY	*QUANTITY*
1st Aviation Brigade	4
1st Cavalry Division	27
1st Infantry Division	11
4th Infantry Division	11
5th Special Forces Group	8
7th Special Forces Group	1
9th Infantry Division	10
11th Armored Cavalry Regiment	3
25th Infantry Division	21
27th Transportation Battalion	1
44th Artillery	1
44th Medical Brigade	1
48th Transportation Group	1
68th Medical Group	1
92d Artillery	1
101st Airborne Division	17
173d Airborne Brigade	13
199th Infantry Brigade	4
Americal Division	11
MACV	4
MACV–Studies and Observation Group	5
Vietnam Training Advisory Group	2
POW	1

U.S. MARINE CORPS (includes U.S. Navy corpsmen)	
1st Marine Air Wing	2
1st Marine Division	28
III Marine Amphibious Force	1
3d Marine Division	28
9th Marine Amphibious Brigade	2
POW	1

U.S. AIR FORCE	*QUANTITY*
1st Air Commando Sqdn	1
3d Special Operations Sqdn	1
20th Special Operations Sqdn	1
20th Tactical Air Support Sqdn	1
21st Tactical Air Suppport Sqdn	1
37th Air Rescue Sqdn	1
38th Aerospace Rescue Sqdn	1
311th Air Commando Sqdn	1
354th Tactical Fighter Sqdn	1
357th Tactical Fighter Sqdn	1
602d Special Operations Sqdn	1
POW	2

U.S. NAVY	
Attack Squadron 192	1
Helicopter Support Sqdn 7	1
River Assault Division 152	1
River Section 531	1
River Squadron 5	1
Seabee Team 1104	1
SEAL Team One	1
MACV–Strategic Technical Directorate	2
POW	1

Vietnam Medal of Honor Recipients

As of December 1, 2004

* Denotes recipient died as a result of his Medal of Honor action

NAME AND RANK	UNIT	DATE OF ACTION	PLACE OF ACTION	HOMETOWN	DATE OF DEATH	BURIAL SITE
*Adams, William E. Maj, USA	1st Aviation Brigade	May 25, 1971	Kontum Province	Craig, CO	May 25, 1971	Ft. Logan National Cem., Denver, CO
*Albanese, Lewis PFC, USA	1st Cavalry Division	Dec 1, 1966	Near Phu Muu, Binh Dinh Province	Seattle, WA	Dec 1, 1966	Evergreen-Washelli Memorial Park, Seattle, WA
*Anderson, James, Jr. PFC, USMC	3d Marine Division	Feb 28, 1967	near Cam Lo, Quang Tri Province	Compton, CA	Feb 28, 1967	Lincoln Memorial Park, Compton, CA
*Anderson, Richard A. LCpl, USMC	3d Marine Division	Aug 24, 1969	Quang Tri Province	Houston, TX	Aug 24, 1969	Forest Park Cemetery Houston, TX
Anderson, Webster SSgt, USA	101st Airborne Division	Oct 15, 1967	near Tam Ky, Quang Tin Province	Winnsboro, SC	Aug 30, 2003	Blackjack Baptist Church, Winnsboro, NC
*Ashley, Eugene, Jr. SFC, USA	5th Special Forces Group	Feb 6–7, 1968	Lang Vei, Quang Tri Province	New York, NY	Feb 7, 1968	Rockfish Memorial Park, Fayetteville, NC
*Austin, Oscar P. PFC, USMC	1st Marine Division	Feb 23, 1969	near Da Nang, Quang Nam Province	Phoenix, AZ	Feb 23, 1969	Greenwood Memorial Park, Phoenix, AZ
Baca, John P. Sp4, USA	1st Cavalry Division	Feb 10, 1970	near Quan Loi, Phuoc Long Province	San Diego, CA	Living	
Bacon, Nicky D. SSgt, USA	Americal Division	Aug 26, 1968	near Tam Ky, Quang Tin Province	Phoenix, AZ	Living	
Baker, John F., Jr. PFC, USA	25th Infantry Division	Nov 5, 1966	near Dau Tieng, Binh Duong Province	Moline, IL	Living	

NAME, RANK	UNIT	DATE OF ACTION	PLACE OF ACTION	HOMETOWN	DATE OF DEATH	BURIAL SITE
Ballard, Donald E. Hosp 2c, USN	3d Marine Division	May 16, 1968	nea Khe Sanh, Quang Tri Province	Kansas City, MO	Living	
*Barker, Jedh C. LCpl, USMC	3d Marine Division	Sep 21, 1967	near Con Thien, Quang Tri Province	Park Ridge, NJ	Sep 21, 1967	George Washington Memorial Park, Paramus, NJ
*Barnes, John A., III PFC, USA	173d Airborne Brigade	Nov 11, 1967	near Dak To, Kontum Province	Dedham, MA	Nov 11, 1967	Brookdale Cemetery, Dedham, MA
Barnum, Harvey C.,, Jr. 1Lt, USMC	3d Marine Division	Dec 18, 1965	Ky Phu, Quang Tin Province	Cheshire, CT	Living	
Beikirch, Gary B. Sgt, USA	5th Special Forces Group	Apr 1, 1970	Dak Seang, Kontum Province	Greece, NY	Living	
*Belcher, Ted Sgt, USA	25th Infantry Division	Nov 19, 1966	Plei Djereng, Pleiku Province	Zanesville, OH	Nov 19, 1966	Greenwood Cemetery, Zanesville, OH
*Bellrichard, Leslie A. PFC, USA	4th Infantry Division	May 20, 1967	Kontum Province	San Jose, CA	May 20, 1967	Oakhill Cemetery, Janesville, WI
Benavidez, Roy P. SSgt, USA	5th Special Forces Group	May 2, 1968	Cambodia	El Campo, TX	Nov 29, 1998	Fort Sam Houston National Cemetery, San Antonio, TX
*Bennett, Steven L. Cpt, USAF	20th Tactical Air Support Sqdn	Jun 29, 1972	over Quang Tri Province	Lafayette, LA	Jun 29, 1972	Lafayette Memorial Park Lafayette, LA
*Bennett, Thomas W. Cpl, USA	4th Infantry Division	Feb 9–11, 1969	Pleiku Province	Morgantown, WV	Feb 11, 1969	East Oak Grove Cem., Morgantown, WV
*Blanchfield, Michael R. Sp4, USA	173d Airborne Brigade	Jul 3, 1969	Binh Dinh Province	Wheeling, IL	Jul 3, 1969	All Saints Cemetery, Des Plaines, IL
*Bobo, John P. 2Lt, USMC	3d Marine Division	Mar 30, 1967	near Con Thien, Quang Tri Province	Niagara Falls, NY	Mar 30, 1967	Gate of Heaven Cemetery, Niagara Falls, NY

NAME AND RANK	UNIT	DATE OF ACTION	PLACE OF ACTION	HOMETOWN	DATE OF DEATH	BURIAL SITE
Bondsteel, James L., SSgt, USA	1st Infantry Division	May 24, 1969	near Lang Sau Binh Long Province	Allen, MI	Apr 9, 1987	Ft. Richardson Nat'l Cem., Ft. Richardson, AK
*Bowen, Hammett L., Jr., SSgt, USA	25th Infantry Division	Jun 27, 1969	Binh Duong Province	Ocala, FL	Jun 27, 1969	Restlawn Memorial Garden, La Grange, GA
Brady, Patrick H. Maj, USA	44th Medical Brigade	Jan 6, 1968	near Chu Lai, Quang Tin Province	Seattle, WA	Living	
*Bruce, Daniel D. PFC, USMC	1st Marine Division	Mar 1, 1969	FSB Tomahawk, Quang Nam Province	Michigan City, IN	Mar 1, 1969	Greenwood Cemetery, Michigan City, IN
*Bryant, William M. SFC, USA	5th Special Forces Group	Mar 24, 1969	Long Khan Province	Newark, NJ	Mar 24, 1969	Raleigh National Cem., Raleigh, NC
Bucha, Paul W. Cpt, USA	101st Airborne Division	Mar 16–19, 1968	near Phuoc Vinh, Binh Duong Province	St. Louis, MO	Living	
*Buker, Brian L. Sgt, USA	5th Special Forces Group	Apr 5, 1970	Chau Doc Province	Albion, ME	Apr 5, 1970	Brown Cemetery, Benton, ME
*Burke, Robert C. PFC, USMC	1st Marine Division	May 17, 1968	Goi Noi Island, Quang Nam Province	Monticello, IL	May 17, 1968	Monticello Cemetery, Monticello, IL
*Capodanno, Vincent R. LT (Chap), USN	1st Marine Division	Sep 4, 1967	Hiep Duc Valley, Quang Tin Province	Staten Island, NY	Sep 4, 1967	St. Peters Cemetery, Staten Island, NY
*Caron, Wayne M. Hosp 3c, USN	1st Marine Division	Jul 28, 1968	Quang Nam Province	Middleboro, MA	Jul 28, 1968	Arlington National Cem., Arlington, VA
*Carter, Bruce W. PFC, USMC	3d Marine Division	Aug 7, 1969	Quang Tri Province	Hialeah, FL	Aug 7, 1969	Vista Memorial Gardens, Hialeah, FL
Cavaiani, Jon R SSgt, USA	Vietnam Training Advisory Group	Jun 4–5, 1971	near Khe Sanh, Quang Tri Province	Ballico, CA	Living	
Clausen, Raymond M., Jr.	1st Marine	Jan 31, 1970	near Da Nang,	Hammond, LA	May 30, 2004	Ponchatoula City Cemetery,

NAME AND RANK	UNIT	DATE OF ACTION	PLACE OF ACTION	HOMETOWN	DATE OF DEATH	BURIAL SITE
*Coker, Ronald L. PFC, USMC	3d Marine Division	Mar 24, 1969	Quang Tri Province	Alliance, NE	Mar 24, 1969	Fairview Cemetery, Alliance, NE
*Connor, Peter S. SSgt, USMC	1st Marine Division	Feb 25, 1966	Quang Ngai Province	South Orange, NJ	Mar 8, 1966	Ft. Rosecrans Nat'l Cem., San Diego, CA
*Cook, Donald G. Cpt, USMC	as POW	Dec 31, 1964 to Dec 8, 1967	Phuoc Tuy and Phuoc Long Provinces	Burlington, VT	Dec 8, 1967	Remains not recovered
*Creek, Thomas E. LCpl, USMC	3d Marine Division	Feb 13, 1969	near Cam Lo, Quang Tri Province	Amarillo, TX	Feb 13, 1969	Llano Cemetery, Amarillo, TX
*Crescenz, Michael J. Cpl, USA	Americal Division	Nov 20, 1968	Hiep Duc Valley, Quang Tin Province	Philadelphia, PA	Nov 20, 1968	Holy Sepulchre Cemetery, Philadelphia, PA
*Cutinha, Nicholas J. Sp4, USA	25th Infantry Division	Mar 2, 1968	near Gia Dinh, Gia Dinh Province	Yulee, FL	Mar 2, 1968	Fort Denaud Cemetery, Fort Denaud, FL
*Dahl, Larry G. Sp4, USA	27th Transport Battalion	Feb 23, 1971	near An Khe, Binh Dinh Province	Seattle, WA	Feb 23, 1971	Willamette Nat'l Cem., Portland, OR
*Davis, Rodney M. Sgt, USMC	1st Marine Division	Sep 6, 1967	Hiep Duc Valley, Quang Tin Province	Macon, GA	Sep 6, 1967	Linwood Cemetery, Macon, GA
Davis, Sammy L. PFC, USA	9th Infantry Division	Nov 18, 1967	FSB Cudgil, Dinh Tuong Province	Martinsville, IN	Living	
Day, George E. Maj, USAF	as POW	Aug 26, 1967 to Mar 14, 1973	North Vietnam	Sioux City, IA	Living	
*DeLaGarza, Emilio A., Jr. LCpl, USMC	1st Marine Division	Apr 11, 1970	near Da Nang, Quang Nam Province	East Chicago, IL	Apr 11, 1970	St. John's Cemetery, Hammond, IN
Dethlefsen, Merlyn H. Cpt, USAF	354th Tactical Fighter Sqdn	Mar 10, 1967	over North Vietnam	Royal, IA	Dec 14, 1987	Arlington National Cem., Arlington, VA
*Devore, Edward A., Jr. Sp4, USA	9th Infantry Division	Mar 17, 1968	near Saigon, Gia Dinh Province	Harbor City, CA	Mar 17, 1968	Green Hills Memorial Pk., San Pedro, CA

NAME AND RANK	UNIT	DATE OF ACTION	PLACE OF ACTION	HOMETOWN	DATE OF DEATH	BURIAL SITE
*Dias, Ralph E. PFC, USMC	1st Marine Divison	Nov 12, 1969	Que Son Mountains, Quang Tin Province	Shelocta, PA	Nov 12, 1969	Oakdale Cemetery, Leetonia, OH
*Dickey, Douglas E. PFC, USMC	3d Marine Division	Mar 26, 1967	near Gio An, Quang Tri Province	Rossburg, OH	Mar 26, 1967	Brook Cemetery, Brook, OH
Dix, Drew D. SSgt, USA	Senior Adviser, IV Corps, MACV	Jan 31–Feb 1, 1968	Chau Phu, Chau Doc Province	Pueblo, CO	Living	
*Doane, Stephen H. 1Lt, USA	25th Infantry Division	Mar 25, 1969	Hau Nghia Province	Walton, NY	Mar 25, 1969	Arlington National Cem., Arlington, VA
Dolby, David C. Sp4, USA	1st Cavalry Division	May 21, 1966	Binh Dinh Province	Philadelphia, PA	Living	
Donlon, Roger H. C. Cpt, USA	7th Special Forces Group	Jul 16, 1964	near Nam Dong, Thua Thien Province	Saugerties, NY	Living	
Dunagan, Kern W. Cpt, USA	Americal Division	May 13–14, 1969	Quang Tin Province	Bishop, CA	Dec 27, 1991	Golden Gate Nat'l Cem., San Bruno, CA
Durham, Harold B., Jr. 2Lt, USA	1st Infantry Division	Oct 17, 1967	Hau Nghia Province	Tifton, GA	Oct 17, 1967	Oakridge Cemetery, Tifton, GA
*English, Glenn H., Jr. SSgt, USA	173d Airborne Brigade	Sep 7, 1970	Binh Dinh Province	Altoona, PA	Sep 7, 1970	Ft. Bragg Post Cemetery, Ft. Bragg, NC
*Estocin, Michael J. Lt Cmdr, USN	Attack Squadron 192	Apr 20 & 26, 1967	over North Vietnam	Turtle Creek, PA	Apr 26, 1967	Remains not recovered
*Evans, Donald W., Jr. Sp4, USA	4th Infantry Division	Jan 27, 1967	near Tri Tam, Kontum Province	Covina, CA	Jan 27, 1967	Oakdale Memorial Park, Glendora, CA
*Evans, Rodney J. Sgt, USA	1st Cavalry Division	Jul 18, 1969	Tay Ninh Province	Florala, AL	Jul 18, 1969	Liberty Hill Cemetery, Florala, AL
Ferguson, Frederick E. CWO, USA	1st Cavalry Division	Jan 31, 1968	Hue, Thua Thien Province	Phoenix, AZ	Living	

NAME AND RANK	UNIT	DATE OF ACTION	PLACE OF ACTION	HOMETOWN	DATE OF DEATH	BURIAL SITE
*Fernandez, Daniel Sp4, USA	25th Infantry Division	Feb 18, 1966	near Cu Chi, Hau Nghia Province	Albuquerque, NM	Feb 18, 1966	Santa Fe National Cem., Santa Fe, NM
Fisher, Bernard F. Maj, USAF	1st Air Commando Sqdn	Mar 10, 1966	A Shau Valley, Thua Thien Province	Kuna, ID	Living	
Fitzmaurice, Michael J. Sp4, USA	101st Airborne Division	Mar 23, 1971	Khe Sanh, Quang Tri Province	Cavour, SD	Living	
*Fleek, Charles C. Sgt, USA	25th Infantry Division	May 27, 1969	Binh Duong Province	Petersburg, KY	May 27, 1969	Petersburg Cemetery, Petersburg, KY
Fleming, James P. 1Lt, USAF	20th Special Ops Squadron	Nov 26, 1968	Cambodia	Sedalia, MO	Living	
Foley, Robert F. Cpt, USA	25th Infantry Division	Nov 5, 1966	near Dau Tieng, Binh Duong Province	Newton, MA	Living	
*Folland, Michael F. Cpl, USA	199th Infantry Brigade	Jul 3, 1969	Long Khanh Province	Richmond, VA	Jul 3, 1969	Glendale National Cem., Richmond, VA
*Foster, Paul H. Sgt, USMC	3d Marine Division	Oct 14, 1967	near Con Thien, Quang Tri Province	San Mateo, CA	Oct 14, 1967	Golden Gate Nat'l Cem., San Bruno, CA
*Fournet, Douglas B. 1Lt, USA	1st Cavalry Division	May 4, 1968	A Shau Valley, Thua Thien Province	Lake Charles, LA	May 4, 1968	McGrill Cemetery, Kinder, LA
*Fous, James W. PFC, USA	9th Infantry Division	May 14, 1968	Kien Hoa Province	Omaha, NE	May 14, 1968	Ft. McPherson Nat'l Cem., Omaha, NE
Fox, Wesley L. 1Lt, USMC	3d Marine Division	Feb 22, 1969	Quang Tri Province	Front Royal, VA	Living	
*Fratellenico, Frank R. Cpl, USA	101st Airborne Division	Aug 19, 1970	near FSB Barnett, Quang Tri Province	Chatham, NY	Aug 19, 1970	Private Cemetery, Chatham, NY

NAME AND RANK	UNIT	DATE OF ACTION	PLACE OF ACTION	HOMETOWN	DATE OF DEATH	BURIAL SITE
Freeman, Edward W. Cpt, USA	1st Cavalry Division	Nov 14, 1965	LZ X-Ray, Pleiku Province	Boise, ID	Living	
Fritz, Harold A. 1Lt, USA	11th Armored Cavalry Regiment	Jan 11, 1969	Binh Long Province	Lake Geneva, WI	Living	
*Gardner, James A. 1Lt, USA	101st Airborne Division	Feb 7, 1966	near My Canh, Pleiku Province	Dyersburg, TN	Feb 7, 1966	Fairview Cemetery, Dyersburg, TN
*Gertsch, John G. SSgt, USA	101st Airborne Division	Jul 15–19, 1969	A Shau Valley, Thua Thien Province	Sheffield, PA	Jul 19, 1969	Northside Catholic Cem., Pittsburgh, PA
*Gonzalez, Alfredo Sgt, USMC	1st Marine Division	Jan 31–Feb 4, 1968	Hue, Thua Thien Province	Edinburg, TX	Feb 4, 1968	Hillcrest Cemetery, Edinburg, TX
*Graham, James A. Cpt, USMC	1st Marine Division	Jun 2, 1967	Hiep Duc Valley, Quang Tin Province	Brandywine, MD	Jun 2, 1967	Arlington National Cem., Arlington, VA
*Grandstaff, Bruce A. PSgt, USA	4th Infantry Division	May 18, 1967	Pleiku Province	Spokane, WA	May 18, 1967	Greenwood-Riverside Cem., Spokane, WA
*Grant, Joseph X. 1Lt, USA	25th Infantry Division	Nov 13, 1966	near Plei Djereng, Pleiku Province	Boston, MA	Nov 13, 1966	Arlington National Cem., Arlington, VA
*Graves, Terrence C. 2Lt, USMC	3d Marine Divisioh	Feb 16, 1968	Quang Tri Province	New York, NY	Feb 17, 1968	Woodlawn Cemetery, Hamilton, NY
*Guenette, Peter M. Sp4, USA	101st Airborne Division	May 18, 1968	near Quan Tan Uyen, Bien Hoa Province	Troy, NY	May 18, 1968	St. John's Cemetery, North Troy, NY
Hagemeister, Charles C. Sp4, USA	1st Cavalry Division	Mar 20, 1967	Binh Dinh Province	Lincoln, NE	Living	
*Hagen, Loren D. 1Lt, USA	Vietnam Training Advisory Group	Aug 7, 1971	Quang Tri Province	Fargo, ND	Aug 7, 1971	Arlington National Cem., Arlington, VA

NAME AND RANK	UNIT	DATE OF ACTION	PLACE OF ACTION	HOMETOWN	DATE OF DEATH	BURIAL SITE
*Hartsock, Robert W. SSgt, USA	25th Infantry Division	Feb 23, 1969	Dau Tieng Base Camp, Hau Nghia Province	Cumberland, MD	Feb 23, 1969	Rocky Gap Veterans Cem., Flintstone, MD
*Harvey, Carmel B., Jr. Sp4, USA	1st Cavalry Division	Jun 21, 1967	Binh Dinh Province	Chicago, IL	Jun 21, 1967	Cedar Park Cemetery, Chicago, IL
Herda, Frank A. PFC, USA	101st Airborne Division	Jun 29, 1968	near Dak To, Kontum Province	Parma, OH	Living	
*Hibbs, Robert J. 2Lt, USA	1st Infantry Division	Mar 5, 1966	Don Dien Lo Ke, Binh Duong Province	Cedar Falls, IA	Mar 5, 1966	Greenwood Cemetery, Cedar Falls, IA
*Holcomb, John N. Sgt, USA	1st Cavalry Division	Dec 3, 1968	near Quan Loi, Binh Long Province	Richland, OR	Dec 3, 1968	Eagle Valley Cemetery, Richland, OR
Hooper, Joe R. Sgt, USA	101st Airborne Division	Feb 21, 1968	near Hue, Thua Thien Province	Moses Lake, OR	May 6, 1979	Arlington National Cem., Arlington, VA
*Hosking, Charles E., Jr. SSgt, USA	5th Special Forces Group	Mar 21, 1967	Phuoc Long Province	Ramsey, NJ	Mar 21, 1967	Valleau Cemetery, Ridgewood, NJ
Howard, Jimmie E. SSgt, USMC	1st Marine Division	Jun 16–18, 1966	Hiep Duc Valley, Quang Tin Province	Burlington, IA	Nov 12, 1993	Ft. Rosecrans Nat'l Cem., San Diego, CA
Howard, Robert L. SFC, USA	MACV-SOG	Dec 30, 1968	Laos	Opelika, AL	Living	
*Howe, James D. LCpl, USMC	1st Marine Division	May 6, 1970	Quang Nam Province	Liberty, SC	May 6, 1970	Liberty Memorial Gardens, Liberty, SC
*Ingalls, George A. Sp4, USA	1st Cavalry Division	Apr 16, 1967	near Duc Pho, Quang Ngai Province	Corona, CA	Apr 16, 1967	Crestlawn Memorial Park, Riverside, CA
Ingram, Robert R. Hosp 3c, USN	3d Marine Division	Mar 28, 1966	Quang Ngai Province	Clearwater, FL	Living	

NAME AND RANK	UNIT	DATE OF ACTION	PLACE OF ACTION	HOMETOWN	DATE OF DEATH	BURIAL SITE
Jackson, Joe M. LTC, USAF	311th Air Commando Sqdn	May 12, 1968	Kham Duc, Quang Tin Province	Newnan, GA	Living	
Jacobs, Jack H. 1Lt, USA	MACV (9th ARVN Inf. Div.)	Mar 9, 1968	Kien Phong Province	Ford, NJ	Living	
Jenkins, Don J. PFC, USA	9th Infantry Division	Jan 6, 1969	Kien Phong Province	Quality, KY	Living	
*Jenkins, Robert H., Jr. PFC, USMC	3d Marine Division	Mar 5, 1969	FSB Argonne, Quang Tri Province	Interlachen, FL	Mar 5, 1969	Sister Spring Baptist Cemetery, Interlachen, FL
Jennings, Delbert O. SSgt, USA	1st Cavalry Division	Dec 27, 1966	Kim Song Valley, Binh Dinh Province	Stockton, CA	Mar 16, 2003	Arlington National Cem., Arlington, VA
*Jimenez, José F. LCpl, USMC	1st Marine Division	Aug 28, 1969	Hiep Duc Valley, Quang Tin Province	Eloy, AZ	Aug 28, 1969	Panteon Municipal Cem., Morelia, Mexico
Joel, Lawrence Sp5, USA	173d Airborne Brigade	Nov 8, 1965	Bien Hoa Province	Winston-Salem, NC	Feb 4, 1984	Arlington National Cem., Arlington, VA
Johnson, Dwight H. Sp5, USA	4th Infantry Division	Jan 15, 1968	near Dak To, Kontum Province	Detroit, MI	Apr 30, 1971	Arlington National Cem., Arlington, VA
*Johnson, Ralph H. PFC, USMC	1st Marine Division	Mar 5, 1968	Quan Duc Valley, Quang Nam Province	Charleston, SC	Mar 5, 1968	Beaufort National Cem., Beaufort, SC
*Johnston, Donald R. Sp4, USA	1st Cavalry Division	Mar 21, 1969	Tay Ninh Province	Columbus, GA	Mar 21, 1969	Ft. Benning Post Cem., Ft. Benning, GA
Jones, William A., III Col, USAF	602d Special Ops Squadron	Sep 1, 1968	over North Vietnam	Charlottesville, VA	Nov 15, 1969	St. John's Church Cem., Warsaw, VA
*Karopczyc, Stephen E. 1Lt, USA	25th Infantry Division	Mar 12, 1967	Kontum Province	Bethpage, NY	Mar 12, 1967	Long Island Nat'l Cem., Farmingdale, NY

NAME AND RANK	UNIT	DATE OF ACTION	PLACE OF ACTION	HOMETOWN	DATE OF DEATH	BURIAL SITE
Kawamura, Terry T. Cpl, USA	173d Airborne Brigade	Mar 20, 1969	Camp Radcliff, Binh Dinh Province	Wahiawa, Oahu, HI	Mar 20, 1969	Mililani Memorial Park, Pearl City, Oahu, HI
Kays, Kenneth M. Pvt, USA	101st Airborne Division	May 7, 1970	FSB Maureen, Thua Thien Province	Fairfield, IL	Nov 25, 1991	Maple Hill Cemetery, Fairfield, IL
*Kedenburg, John J. Sp5, USA	MACV-SOG	Jun 13, 1968	Laos	Brooklyn, NY	Jun 14, 1968	Long Island Nat'l Cem., Farmingdale, NY
*Keith, Miguel LCpl, USMC	CAP 1-3-2 III MAF	May 8, 1970	Quang Ngai Province	Omaha, NE	May 8, 1970	Forest Lawn Cemetery, Omaha, NE
Keller, Leonard B. Sgt, USA	9th Infantry Division	May 2, 1967	near Ap Bac, Long An Province	Rockford, IL	Living	
Kelley, Thomas G. Lt, USN	River Assault Div 152	Jun 15, 1969	Kien Hoa Province	Boston, MA	Living	
Kellogg, Allan J., Jr. SSgt, USMC	1st Marine Division	Mar 11, 1970	Quang Nam Province	Bethel, CT	Living	
Kerrey, Joseph R. Lt, USN	SEAL Team One	Mar 14, 1969	Nha Trang Bay, Khanh Hoa Province	Lincoln, NE	Living	
Kinsman, Thomas J. PFC, USA	9th Infantry Division	Feb 6, 1968	near Vinh Long, Vinh Long Province	Onalaska, WA	Living	
Lambers, Paul R. SSgt, USA	25th Infantry Division	Aug 20, 1968	Tay Ninh Province	Holland, MI	Dec 1, 1970	Remains not recovered
Lang, George C. Sp4, USA	9th Infantry Division	Feb 22, 1969	near Ben Tre, Kien Hoa Province	Hicksville, NY	Living	
*Langhorne, Garfield M. PFC, USA	1st Aviation Brigade	Jan 15, 1969	near Plei Djereng, Pleiku Province	Riverhead, NY	Jan 15, 1969	Riverhead Cemetery, Riverhead, NY
*LaPointe, Joseph G., Jr. Sp4, USA	101st Airborne Division	Jun 2, 1969	Quang Tin Province	Dayton, OH	Jun 2, 1969	Riverside Cemetery, West Milton, OH

NAME AND RANK	UNIT	DATE OF ACTION	PLACE OF ACTION	HOMETOWN	DATE OF DEATH	BURIAL SITE
Lassen, Clyde E. Lt, USN	Helicopter Spt Squadron 7	Jun 19, 1968	North Vietnam	Venice, FL	Apr 1, 1994	Barrancas National Cem., Pensacola, FL
*Lauffer, Billy L. PFC, USA	1st Cavalry Division	Sep 21, 1966	near Bong Son, Binh Dinh Province	Tucson, AZ	Sep 21, 1966	Murray Memorial Cem., Murray, KY
*Law, Robert D. Sp4, USA	1st Infantry Division	Feb 22, 1969	Binh Long Province	Ft. Worth, TX	Feb 22, 1969	Mt. Olivet Cemetery, Ft. Worth, TX
Lee, Howard V. Cpt, USMC	3d Marine Division	Aug 8–9, 1966	near Cam Lo, Quang Tri Province	The Bronx, NY	Living	
*Lee, Milton A. PFC, USA	101st Airborne Division	Apr 26, 1968	near Phu Bai, Thua Thien Province	San Antonio, TX	Apr 26, 1968	Ft. Sam Houston National Cemetery, San Antonio, TX
*Leisy, Robert R. 2Lt, USA	1st Cavalry Division	Dec 2, 1969	Phuoc Long Province	Seattle, WA	Dec 2, 1969	Evergreen-Washelli Memorial Park, Seattle, WA
Lemon, Peter C. Sp4, USA	1st Cavalry Division	Apr 1, 1970	Tay Ninh Province	Tawas City, MI	Living	
*Leonard, Matthew PSgt, USA	1st Infantry Division	Feb 28, 1967	near Suoi Da, Tay Ninh Province	Birmingham, AL	Feb 28, 1967	Shadow Lawn Cemetery, Birmingham, AL
Levitow, John L. Arnn 1c, USAF	3d Special Ops Squadron	Feb 24, 1969	over Long Binh, Bien Hoa Province	Glastonbury, CT	Nov 8, 2000	Arlington National Cem., Arlington, VA
Liteky, Angelo J. Cpt (Chap), USA	199th Infantry Brigade	Dec 6, 1967	near Phuoc Loc, Bien Hoa Province	Jacksonville, FL	Living	
Littrell, Gary L. SFC, USA	MACV (2d ARVN Ranger Group)	Apr 4–8, 1970	Kontum Province	Henderson, KY	Living	

NAME AND RANK	UNIT	DATE OF ACTION	PLACE OF ACTION	HOMETOWN	DATE OF DEATH	BURIAL SITE
Livingston, James E. Cpt, USMC	9th Marine Amphib Brigade	May 2, 1968	Dai Do, Quang Tri Province	McRae, GA	Living	
*Long, Donald R. Sgt, USA	1st Infantry Division	Jun 30, 1966	near Loc Ninh, Binh Long Province	Blackfork, OH	Jun 30, 1966	Union Baptist Church Cemetery, Blackfork, OH
*Lozada, Carlos J. PFC, USA	173d Airborne Brigade	Nov 19, 1967	near Dak To, Kontum Province	Brooklyn, NY	Nov 19, 1967	Long Island Nat'l Cem., Farmingdale, NY
*Lucas, Andre C. LTC, USA	101st Airborne Division	Jul 1–23, 1970	FSB Ripcord, Thua Thien Province	Seattle, WA	Jul 23, 1970	U.S. Military Academy Cemetery, West Point, NY
Lynch, Allen J. Sp4, USA	1st Cavalry Division	Dec 15, 1967	near My An 2, Binh Dinh Province	Dolton, IL	Living	
Marm, Walter J., Jr. 2Lt, USA	1st Cavalry Division	Nov 14, 1965	LZ X-ray Pleiku Province	Washington, PA	Living	
*Martini, Gary W. PFC, USMC	1st Marine Division	Apr 21, 1967	Hiep Duc Valley, Quang Tin Province	Charleston, WV	Apr 21, 1967	Rosewood Cemetery, Lewisburg, WV
*Maxam, Larry L. Cpl, USMC	3d Marine Division	Feb 2, 1968	near Cam Lo, Quang Tri Province	Burbank, CA	Feb 2, 1968	Nat'l Memorial Cemetery of the Pacific, Honolulu, Oahu, HI
McCleery, Finnis D. PSgt, USA	Americal Division	May 14, 1968	near Tam Ky, Quang Tin Province	San Angelo, TX	Jul 11, 2002	Belvedere Cemetery, San Angelo, TX
*McDonald, Phill G. PFC, USA	4th Infantry Division	Jun 7, 1968	near Kontum, Kontum Province	Greensboro, NC	Jun 7, 1968	Guilford Memorial Park, Greensboro, NC
McGinty, John J., III SSgt, USMC	3d Marine Division	Jul 18, 1966	Song Ngan Valley, Quang Tri Province	Louisville, KY	Living	

NAME AND RANK	UNIT	DATE OF ACTION	PLACE OF ACTION	HOMETOWN	DATE OF DEATH	BURIAL SITE
*McKibben, Ray Sgt, USA	1st Aviation Brigade	Dec 8, 1968	near Song Mao, Pleiku Province	Felton, GA	Dec 8, 1968	Center Baptist Cemetery, Felton, GA
*McMahon, Thomas J. Sp4, USA	American Division	Mar 19, 1969	Quang Tin Province	Lewiston, ME	Mar 19, 1969	Mount Hope Cemetery, Lewiston, ME
McNerney, David H. 1st Sgt, USA	4th Infantry Division	Mar 22, 1967	near Polei Doc, Pleiku Province	Houston, TX	Living	
*McWethy, Edgar L., Jr. Sp5, USA	1st Cavalry Division	Jun 21, 1967	Binh Dinh Province	Leadville, CO	Jun 21, 1967	Pence Cemetery, Baxter Springs, KS
*Michael, Don L. Sp4, USA	173d Airborne Brigade	Apr 8, 1967	Tay Ninh Province	Lexington, AL	Apr 8, 1967	Mount Pleasant Cem., Lexington, AL
Miller, Franklin D. SSgt, USA	MACV-SOG	Jan 5, 1970	Laos	Santa Fe, NM	Jun 30, 2000	Cremated
*Miller, Gary L. 1Lt, USA	1st Infantry Division	Feb 16, 1969	Binh Duong Province	Covington, VA	Feb 16, 1969	Allegheny Memorial Park, Covington, VA
Modrzejewski, Robert J. Cpt, USMC	3d Marine Division	Jul 15–18, 1966	Song Ngan Valley, Quang Tri Province	Milwaukee, WI	Living	
*Molnar, Frankie Z. SSgt, USA	4th Infantry Division	May 20, 1967	Kontum Province	Logan, WV	May 20, 1967	Highland Memorial Gardens, Logan, WV
*Monroe, James H. PFC, USA	1st Cavalry Division	Feb 16, 1967	near Bong Son, Binh Dinh Province	Wheaton, IL	Feb 16, 1967	Wheaton Cemetery, Wheaton, IL
*Morgan, William D. Cpl, USMC	3d Marine Division	Feb 25, 1969	Laos	Pittsburgh, PA	Feb 25, 1969	Mt. Lebanon Cemetery, Pittsburgh, PA
Morris, Charles B. Sgt, USA	173d Airborne Brigade	Jun 29, 1966	Long An Province	Galax, VA	Aug 20, 1996	Morris Family Cemetery, Galax, VA
*Murray, Robert C. SSgt, USA	American Division	Jun 7, 1970	Hiep Duc Valley, Quang Tin Province	Tuckahoe, NY	Jun 7, 1970	Gate of Heaven Cemetery, Hawthorne, NY

NAME AND RANK	UNIT	DATE OF ACTION	PLACE OF ACTION	HOMETOWN	DATE OF DEATH	BURIAL SITE
*Nash, David P. PFC, USA	9th Infantry Division	Dec 29, 1968	Dinh Tuong Province	Whitesville, KY	Dec 29, 1968	St. Mary's of the Woods, Whitesville, KY
*Newlin, Melvin E. PFC, USMC	1st Marine Division	Jul 4, 1967	Nong Son, Quang Nam Province	Wellsville, OH	Jul 4, 1967	Spring Hill Cemetery, Wellsville, OH
*Noonan, Thomas P., Jr. LCpl, USMC	3d Marine Division	Feb 5, 1969	Quang Tri Province	Woodside, NY	Feb 5, 1969	First Calvary Cemetery, Woodside, NY
Norris, Thomas R. Lt, USN	MACV-STD	Apr 10–13, 1972	near Cam Lo, Quang Tri Province	Silver Spring, MD	Living	
Novosel, Michael J. CWO, USA	68th Medical Group	Oct 2, 1969	Kien Tuong Province	Etna, PA	Living	
*Olive, Milton L. PFC, USA	173d Airborne Brigade	Oct 27, 1965	near Phu Cuong, Binh Duong Province	Chicago, IL	Oct 27, 1965	West Grove Cemetery, Lexington, MS
*Olson, Kenneth L. Sp4, USA	199th Infantry Brigade	May 13, 1968	Long An Province	Paynesville, MN	May 13, 1968	Paynesville Cemetery, Paynesville, MN
O'Malley, Robert E. Cpl, USMC	3d Marine Division	Aug 18, 1965	near An Cuong 2, Quang Ngai Province	New York, NY	Living	
*Ouellet, David G. Seaman, USN	River Squadron 5	Mar 6, 1967	Mekong River, Kien Hoa Province	Wellesley, MA	Mar 6, 1967	Woodlawn Cemetery, Wellesley, MA
Patterson, Robert M. Sp4, USA	101st Airborne Division	May 6, 1968	near La Chu, Phuoc Long Province	Fayetteville, NC	Living	
*Paul, Joe C. LCpl, USMC	1st Marine Division	Aug 18, 1965	near An Cuong 2, Quang Ngai Province	Vandalia, OH	Aug 18, 1965	Memorial Park, Dayton, OH
Penry, Richard A. Sgt, USA	199th Infantry Brigade	Jan 31, 1970	Binh Tuy Province	Petaluma, CA	May 9, 1994	Cypress Hills Memorial Park, Petaluma, CA

NAME AND RANK	UNIT	DATE OF ACTION	PLACE OF ACTION	HOMETOWN	DATE OF DEATH	BURIAL SITE
*Perkins, William T., Jr. Cpl, USMC	1st Marine Division	Oct 12, 1967	Quang Tri Province	Sepulveda, CA	Oct 12, 1967	San Fernando Mission Cemetery, San Fernando, CA
*Peters, Lawrence D. Sgt, USMC	1st Marine Division	Sep 4, 1967	Hiep Duc Valley, Quang Tin Province	Binghamton, NY	Sep 4, 1967	Chenango Valley Cem., Binghamton, NY
*Petersen, Danny J. Sp4, USA	25th Infantry Division	Jan 9, 1970	Tay Ninh Province	Horton, KS	Jan 9, 1970	Netawaka Cemetery, Netawaka, KS
*Phipps, Jimmy W. PFC, USMC	1st Marine Division	May 27, 1969	near An Hoa, Quang Nam Province	Santa Monica, CA	May 27, 1969	Woodlawn Cemetery, Santa Monica, CA
*Pierce, Larry S. Sgt, USA	173d Airborne Brigade.	Sep 20, 1965	near Ben Cat, Binh Duong Province	Taft, CA	Sep 20, 1965	Wasco Cemetery, Wasco, CA
*Pitsenbarger, William H. Amn 1c, USAF	38th Aerospace Rescue Sqdn	Apr 11, 1966	Phuoc Tuy Province	Piqua, OH	Apr 11, 1966	Miami Memorial Park, Covington, OH
Pittman, Richard A. LCpl, USMC	1st Marine Division	Jul 24, 1966	Quang Tri Province	Stockton, CA	Living	
*Pitts, Riley L. Cpt, USA	25th Infantry Division	Oct 31, 1967	near Ap Dong, Tay Ninh Province	Oklahoma City, OK	Oct 31, 1967	Hillcrest Memorial Gardens, Spencer, OK
Pless, Stephen W. Cpt, USMC	1st Marine Air Wing	Aug 19, 1967	near Duc Pho, Quang Ngai Province	Newnan, GA	Jul 20, 1969	Barrancas National Cem., Pensacola, FL
*Port, William D. PFC, USA	1st Cavalry Division	Jan 12, 1968	Hiep Duc Valley, Quang Tin Province	Petersburg, PA	Nov 27, 1968	Arlington National Cem., Arlington, VA
*Poxon, Robert L. 1Lt, USA	1st Cavalry Division	Jun 2, 1969	Tay Ninh Province	Detroit, MI	Jun 2, 1969	Forest Lawn Cemetery, Detroit, MI

NAME AND RANK	UNIT	DATE OF ACTION	PLACE OF ACTION	HOMETOWN	DATE OF DEATH	BURIAL SITE
*Prom, William R. LCpl, USMC	3d Marine Division	Feb 9, 1969	near An Hoa, Quang Nam Province	Pittsburgh, PA	Feb 9, 1969	Allegheny County Memorial Park, Pittsburgh, PA
*Pruden, Robert J. SSgt, USA	American Division	Nov 29, 1969	Quang Ngai Province	St. Paul, MN	Nov 29, 1969	Ft. Snelling Nat'l Cem., Minneapolis, MN
*Rabel, Laszlo SSgt, USA	173d Airborne Brigade	Nov 13, 1968	Binh Dinh Province	Minneapolis, MN	Nov 13, 1968	Arlington National Cem., Arlington, VA
Rascon, Alfred V. Sp4, USA	173d Airborne Brigade	Mar 16, 1966	Binh Duong Province	Oxnard, CA	Living	
*Ray, David R. Hosp 2c, USN	1st Marine Division	Mar 19, 1969	Phu Loc 6, Quang Nam Province	McMinnville, TN	Mar 19, 1969	Mountain View Cemetery McMinnville, TN
Ray, Ronald E. 1Lt, USA	25th Infantry Division	Jun 19, 1966	Ia Drang Valley, Pleiku Province	Auburndale, FL	Living	
*Reasoner, Frank S. 1Lt, USMC	3d Marine Division	Jul 12, 1965	near Da Nang, Quang Nam Province	Kellogg, ID	Jul 12, 1965	Greenwood Cemetery, Kellogg, ID
*Roark, Anund C. Sgt, USA	4th Infantry Division	May 16, 1968	Kontum Province	San Diego, CA	May 16, 1968	Ft. Rosecrans Nat'l Cem., San Diego, CA
Roberts, Gordon R. Sp4, USA	101st Airborne Division	Jul 11, 1969	Thua Thien Province	Lebanon, OH	Living	
*Robinson, James W., Jr. Sgt, USA	1st Infantry Division	Apr 11, 1966	Phuoc Tuy Province	Cicero, IL	Apr 11, 1966	Clarendon Hills Cemetery, Westmont, IL
Rocco, Louis R. SFC, USA	MACV–Advisory Team 162	May 24, 1970	Cambodia	Albuquerque, NM	Oct 31, 2002	Ft. Sam Houston National Cemetery, San Antonio, TX
Rogers, Charles C. LTC, USA	1st Infantry Division	Nov 1, 1968	FSB Rita, Tay Ninh Province	Mt. Hope, WV	Sep 21, 1990	Arlington National Cem., Arlington, VA

NAME AND RANK	UNIT	DATE OF ACTION	PLACE OF ACTION	HOMETOWN	DATE OF DEATH	BURIAL SITE
*Rubio, Euripides Cpt, USA	1st Infantry Division	Nov 8, 1966	Tay Ninh Province	Ponce, Puerto Rico	Nov 8, 1966	Puerto Rico Nat'l Cem., Bayamón, Puerto Rico
*Santiago-Colon, Hector Sp4, USA	1st Cavalry Division	Jun 28, 1968	Quang Tri Province	Salinas, Puerto Rico	Jun 28, 1968	Salinas Municipal Cem., Salinas, Puerto Rico
*Sargent, Ruppert L. 1Lt, USA	25th Infantry Division	Mar 15, 1967	Hau Nghia Province	Hampton, VA	Mar 15, 1967	Hampton National Cem., Hampton, VA
Sasser, Clarence E. PFC, USA	9th Infantry Division	Jan 10, 1968	Dinh Tuong Province	Angleton, TX	Living	
*Seay, William W. Sgt, USA	48th Trans Group	Aug 25, 1968	near Ap Nhi, Tay Ninh Province	Brewton, AL	Aug 25, 1968	Weaver Cemetery, Brewton, AL
*Shea, Daniel J. PFC, USA	Americal Division	May 14, 1969	Quang Tri Province	Norwalk, CT	May 14, 1969	St. John's Cemetery, Norwalk, CT
*Shields, Marvin G. CM3, USN	Seabee Team 1104	Jun 10, 1965	Dong Xoai, Phuoc Long Province	Port Townsend, WA	Jun 10, 1965	Gardiner Cemetery, Gardiner, WA
*Sijan, Lance P. Cpt, USAF	as POW	Nov 9, 1967 to Jan 21, 1968	North Vietnam	Milwaukee, WI	Jan 22, 1968	Arlington Park Cemetery, Milwaukee, WI
Sims, Clifford C. SSgt, USA	101st Airborne Division	Feb 21, 1968	near Hue, Thua Thien Province	Port St. Joe, FL	Feb 21, 1968	Barrancas National Cem., Pensacola, FL
*Singleton, Walter K. Sgt, USMC	3d Marine Division	Mar 24, 1967	near Gio Linh, Quang Tri Province	Memphis, TN	Mar 24, 1967	Memory Hills Garden Cemetery, Memphis, TN
*Sisler, George K. 1Lt, USA	MACV-SOG	Feb 7, 1967	Laos	Dexter, MO	Feb 7, 1967	Dexter Cemetery, Dexter, MO
*Skidgel, Donald S. Sgt, USA	1st Cavalry Division	Sep 14, 1969	near Song Be, Binh Long Province	Plymouth, ME	Sep 14, 1969	Sawyer Cemetery, Plymouth, ME

NAME AND RANK	UNIT	DATE OF ACTION	PLACE OF ACTION	HOMETOWN	DATE OF DEATH	BURIAL SITE
*Smedley, Larry E. Cpl, USMC	1st Marine Division	Dec 21, 1967	near Phuoc Ninh 2, Quang Nam Province	Union Park, FL	Dec 21, 1967	Arlington National Cem., Arlington, VA
*Smith, Elmelindo R. SSgt, USA	4th Infantry Division	Feb 16, 1967	Kontum Province	Honolulu, Oahu, HI	Feb 16, 1967	Nat'l Memorial Cemetery of the Pacific, Honolulu, Oahu, HI
Sprayberry, James M. 1Lt, USA	1st Cavalry Division	Apr 25, 1968	Thua Thien Province	Sylacauga, AL	Living	
*Steindam, Russell A. 1Lt, USA	25th Infantry Division	Feb 1, 1970	Tay Ninh Province	Plano, TX	Feb 1, 1970	Restland Memorial Park, Dallas, TX
*Stewart, Jimmy G. SSgt, USA	1st Cavalry Division	May 18, 1966	near An Khe, Binh Dinh Province	Middleport, OH	May 18, 1966	Riverview Cemetery, Middleport, OH
Stockdale, James B. Cpt, USN	as POW	Sep 4, 1969	Hoa Lo Prison, Hanoi, North Vietnam	Abingdon, IL	Living	
*Stone, Lester R., Jr. Sgt, USA	Americal Division	Mar 3, 1969	LZ Liz, Quang Tin Province	Harpursville, NY	Mar 3, 1969	Chenango Valley Cem., Binghamton, NY
*Stout, Mitchell W. Sgt, USA	44th Artillery	Mar 12, 1970	Khe Gio Bridge, Quang Tri Province	Lenoir City, TN	Mar 12, 1970	Virtue Cemetery, Concord, TN
*Stryker, Robert F. Sp4, USA	1st Infantry Division	Nov 7, 1967	near Loc Ninh, Binh Long Province	Throop, NY	Nov 7, 1967	Pine Hill Cemetery, Throopsville, NY
Stumpf, Kenneth E. Sp4, USA	25th Infantry Division	Apr 25, 1967	near Duc Pho, Quang Ngai Province	Menasha, WI	Living	
*Swanson, Jon E. Cpt, USA	1st Cavalry Division	Feb 26, 1971	Cambodia	Boulder, CO	Feb 26, 1971	Arlington National Cem., Arlington, VA
Taylor, James A. 1Lt, USA	Americal Division	Nov 9, 1967	Hiep Duc Valley, Quang Tin Province	Arcata, CA	Living	

NAME AND RANK	UNIT	DATE OF ACTION	PLACE OF ACTION	HOMETOWN	DATE OF DEATH	BURIAL SITE
*Taylor, Karl G., Sr. SSgt, USMC	3d Marine Division	Dec 8, 1968	Quang Tri Province	Laurel, MD	Dec 8, 1968	Independence Cemetery, Independence, PA
Thacker, Brian M. 1Lt, USA	92d Artillery	Mar 31, 1971	Kontum Province	Columbus, OH	Living	
Thornton, Michael E. EN2c, USN	MACV-STD	Oct 31, 1972	near Cua Viet, Quang Tri Province	Spartanburg, SC	Living	
Thorsness, Leo K. Maj, USAF	357th Tactical Fighter Sqdn	Apr 19, 1967	over North Vietnam	Walnut Grove, MN	Living	
Vargas, Jay R. Cpt, USMC	9th Marine Amphib Bde	Apr 30 – May 2, 1968	Dai Do, Quang Tri Province	Winslow, AZ	Living	
*Versace, Humbert R. Cpt, USA	as POW	Oct 23, 1963 to Sep 26, 1965	U Minh Forest, An Xuyen Province	Alexandria, VA	Sep 26, 1965	Remains not recovered
*Warren, John E., Jr. 1Lt, USA	25th Infantry Division	Jan 14, 1969	Tay Ninh Province	Brooklyn, NY	Jan 14, 1969	Long Island Nat'l Cem., Farmingdale, NY
*Watters, Charles J. Maj (Chap), USA	173d Airborne Brigade	Nov 19, 1967	near Dak To, Kontum Province	Jersey City, NJ	Nov 19, 1967	Arlington National Cem., Arlington, VA
*Wayrynen, Dale E. Sp4, USA	101st Airborne Division	May 18, 1967	Quang Ngai Province	McGregor, MN	May 18, 1967	Rice River Lutheran Cem., McGregor, MN
*Weber, Lester W. LCpl, USMC	1st Marine Division	Feb 23, 1969	near Bo Ban, Quang Nam Province	Hinsdale, IL	Feb 23, 1969	Clarendon Hills Cemetery, Westmont, IL
Wetzel, Gary G. PFC, USA	1st Aviation Brigade	Jan 8, 1968	near Ap Dong, Binh Long Province	Oak Creek, WI	Living	
*Wheat, Roy M. LCpl, USMC	1st Marine Division	Aug 11, 1967	near An Hoa, Quang Nam Province	Moselle, MS	Aug 11, 1967	Eastabuchie Cemetery, Eastabuchie, MS

NAME AND RANK	UNIT	DATE OF ACTION	PLACE OF ACTION	HOMETOWN	DATE OF DEATH	BURIAL SITE
*Wickam, Jerry W. Cpl, USA	11th Armored Cavalry Regiment	Jan 6, 1968	near Loc Ninh, Binh Long Province	Leaf River, IL	Jan 6, 1968	Lightsville Cemetery, Leaf River, IL
*Wilbanks, Hilliard A. Cpt, USAF	21st Tactical Air Sprt Sqdn	Feb 24, 1967	near Dalat, Tuyen Duc Province	Cornelia, GA	Feb 24, 1967	Fayette Methodist Cem., Fayette, MS
*Willett, Louis E. PFC, USA	4th Infantry Division	Feb 15, 1967	Kontum Province	Brooklyn, NY	Feb 15, 1967	St. John's Cemetery, Middle Village, NY
Williams, Charles Q. 2Lt, USA	5th Special Forces Group	Jun 9–10, 1965	Dong Xoai, Phuoc Long Province	Vance, SC	Oct 15, 1982	Arlington National Cem., Arlington, VA
*Williams, Dewayne T. PFC, USMC	1st Marine Division	Sep 18, 1968	Quang Nam Province	St. Clair, MI	Sep 18, 1968	St. Mary's Cemetery, St. Clair, MI
Williams, James E. BM1c, USN	River Section 531	Oct 31, 1966	near My Tho, Dinh Tuong Province	Charleston, SC	Oct 12, 1999	Florence Nat'l Cem., Florence, SC
*Wilson, Alfred M. PFC, USMC	3d Marine Division	Mar 3, 1969	FSB Cunningham, Quang Tri Province	Odessa, TX	Mar 3, 1969	Sunset Memorial Park, Odessa, TX
*Winder, David F. PFC, USA	Americal Division	May 13, 1970	Quang Ngai Province	Mansfield, OH	May 13, 1970	Mansfield Memorial Park, Mansfield, OH
*Worley, Kenneth L. LCpl, USMC	1st Marine Division	Aug 13, 1968	Bo Ban, Quang Nam Province	Farmington, NM	Aug 13, 1968	Westminster Memorial Park, Westminster, CA
Wright, Raymond R. Sp4, USA	9th Infantry Division	May 2, 1967	near Ap Bac, Long An Province	Mineville, NY	Sep 23, 1999	Saratoga National Cem., Saratoga Springs, NY
*Yabes, Maximo 1st Sgt, USA	25th Infantry Division	Feb 26, 1967	near Phu Hoa Dong, Hau Nghia Province	Oak Ridge, OR	Feb 26, 1967	Fort Logan National Cem., Denver, CO
*Yano, Rodney J.T. SFC, USA	11th Armored Cavalry Regiment	Jan 1, 1969	over Bien Hoa, Bien Hoa Province	Kealakekua, Oahu, HI	Jan 1, 1969	Nat'l Memorial Cemetery of the Pacific, Honolulu, Oahu, HI

Bibliography

Anderson, William C. *Bat 21*. New York: Bantam Books, 1980.

Benavidez, Roy P., with Oscar Griffin. *The Three Wars of Roy Benavidez*. San Antonio, TX: Corona Publishing, 1986.

Donlon, Roger H. C. *Outpost of Freedom*. New York: Avon Books, 1966.

Hildreth, Ray, and Charles W. Sasser. *Hill 488*. New York: Pocket Books, 2003.

Johnson, James D. *Combat Chaplain*. Denton, TX: University of North Texas Press, 2001.

Kayser, Hugh F. *The Spirit of America*. Palm Springs, CA: ETC Publications, 1982.

Lowry, Timothy S. *And Brave Men, Too*. New York: Crown Publishers, 1985.

McConnell, Malcolm. *Into the Mouth of the Cat: The Story of Lance Sijan, Hero of Vietnam*. New York: W. W. Norton, 1985.

McKeown, Bonni. *Peaceful Patriot: The Story of Tom Bennett*. Capon Springs, WV: Peaceful Patriot Press, 1980.

Miller, Franklin D., with Elwood J. C. Kureth. *Reflections of a Warrior*. Novato, CA: Presidio Press, 1991.

Mode, Daniel L., Fr. *The Grunt Padre*. Oak Lawn, IL: CMJ Marian Publishers, 2000.

Nicholas, John B., and Barrett Tillman. *The Naval Air War over Vietnam*. Annapolis, MD: U.S. Naval Institute Press, 1987.

Nolan, Keith W. *Battle for Hue, Tet 1968*. Novato, CA: Presidio Press, 1983.

———. *Death Valley: The Summer Offensive, I Corps, August 1969*. Novato, CA: Presidio Press, 1987.

———. *The Magnificent Bastards: The Joint Army-Marine Defense of Dong Ha, 1968*. Novato, CA: Presidio Press, 1994.

———. *Operation Buffalo: USMC Fight for the DMZ*. Novato, CA: Presidio Press, 1991.

Novosel, Michael J. *Dustoff*. Novato, CA: Presidio Press, 1999.

Plaster, John L. *SOG: The Secret Wars of America's Commandos in Vietnam*. New York: Simon & Schuster, 1997.

Schneider, Donald K. *Air Force Heroes in Vietnam*. San Antonio, TX: Air University, Air Power Research Institute, 1980.

Smith, Larry. *Beyond Glory*. New York: W. W. Norton, 2003.

Tillman, Barrett. *Above and Beyond: The Aviation Medals of Honor.* Washington, DC: Smithsonian Institution Press, 2002.

Vetter, Lawrence C., Jr. *Never without Heroes: Marine 3d Reconnaissance Battalion in Vietnam, 1965–1970.* New York: Ballantine Books, 1996.

Whitcomb, Darrel D. *The Rescue of Bat 21.* New York: Dell Publishing, 1998.

Index